ISBN: 9781313559911

Published by:
HardPress Publishing
8345 NW 66TH ST #2561
MIAMI FL 33166-2626

Email: info@hardpress.net
Web: http://www.hardpress.net

DATE DUE

MY LIFE AND MY LECTURES

MY LIFE AND MY LECTURES

BY

LAMAR FONTAINE, C. E., Ph. D.

NEW YORK AND WASHINGTON

THE NEALE PUBLISHING COMPANY

1908

CONTENTS

3

VI

VII

VIII

IX

X

XI

CONTENTS

INTRODUCTION

In offering this book to the public I have been impelled by no desire to attain notoriety or hope of making money out of it, but as garbled accounts of many of the incidents I shall herein relate have long been public property, and read and reread in many lands, I feel it a duty I owe, not only to the reading public, but to myself and descendants, that I give the cold facts just as they occurred. I shall make no attempt to write history, or give details of great battles. I shall narrate what I saw with my own eyes and what occurred to me individually, and I will be as brief with each event as possible, and where they are of great importance to me personally I shall be minute in my word painting, and truthfully convey the scene and incident to the mind of the reader.

For more than a third of a century I have been urged and entreated by my legions of friends to give these incidents to the public, but until now I have been restrained from the fear that I would be looked upon as an egotistical braggart—for my long life, of more than three-quarters of a century, has been a busy and eventful one, and filled with adventures in every clime under the sun. And whether in early childhood as a schoolboy, or as an Indian, a captive, on the wild Western plains of my own native State, as sailor, soldier, explorer, hunter, or civil engineer, I have been guided by devotion, concentration, and absolute persistence in the duties involved in whatever enterprise or calling I at the time engaged in. I always tried to excel in whatever I undertook. I was taught in my early childhood by one of the best of mothers that whatever was worth doing was worth doing well, and this idea has always been uppermost in my mind, and has been my guide through life.

An old Latin idiom in early life appealed to me, and

I adopted it, "*Aut viam, inveniam, aut faciam.*"
Broadly translated, " I will find a way, or make one."
This has carried me through many a wilderness, and
cheered me and forced paths over seemingly insur-
mountable difficulties, and brought me to havens of
safety through many storms.

In my explorations I followed no guides.   I led the
way and blazed the paths.   In hunting the wild animals of the jungle I made no haphazard shots at
them, I shot to kill.   In battle I saw my country's
foes, those whose duty it was to slay me or my companions, and to slay them was the duty I had to perform.   Hence, I loaded my rifle to kill.   And, when
I came in contact with those vast hordes of foreign
hirelings who entered the Federal Army during the
great "Confederate War" for gold alone, and not
from patriotism or love of country, I felt it a solemn,
a God-given duty, a privilege to kill them; and I
thanked my Creator that he had given me steady hands
and good eyes to hold and direct my missiles of death,
for they were only fit to feed the buzzards of our
Southland.   They had sold their very souls for gold,
and I took delight in piling their carcases in mounds
to feed the fowls of the air.   And I would do it again,
under the same conditions, a thousand times over.

My early training and life with the Comanche Indians imbued me with a spirit that made me never forget an enemy or desert a friend, hence I always smote
my enemies and loved and helped my friends, and did
my duty as my God-given conscience dictated and
approved.

And here, to-day, in my little, humble cottage home
in the village of Lyon, in the beautiful and most fertile
region of earth near the banks of the Sunflower River,
in the great plain of the Yazoo Delta of the Mississippi
Valley, where the whir and hum of the mighty wheels
of that far-reaching, civilizing, and educating railroad,
the Illinois Central, daily and hourly reminds me of
the busy outside world, I sit and dream over the past,
enjoying the confidence and esteem of friends and
neighbors, and, above all, blest with the love of a truly

womanly woman, whose tender touch and devout ministrations for forty years have smoothed the wrinkles from my brow, and have made my pathway, once so rugged and bloodstained, smooth and level, and covered the dark, crimson-dyed spots on it with pure white lilies-of-the-valley, and filled my vase with the perfume of star jasmine and violets. And with my brow still caressed by her loving hand, and my lips kissed by hers and those of my loved children and grandchildren, I feel at peace with all the world.

For the part I took in the war I feel a just pride, and have no apologies to make. I leave my acts and deeds a legacy to my loved ones and their descendants; and were I to go over the same long four years of bloody warfare again, as in the sixties, I would not alter a single step, but pursue the same pathways to the end. I love my sunny Southland as only a son can love a mother. And to those dear old comrades with whom I ate, drank, slept, marched, fought, and shared the prison fare I tender a comrade's love. I feel that if we meet no more on earth we shall soon do so in the " Bivouac beyond the Stars," and that we shall rest in the beautiful vales of Paradise and enjoy the smiles of a just, approving God.

CHAPTER I

Birthplace—Personal appearance—Educated in early years by a Polish exile—Sent to Onion Creek school—Ran away from home—Stolen by Indians.

I WAS born in Captain John Christman's tent, on Laberde Prairie, on the headwaters of the Yegua River, near where the small village of Gay Hill was afterward built, in what is now Washington County, Texas, on the 10th of October, 1829. My mother has often told me that at my birth I weighed only three pounds, clothes and all, and that when a week old she slipped her wedding ring over my hand up to my shoulder. At sixteen years of age I weighed only fifty-eight pounds.

At the beginning of the war in 1861 I was six feet and one-quarter of an inch in height, and weighed one hundred and sixty pounds, and my face was as smooth as a girl's, and as free from whiskers. In my babyhood days and early childhood my father determined that I should be a preacher, a missionary to some foreign clime, and he wished me educated with this end in view. I was taught my letters from a Latin grammar, and began the study of that language as soon as I mastered the alphabet. Greek and Hebrew followed.

When but three years of age there came into our camp an old man, a Polish exile, a baron of German birth, by the name of Homvosky. He was a graduate of Heidelberg, and was a general in the Polish Army, and had been banished from Europe upon the downfall of Poland.

This old man took a great fancy to me, and for years I slept with him. He would wash and dress me, and I almost worshiped him. He taught me my Latin, Greek, and Hebrew lessons, and, what I liked best, how

12

to box, wrestle, fence, with both foil and saber, and how to ride, and shoot the rifle and pistol. Many a long ride over the prairies, on his shoulders, have I taken, when in search of deer, or turkeys, or wild animals of that region.

When on these tramps he would fill my youthful mind with history of great events that had occurred in ages past. Under his kind and steady hand, for nearly seven years, my young mind expanded rapidly, and I was almost as well versed in the languages and ancient histories, and almost as far advanced in mathematics as many of our college graduates of to-day.

Just before my tenth birthday my old friend passed into the " Great Beyond," and left a void in my life— my first great sorrow.

At that time we were in camp where the city of Austin now stands. There were not enough children in our camp to employ a teacher, but about seven miles south of Austin, on the banks of Onion Creek, was a larger settlement, known as the Tom McKinney branch of Austin's colony. Here, in a wooden-framed, cloth-covered schoolhouse, some twenty or more of the colonists' children daily studied under the tutelage of an old red-headed, Scotch-Irish, Presbyterian schoolmaster.

Soon after the death of my grand old Baron-exiled friend and teacher I was sent to the Onion Creek school by my father. I had to ford the Colorado River, and ride across a wide prairie studded with live-oaks and dogwood thickets, and here and there a few post-oaks. Many of the live-oaks were draped in mustang grape vines, on which hung great clusters of these fragrant, luscious, and juicy fruit. The landscape was one to awake all the poetry in the soul of a young and ardent lover of nature.

Each morning and evening, on my Indian pony, I rode the seven miles that lay between the school and my home. I did not fancy my teacher—our spirits were not in accord. He was as far off from my old exiled friend in intellect and soul as the earth from the sun, and he was a stern and strict disciplinarian. He did not believe in sparing the rod and spoiling the child, as he held a switch ever ready in his hand, and upon the least provocation, from boy or girl, he let it fall upon the offender with force, or gently as a reminder. I could feel neither love nor respect for him.

Among the pupils was a young girl just budding into womanhood, a Miss Mary Stone, whose father had been captured by Mexicans in what is known in Texas history as the Mier expedition. These men, some two hundred and fifty strong, had made a raid into Mexico, and been captured by the soldiers of Santa Anna and confined in the castle of San Perote, down in Mexico, and every tenth man condemned to die. They were not chosen by name or number by their captors, but their selection left to the chance of drawing from twenty-five black beans and two hundred and twenty-five white. Each prisoner was required to step up and draw a bean from the hat, where they had all been placed. Those drawing black ones were shot.

Mary's father drew a white one, and thus for the present was safe, though still a prisoner, and suffering all the tortures that a half-civilized people inflict on helpless men when in their power.

My sympathy and love went out to Mary in her distress at the uncertainty of her father's fate. She would take me in her lap, and curl my long hair, kiss me, and call me her little sweetheart, and I almost worshiped her. She was beginning the study of Latin, and I would write her exercises, and thus keep her at the head of her class. One evening, just at recess, someone informed the teacher that I aided Mary and kept her at the head of the class. Without any warning he carried me down to the spring, which was just under the bluff, a short distance from the tent-house in which he taught, and near the spring, in the shadow of an old cottonwood log, he repeated a verse from the Bible, about sparing the rod and spoiling the child; he then knelt, and prayed a short prayer, in which he asked his Heavenly Father to forgive the awful crime of which I had been guilty, and then rose, and catching me by my long hair, almost lifting me from the ground, he administered an awful whipping, such as I had never felt before.

The first terrible blow from the lash almost took my breath, and the sting of it sent a thrill through every fiber of my being. I started to scream, but caught my breath and shut my teeth together, and let every muscle grow rigid, and made no sound. He might have cut me in two and I would not have flinched.

Such feelings as crept over me are indescribable. I determined to have revenge on him for the outrage and pain inflicted, and I grew as calm and stolid as if made of stone.

When he had finished I saw the blood trickling down my feet from his cruel blows. I started straight up the bluff, my feet and hands clasping the limestone steps that we boys had cut in the soft rock to aid us in climbing its perpendicular sides. My intentions were to reach and saddle my pony, and gallop away toward my home before my teacher could reach the school grounds, and prevent me, as he would have to go down the creek, some hundred yards, before he could get up on the bluff, and by the time he reached the tent I would be on my pony and flying across the prairie out of his reach.

Just as I got to the top of the bluff I looked down and saw him climbing up close behind me. I did not hesitate a moment; I gathered a stone, sharp and jagged-edged, and with all the strength and pent-up anger I felt I sent it at his head, and struck him fair in the forehead just as he was lifting his eyes to see how near he was to the top.

As my stone struck, he dropped like a dead man to the bottom. I felt a great load, as it were, lifted from my soul; I felt that I had fully avenged my wrongs without aid from anyone. I took my bucket and books, saddled my pony, and without saying a word to anyone I mounted, and with a light heart rode home.

Some two or three hours after my arrival I was chagrined and surprised to see the old fellow, all covered with soot and blood, ride up to our tent, dismount, and go in. In a few moments I was called by my father, and I saw my old teacher, covered with blood and his head bound in cobwebs and soot, and his brown linen suit, that had been washed and bleached until white, showed him up as the bloodiest man I had ever seen alive.

I found that he had given my father his side of the controversy, and I made no defense. I aimed to kill him as he climbed the bluff behind me, and had failed, and I was disappointed.

My father gave me another terrible whipping in the presence of my teacher, and I bore it with the same unflinching stoicism, and without a sound. But I made up my mind, while the lash burned my tender skin, that never again would I attend school under the old Scotchman. Yes, I would die first.

I there determined to run away from home the next day, and go to Mexico, to Castle San Perote, where Mary's father was a prisoner, and live with the Mexicans, where neither my father nor teacher would dare to come to hunt me.

That night I molded bullets, with two negro boys, until late in the night, and secured a large buffalo horn, containing five pounds of powder, for my little rifle. The rifle was a present from General M. B. Lamar, and my shotpouch a gift from General Sam Houston. I put my bullets in one end and my powder-horn in the other of a rawhide sack or wallet, as they were called in those days, and hid them in a crevice of a bluff on the river, just above the ford on the bank of the Colorado, where I daily crossed it on my way to school. The next morning I took my rifle, and a few charges of powder in the horn attached, and my bucket of lunch, and satchel of books, and, giving my mother an extra hug and kiss, I mounted my pony and rode away. As soon as I crossed the divide between the river and Onion Creek I set my satchel of books and bucket in the trail, and turning southwest I put my pony in a lope, and struck the trail that led from Austin to San Antonio, entering the latter near Manchac Spring, about twelve miles from Austin. I turned down the trail in a gallop, and rode up on the bluff that overlooks the San Marcos Springs. The trail makes a sudden turn to the east and follows down the river on top of the bluff for some distance, before descending to the ford. Just as I made the turn I saw, standing directly in front of me in the trail, an Indian in his war paint, and with his bow at a ready. My first impulse was to raise my rifle and kill him before he could shoot me, but my gun was in its sling and swung to the pommel of my saddle, so I merely checked the speed of my pony and rode straight up to him.

As I approached the thought entered my brain, " Why not go with the Indians, instead of the Mexicans? " and I made up my mind at once to go with them. I rode up and stopped, and he said in very good English:

" Where going? "

Without hesitation or the least embarrassment I answered, " With the Indians."

" That's good, give me gun."

I handed him my rifle, and as I did so I glanced back up the trail, and at the very spot from which I would have tried to shoot my captor about thirty other warriors had risen out of tall mesquite grass. They came in a body down the road, and each took a good look at me, several saying in very good English:

" How do? "

They exchanged my pony for a fresher one, as my long gallop of some seventeen or eighteen miles had begun to tell on him, and mounted me on one of theirs, and we started off in a northwesterly direction.

CHAPTER II

Parentage—Escapade with wild cats—Exploding " ghost "
and " witch " theories—Visits to grandparents—partnership of my father with William Jacob Thompson—
Protecting the government archives—Life with the Indians.

BEFORE going into the details of my long captivity
of four years and three months among them, the reader
must indulge me for a while, as I give a short history
of myself and parents prior to my life among this
fierce band of Comanches.

Both of my parents were natives of Virginia. Father
was born in Henry County, at the old family residence
of Patrick Henry, who was his great-grandfather on
his father's side. John Fontaine, his grandfather, married Martha, the oldest daughter of Patrick Henry,
and they named their first-born after Patrick Henry,
and Patrick Henry Fontaine married Nancy Dabney
Miller, and my father, Rev. Edward Fontaine, was the
oldest child, and first great-grandson of the immortal
Patrick Henry.

My father was born on Leatherwood Creek, in
Henry County, on the 5th of August, 1800.

My mother was born at the old homestead of the
Maurys, in Albemarle County, Virginia, on September
13, 1805. Her father moved to Tennessee when she
was an infant, and Maury County was named after
him.

On the 10th of September, 1828, they were married
at the old homestead near Columbia, in Maury County,
and went at once to Texas with Stephen F. Austin,
who had received valuable grants of land, and other
inducements, from the Mexican authorities to induce
emigration and the colonization of the territory.

My grandfather took up his residence at Pontotoc,
in Pontotoc County, Mississippi, in 1834, and for several years, under President Jackson's Administration,

was surveyor general of public lands south of Tennessee, and had his land office at Pontotoc.

When a child only six years old I was carried to see my grandparents, aunts, uncles, and kinfolks in and around Pontotoc.

I well remember the looks of the great logs the negroes were hewing in long straight lines to build the houses to live in. They were a novelty to me, as my home had ever been a tent, and I asked my grandfather how he was going to take all those great logs with him when he went to move his tent? This, of course, provoked a laugh at my expense, and exposed my ignorance to the crowd, and my mother had to tell them that I had never lived in a house, but always in a tent that could be moved about to suit our nomadic life on the prairies of our Texas home.

I had several boyish escapades that were somewhat ludicrous, while we stayed at grandfather's. One I well remember.

Grandpa was very fond of cats, and he had a dozen or more that at each meal he would feed out on the brick walk at the front porch; and there were a number that lived out on the lot around the stables and barns, and these were wild and would not come about the house. Grandma constantly complained that cats destroyed the young chickens, and ought to be destroyed; so, at her suggestion, grandpa offered us a picayune for each pair of cat ears we would bring him. Under the guidance of Billy Bradford, my uncles, Edmund Winston and Charles Fontaine, we organized a brigade of "cat hunters," and proceeded to destroy all the cats we could find around and about the barns and stables. But the cats seemed to have had warning of our intentions, and only two or three yielded us their ears, after a long and exciting chase. But nearer the house we found several tame ones; these we did not kill, but merely cut off their ears.

That night I offered the spoils of the chase to my grandfather, and received fifty cents in picayunes for my reward. But the next morning, when the old man went to feed his pets, seven hoisted their tails and came rushing up to him, bloody around their heads and minus their ears.

He said nothing on the porch as he gazed at his shorn pets, but he walked out to a young, long-limbed elm and cut a nice keen switch, went into his office, and called me in. I had to obey. As I entered he asked if I still had the money he paid me for catching the wild cats out at the barn?

" Yes, sir," I said.

" Well, give it back to me, I paid you too much."

He held out his hand and I dropped the picayunes one by one into it. He took out seven, and then handed me back the rest, and I started to go, but he said:

" I am not through my settlement with you yet; don't I owe you something else? "

I knew by intuition what was coming—my conscience told me this, and I answered:

" No, sir."

" But I do," he said, " and I am going to pay you now."

And he did, and it made an impression on me that has never been effaced.

Upon another occasion, to get revenge for this whipping, I played a practical joke on him that was cruel in the extreme.

Every afternoon, after dinner, he would take a nap for a few minutes, and then get up and go in his garden and weed or work among his vegetables for exercise and recreation. On the day I remember so well it was washday, and the women had been washing. They had stretched a clothes line from the posts around the well to another in front of the back window of the office in which grandpa took his nap. I heard him snoring, and knew that he was sound asleep. I caught two of the largest old tomcats that were asleep on the gallery, and handling them gently I tied their tails together, and slipped up to the clothes line and threw them across it, and then hid behind the well curb and shed to watch the outcome. The cats at once made their presence known, and soon I heard grandpa say

"Scat!" in no uncertain tones; but his voice only increased the din of the warring cats, and brought grandpa to the window to see the meaning of the turmoil. I was peeping from my hiding-place enjoying the fun, and he got a glimpse of me, and out in his slippers he came, cut the strings that bound the cats, and came straight to my hiding-place. He stripped a limb from a young peach tree, and for a minute or two I had some sure enough "fun" in the most exaggerated form.

On one occasion my curiosity was aroused by hearing the negroes talking about ghosts. I wanted to see one, and old Anthony, one of the oldest of the negroes, told me that I would have to go to a graveyard, among the dead people, and sit right still until midnight, and a ghost would come right up to me, and I could see him in the dark, as he would be white. So one night I slipped out of my trundlebed and went across the orchard, and into the graveyard, and got up on a tombstone and waited. How long I sat I have no idea, but presently I was aroused by the shaking of a bush that hung over the gravestone and touched me, and saw something white, seemingly, bowing to me and almost in reach. It came a little nearer, and I made a spring and grabbed it. It gave a quick whirl, and lunged forward with a loud "Baa-baa," and revealed by its bleat an old billygoat that I was familiar with around the lot. My disappointment was intense, and from that day to this I have had my doubts about there being any real ghosts.

I had another "witch theory" exploded in a somewhat similar way not long after my ghost adventure. Only a few miles from grandpa's there lived two very old people, kind, gentle, and as hospitable as could be found. They lived alone in a large, rambling house, with upstairs rooms. The children of this old couple were married and scattered around, and frequently with their children would spend days and weeks at the old homestead. I paid them a visit one evening, and a storm came up, and darkness, and they kept me until morning. When bedtime came they sent a servant with me upstairs, and put me to bed in a large room with an old high-post tester-covered bedstead, hung all round with heavy curtains above and below the place I lay on. The negro helped me to undress, and put on my nightrobe, which was much too large for me, lifted me up into the tall bed, drew the curtains together, and left me alone. I heard her footsteps echoing down the stairs, then all was silent as death. I lay for a long time thinking of all the stories I had heard the negroes tell about ghosts, and about this old woman, in whose house I now was, being a cruel witch that liked to ride horses at night, and take bad boys away from their homes, and not let them see their mother or father any more. I was satisfied on the ghost question, but the witch was a known quantity, for I had read of the Witch of Endor in the Bible, and I had no doubts on that line, and here I was, all alone, in a real witch's house, and miles from home.

I had been told by Nancy Ann and old Anthony, and other negroes at grandpa's, that as long as I worked my big toe on my right foot that the witches would not and could not bother me. I thought of these things in a wide-awake state for some time, when all of a sudden I was roused by the sound of footsteps coming up to my room. They were not those of a human being, for these feet had claws——I could hear them strike the steps as they ascended the stairs. I was satisfied that the witch had transformed herself into some great animal and was coming to take me away. I worked my big toe with wonderful rapidity, but it did not seem to have the desired effect. The witch came on right to my chamber door, and I heard it screech, as she pushed it open, and I heard her claws strike the floor as she approached the bed, and felt the curtains part, and heard her heavy breathing as she seemed to stand and look down upon me. It was very dark, and I could see nothing. All of a sudden, as I was doing my best working my toe, a tremendous body lit upon me, nearly mashing me down through the bed, and I could feel the quick throb of the witch's heart beat. Mine almost ceased.

I lay like a dead being for some time, with the panting witch lying heavily upon me, and making no effort to do me an injury. I took my head from under the cover and stretched my hand out to feel her. The relief I experienced was beyond expression, for, instead of being grabbed by the long bony claws of a horrid witch, I was greeted by the warm breath of old Ossian, our big Newfoundland dog. I grabbed him and drew him under the cover, and in a few minutes I was safe in the land of Nod.

My dog had missed me and followed my pony's track, and was at the house before the storm, and when night came on he made so much noise that the servant let him in. He came right up to me, and thus for all time ended my belief in witches.

We spent several months with my grandparents, and I think that they were glad to bid me good-by. Upon returning to my prairie home and my old Polish exile, I practiced daily with my rifle at the deer, turkeys, and prairie chickens that were in herds and flocks on every hand, and became wonderfully expert with it. Under my old tutor I made progress with my lessons in mathematics and all the higher branches that he taught by the text and by lectures.

In 1837 we paid my grandparents another visit, and my father and the Hon. Jacob Thompson, who was afterward Secretary of the Interior under President Buchanan, with William Bradford, formed a law partnership at Pontotoc. My father and Jacob Thompson entered some large tracts of land in the Mississippi bottom, on what is now known as Bear Lake, in Tunica County, and in the winter of 1837 and 1838 they took a surveyor and a large force of negroes, wagons, and mules, and four Chickasaw Indians—the latter as hunters to keep them in fresh meat.

We camped on some mounds just south and west of the present station of Dundee, on the Yazoo and Mississippi Valley Railroad, on the east bank of Bear Lake. Here, with "Fat Bob" as my Indian companion and guide, I hunted as far south as Ward Lake.

Father and "Jake" Thompson followed the surveyors' trails and superintended the deadening of the lands.

Returning to Texas in 1838, we moved up the Colorado River to the present site of the city of Austin, and laid it out. Our tent was pitched in the center of what is now Pecan Avenue, and in laying off the city a small triangle was left to mark the spot, as ours was the first tent pitched, and ours the first horses ever staked by a white man's hand in that region.

Being the first male child born in the colony, I was allowed to hold and help drive the first tent pin, and to aid in staking the first horse on the site of what was to be the capital city of the largest and greatest State in the grandest republic the world has even known.

It was on this occasion that I first felt that I had a place in the world.

In 1839 we built a substantial, double-walled, four-room, auditor's, comptroller's, and treasurer's log-house, and a heavy double-walled house, lined with earth, eight inches thick, of hand-sawed boards, for a general land office, and a large, roomy capitol building of hand-sawed boards. We then stored all the archives of the State away nicely for the officers in charge whenever their services should be required.

President Sam Houston, concluding that Austin was too far out on the confines of civilization for their safety, decided that he would remove them back to Washington, where they would not be so exposed. So he sent some commissioners, headed by old "Deaf Smith," to remove them. But they met a snag and did not carry out Sam Houston's directions.

All the men were absent from the city upon their arrival, on an Indian scout, and only seven grown women, and five boys, myself the oldest boy, and one girl composed the whole white population of the city when the commissioners appeared. Mrs. Crosby, Mrs. Haynie, and Mrs. Swisher had the keys to the buildings, and they told the commissioners that they could not get the archives, nor could they enter the buildings, until the men returned. The commissioners became indignant at the delay, and said that they would break the doors down and remove them anyhow, as they were clothed with the power and had the authority to do so from the President.

My mother replied that when they broke open those doors and removed those records it would be over the dead bodies of every woman and child in that place.

The ladies loaded a small six-pound cannon and sighted it at the entrance to the land office, and gave me and three other boys rifles, and lit a piece of hemp rope, and primed the cannon, ready to defend the archives of the State from being removed, and, as "Deaf Smith" stepped upon the front porch into the vestibule of the land office, they touched the match to the cannon and the ball entered the building just in front of "Deaf Smith," covering him with dust and splinters. We boys lay behind a small breastwork ready to fire with deadly aim at the word, but it never came. The commissioners beat a hasty retreat, and the archives were saved.

The hole made in the wall of the old land office by the six-pound shot on that fateful morning was afterward closed up, and a metal tablet marked the place, with the history of the occurrence engraved thereon to perpetuate the event to the coming generations.

The men upon their return thanked the gallant women for their brave acts, and said that it was better than they could have done, as they would have had to obey the President and give the archives up.

It is a pleasure to me now, at this distant day, to recall those stirring times in the early days of my native State, the founders of which had in their veins the best and purest blood of this great nation. It was among these noble men and women that my early childhood was spent, and the memory of them clings to me, and cannot be obliterated.

Turning again to that fateful morn, the 10th of September, 1839, when I handed my gun to my Indian captor, and upon a fresh pony was carried into a little over four years of Indian life, I will try to give you a brief history.

My captors placed my saddle on a fresh pony, took my gun and ammunition, and we started on what was to me a long and tiresome ride. About four o'clock in the evening two of the "bucks" dismounted at the top of a high ridge, while the rest of us rode on down into a beautiful valley, a mile or more from the ridge. Here we dismounted, let our stake ropes drag, and hoppled some of the ponies with rawhide thongs, coupling their front feet close together. After watering them, we turned them out thus fastened to graze. About sundown the two Indians left on the ridge came up, and we again mounted and continued our march, which lasted through the night. I went to sleep on my pony and when I awoke I found myself in the arms of an Indian—and thus I rode until sun-up.

We then dismounted, ate a strip of dried venison or buffalo meat, and watered and grazed our horses for an hour or two, then rode until four in the evening. Some time in the night we remounted, and rode until daylight, myself in the arms of an Indian. We continued thus for many days—I don't know how long. I lost my hat the first night, and I thought that maybe someone would find it and thus get a clue to the way I had gone.

One evening we came in sight of a very large camp where there seemed to be from thirty to forty thousand men, women, and children (we numbered only about a hundred), and when we rode into their midst they made quite a din. I was given in charge of an Indian woman, about forty-five years of age, who put her arms around me, gave me a hearty squeeze, and made signs that I belonged to her. I went into her teepee, and was soon fast asleep. How long I slept I have no idea. When I awoke the sun was nearly an hour high, and the morning bright and clear.

My foster mother gave me a breakfast of fresh venison, roasted on the coals, some jerked buffalo meat, and dried turkey, and a gourd of water before I left the tent.

As I walked out into the campus all the little Indians around came up and took a good look at me.

One little tot about my size walked up and gave me a sharp rap square in the face. I stood still and looked him in the eye. He came up again laughing, and as he attempted to repeat the blow I warded it off, let drive at him, and laid him out on the ground, flat on his back, with the breath almost knocked out of him.

Another, a shade larger, came up and struck at me. I parried the blow and sent him to earth also. Then several rushed at me and I got some heavy licks about the head and ears, but every blow I struck would send my victim to the ground. They were coming at me in crowds, and I was fast getting winded when my foster mother, hearing the mêlée, came rushing to my aid and carried me into her tent. After resting for an hour or two, I again left my quarters and the battle was renewed.

This routine I had to go through two or three times a day for more than a week, until I think that every little Indian in the camp that was near my size had had a taste of my fist. As I always came out victorious when in single combat, they ceased to torment me, and I was looked up to as a " good warrior," as I was a victor in full three hundred encounters.

CHAPTER III

Prestige as a marksman—The Flat-Headed Indians—My encounter with a grizzly—Finding evidences of the " Cliff-Dwellers "—Walk home a distance of 750 miles after living three years with the Comanches.

AFTER living with my captors for about three months and sharing all of their sports and games, swimming, running, wrestling, and ball playing, I was given back my rifle and a small amount of ammunition, and told to go and kill a deer for my mother. My own pony was returned, and two nearly grown warriors were sent with me to the hunting grounds.

After riding several miles down a lovely valley, we came up on a wide, level plain, with here and there a few mesquite trees, and occasionally a thicket of dogwood or " shin-oak." Just before we reached the end of one of these dwarf shin-oak thickets, a very large buck leaped out in front of me only a few yards away and dashed off at his best speed. I raised my rifle, let drive at him and broke his neck. I saw a look of surprise on my companions' faces, but they said nothing. They were only armed with bows and arrows. They dismounted and hung my deer high up in a mesquite tree above the reach of a wolf, and we continued our hunt. As we approached another thicket we separated, they a little in advance and on the right side of me. I had only ridden a few yards when another deer sprang into the open in front of me and I repeated my first shot. They hung him up just as they did the first. Not half a mile was passed when several deer dashed out of a thicket and I broke the neck of another. Neither of my companions had had even a shot, for I did not wait for the deer to stop so that they could stalk and creep up on them, but killed them while at full speed, a proceeding they had never before witnessed, and they could not comprehend the power that I held.

Putting a deer up behind each of us, we turned back to camp. They laid the three deer down before my foster mother's door and rode off. Soon, from the gestures and the language of many around the camp, I noticed that there was something wrong. I saw my comrades show that I had killed all three of the deer while sitting on my horse, that I had broken each of their necks while they were at full speed, and it was plain to see that they did not believe this. All eyes were turned on me, and by gestures they asked me if I did kill them while running, and without getting off my horse. I answered in the affirmative. Fully a dozen or more gray-haired warriors came up and made a close inspection of the deer, turning them about in different directions, then, leaving, they returned with the chief. He also turned the deer about, made a careful and critical examination of them, gave a grunt of incredulity, and left. He had made the two young men who were with me go through the same pantomime that the others had, showing how I sat my horse, how the deer ran, and how I threw my gun up and shot; how the deer were hit and how they fell.

After some consultation and the elapse of an hour or so, they brought my pony out, and several hundred men assembled, including my two comrades of the morning without their arms, and the chief, and mounting their horses the whole cavalcade moved up the valley in an opposite direction from our course of the morning.

I was placed in front and my two comrades just behind me. After riding a mile or so we came to a clump of cottonwood trees on the bank of the stream upon which we were camped. On the opposite side of the river was a high bluff. The party halted, and my two comrades rode some two or three hundred yards in front of the crowd. Some prairie chickens flew up and I started to throw up my rifle and shoot, but they caught my gun and stopped me. After a silent ride of a mile or more farther a fine drove of wild turkeys flew up from under the lower bank of the river and one sailed across in front of me. I raised my rifle and fired, cutting him down. My two companions yelled, whirled round, and rode back in a gallop through the crowd that was following, and never halted until they reached the camp. The whole cavalcade rode up to me, and the chief took me and my gun in his arms from off my pony, and said many times " How do! How do!" and I think I shook hands with every member of the party.

My turkey was borne in triumph on the point of a lance into camp, and laid at the door of my foster mother's tent. My prestige as a marksman and hunter was never again doubted from that day until I left them four years after. I had their full esteem and confidence, and was always awarded the leadership in all juvenile expeditions, and was made chief of the young ball players and their games. From my decisions there was no appeal.

My life among these Indians was very pleasant for four years. In the spring, as soon as the calves of the buffaloes were old and strong enough, these animals would begin to move northward. This was the signal for the Indians to break up their winter camps and follow them, as the buffaloes furnished them their meat and their houses. We would follow them to the shores of Manitoba. I have killed them on the Yellowstone, far up on the Platte, the Sioux, and in the valley of the Red River of the North, when not a human being of my own race inhabited those wild regions, sixty odd years ago.

The buffaloes do not feed like any other animals of the plains—they stretch out in long lines, one behind the other, and make beaten trails, which they follow until paths are worn so deep into the soil that they touch their sides, and the young can scarce reach the grass that grows along the edges. At the head of the moving column are the young and powerful bulls and the young heifers, next come the cows and their calves, and last the aged patriarchs of the herd. The latter act as guards for the young and helpless. All feed as they march along the narrow roads.

They reach their long tongues as far out as possible and grasp a huge mouthful of grass, then slowly chew it for some time before they take another bite. Thus there is always left a bunch for those following behind.

On one occasion, as I was out in the foothills of the Rocky Mountains with a small party of young boys and girls on a frolic, we got far out of the regular line of march and were lost. We fell into the hands of a tribe of Flat Head, or Digger Indians, and they took all the care of us they could. We could not speak their language, but all tribes have a universal sign language that is understood. These Indians are the poorest and the lowest in the scale of humanity of all the North American tribes that inhabit the plains. They live on roots, acorns, grasshoppers, lizards, and various kinds of small birds that are easy to trap. They catch large quantities of grasshoppers, and a small white rock lizard. These they store away in straw bunks or pumps, after drying them in the sun. They are very fond of a small, sweet, black acorn of the live-oak, and the pecan is as great a delicacy as candy to a city-bred child.

Their mode of cooking was crude in the extreme. They hollow out a basin with their knives in the soft limestone rocks, and fill the hole with water, in which they place their dried grasshoppers, lizards, and powdered acorns. Then they build a fire near by and in it place rocks. When these are heated to a very hot temperature, they remove them and dip them into the water that contains the mass of lizards and other ingredients. As soon as the hot rock quits sizzling, they remove it and put in another. This is repeated until the stuff is boiled to their taste. We ate this grasshopper and lizard soup for at least a week, when we were rescued by our own tribe. This lizard dish is quite palatable and tastes like a "crab gumbo" prepared by a French cook. It would be enjoyed by many, as far as taste is concerned, if its composition was unknown.

During my four years of captivity I learned much of the habits, the modes, manners, and customs of the

wild, nomadic tribes of these yellow savages that profited me in after wanderings in other lands and other
climes.   I never led as free, untrammeled a life as I here
enjoyed among these Indians.   My thin summer clothing that I wore when captured was soon in rags, and
I discarded the remnants, and in a state of nudity I
roamed the rest of the days and years of my captivity.
Every part of my body became as impervious to heat
and cold as was my face.   I felt far more comfortable
and free.   My skin was like a tanned buckhide, my hair
long, and my eyesight as keen as that of an eagle.   I
was never sick a day, and my muscles were like steel.

I often rode alone far away from our camps or
trails, exploring and examining the country, and my
old foster mother always had a large store of provisions, due to my skill with the rifle.   I met with one
adventure that is worth relating, as I thought at the
time it was the last that I would ever be the hero of.

I was about five miles from our trail, had dismounted,
and was stalking a large buck antelope that stood
on guard on an eminence, under which a large herd
was feeding.   It was not more than a mile from the
high bluffs that overshadowed the plains.   My antelope was not paying much attention to my signals,
but seemed to have his attention fixed in an opposite direction.   I saw this, took advantage of it, and
was soon in shooting distance.   I fired and he fell.   I
reloaded my rifle and was priming it as I approached
to cut his throat and prepare the body for transportation to my camp.   As I reached the top of the elevation
and was within a few feet of him, the whole herd, of
which he was the guardian, came by with a rush, and
right behind them one of the largest grizzly bears that
I had ever seen, dead or alive.   My dead deer lay between us, my horse was half a mile away, and there
was not a spot of safety or place of retreat in the
whole range of my vision.   I was about ten feet from
my antelope and I thought that maybe the bear would
be satisfied with it, and let me alone.   This hope was
soon dispelled, for he came up to it, smelt it, turned it
over, licked the blood, and looked at me.

I stood perfectly still and made up my mind that the only spot my little ball could have any effect on his huge carcass was in his eye, and the only hope I had was to find his brain in that opening. All of a sudden he quit licking the blood, looked toward the bluffs, gave a low growl, and turning toward me raised on his hind feet until it seemed that he was as tall as the bluffs. I saw that his intentions were to destroy me, and I had to act quickly or it would be too late.

As he rose and faced me, I raised my rifle and fired directly at his throat, as I knew that a blow near or upon "Adam's apple" always knocked a man down or stunned him. My little ball went true and the giant fell at my very feet. I loaded as quickly as I could, and put another bullet in the hollow of his ear, but this was needless, as the first shot had killed him.

I reloaded, and in a moment after I was very weak and could hardly stand. The sudden revulsion of feeling from a nightmare of death to the enchanted ground of perfect safety was too great, and I had to sit down and recover.

My pony was frightened by the stampede of the herd of antelope and the scent of the grizzly, and galloped across the prairie toward our camp, leaving me alone with my dead. I knew, however, that when my pony reached the camp that my friends would begin a search for me, and I did not feel the least alarm. I took out my flint and steel from my shot pouch, and gathered some "buffalo chips" and dry grass, and kindled a fire, then took a steak from my buck and soon had a savory meal. I built a large blaze so that my friends could see where I was, and to protect me from the wolves, that I knew would put in their appearance as soon as night came on.

I was sound asleep when a band of searchers awoke me, and their exclamations of admiration at the prowess I had shown in killing the great grizzly with one small bullet sent a thrill of pleasure to my young heart. Several horses were hitched to the bear, I mounted my pony, which they had brought with them, and we rode into camp.

The next morning they examined the bear, the track of the bullet, cut him up, and gave the flesh to my foster mother. They cut the claws from the hide, cleaned and polished them beautifully, and mounted them on a band. The war chief put the band around my hair, and told me that I belonged to him and was one of his warriors.

Of course I felt proud of the distinction, as I was the smallest and youngest of the tribe who had ever been thus honored.

While with the Indians I was a constant student of nature, and learned much of the habits and nature of wild animals. I could follow their trails swiftly over any kind of ground as unerringly as a trained hound could by scent. I wandered among the ruined cities of the ancient " cliff-dwellers," and climbed the steep sides of the great " mesas " of the Zuni plateaux, and played hide-and-seek in the chambers of these, the first civilized people in the world—the very first that carved stones and lived in stone houses, and understood the art of making glazed porcelain ware.

I have often carried beautiful, small, glazed, and colored cups, vases, and bowls of different patterns from these great elevated rock-hewed houses of a hundred rooms to my Indian mother, to use in our camp in her domestic pursuits, and I taught her the use of many of them. She would never carry them from one camp to another, but would either break them or leave them where they were last used. I suppose she was superstitious regarding them, as she would not give me any reason why.

I remember that in one of the rooms, in a residence that was over a thousand feet above the level of the surrounding plain, I found a number of skeletons of a small, straight-boned people with high foreheads, who were nothing like the Indian skeletons. They had been murdered by a people using the chipped, rough stone arrows and spears, and some of the stones were still imbedded in their skulls.

These skeletons were covered with dust from two to three feet deep, beneath which their outlines were plainly visible. When uncovered their bones were too soft to handle—they, too, were but dust and crumbled at my touch. Their implements were all of polished stone and colored pottery. I have seen my little Indian playmates throw hundreds of the large and small vessels of this pottery ware over the bluffs, from the doors of these chambers, and watch them fall and fly into a thousand fragments below. How often in later years have I regretted this wanton destruction, which at the time was great fun to us!

But to recount my various adventures while with these Indians would only tire you. To the northwest of the largest of one of these prehistoric cities of the first civilized people of earth there is a lovely canyon, and in a day and a half's ride you will pass under three long, high " natural bridges." The one nearest the mouth of the canyon is about 150 feet high, over 400 feet long, and 100 feet wide; the second is fully 250 feet high, 150 feet wide, and is fully 500 feet long; the third is a magnificent structure over 500 feet above the bottom of the dry bed of the canyon, 300 feet wide and 700 feet in length.

I have passed under these great works of nature in our hunting expeditions into the mountains after bear. I call attention to these great " natural bridges " here to cause some adventurer to visit and photograph these wonders of nature.

I have, in these same regions, passed over beautiful tesselated pavements of white and black stone for several miles in extent, and through forests of petrified trees that are of the most beautiful colors. It is worth a journey across those trackless wastes to see them. In the rooms of the cliff-dwellers you can see upon the plastering, to this day, the prints of their hands, the lines of the epidermis yet clear and distinct, and by the art pursued by Bertillon you could get a very good idea of the people who once inhabited this region. The phrenologist and the anatomist, in the modern light of science, could give us pictures of these vanished and long-ago forgotten civilized people.

Toward the close of my third year of captivity with

the Comanches I asked the chief if he would not let me go back to my home and see my mother and my people. He said yes, if I would walk.

This reply put a damper on my undertaking the journey, as it was at least seven hundred and fifty or more miles in an air line, across a trackless waste, to my home, and on the route there was a desert of eighty miles, without a drop of water in its whole extent. There was not a white man nor white settlement on those wild wastes between the city of Austin and the Pacific Ocean at that time. So, with a desert in front of me of eighty miles in extent and no pony to ride, I hesitated and did not accept his offer. But upon our return the next year I renewed my request, and received the same answer. I then determined to make the attempt on foot, and so informed my foster mother.

The next day I made preparations for my long and lonely journey. My foster mother did all she could to deter me from the undertaking, but I was firmly resolved on making the trip. She made me several pairs of heavy-soled moccasins that reached far above my knees, to prevent the long coarse grass from cutting my skin, as I waded through it across the buffalo trails. She also prepared some shredded, dried turkey breast and venison in a buckskin pouch, filled my quiver with a supply of fresh arrows, and a new deer sinew string to my bow, and, after putting her mark carefully upon each arrow, she told me to " be good." I bade her farewell, and, alone and on foot, I set out on my long journey homeward.

Reader, can you imagine a child scarce fourteen years of age (who at sixteen only weighed fifty-eight pounds), on a bald prairie, seven hundred and fifty miles from home, without a companion, without a horse, without a guide, surrounded by wild animals, and some parts of his way not within eighty miles of a drop of water? This was my condition. Only the hope of seeing my mother at the end of my long tramp gave me strength.

I knew that all the water courses that had their sources on the southern and eastern slope of the Rocky

Mountains flowed into the Gulf of Mexico, and that by following any of them I would strike the Gulf somewhere. When I came to the desert, or waterless region, game became scarce. I carried a deer hide across it, and in the morning I would spread it out, shake the dew from the grass on to it, and gather the ends up, and thus get a supply sufficient to last me all that day. Thus I succeeded in keeping water. My rifle kept me in a good supply of food—the jerked or dried venison and the shredded turkey breasts I used as bread.

At night I would kindle a fire of the dry buffalo chips, broil my fresh meat, eat a hearty meal of it, and then lie down by my fire and sleep as sound as a tired child only can. Sometimes the coyotes and larger wolves would make some trouble with their howling and snarling. If they got too bold I would send a ball or an arrow into the nearest and most bold, and he would leap off with a howl and the rest would scatter.

I did not see a human being on my whole journey, and I don't think that I was ever in any great danger from any wild animal. I felt that a special guardian angel watched over my pathway, and guided my every step. The first water course I struck, after crossing the Rio Grande and Pecos, was the Conchas, a tributary of the Colorado, the very stream on which the city of Austin was located, and on which was my home. But I did not know it, and did not recognize it until I reached the junction of the San Saba and the Colorado. There I saw the remains of one of our camping places of more than four years before. My heart gave a great bound when I saw the first marks of a civilized people, and knew that I was not more than seventy-five miles from home.

The day was bright and clear and the moon was but a day old, and, had I had moonlight I think that I would have been tempted to travel all night, I was so elated.

One evening just after sundown I had built my campfire on the eastern slope of a mountain, on the south side of the river, and was looking off down it, when I caught the glimmer of a light. It shone out bright and clear, and twinkled like a star. I watched it until my eyes grew weary and heavy with sleep, and I drifted into the Land of Nod with its sheen upon my lids. This mountain was only twenty miles from my home, and the light was in my mother's room.

CHAPTER IV

Arrival home—Mistaken for an Indian—Tortured by wearing clothing and sleeping in beds—Jeers of neighborhood children—Sent to Professor Bingham's school.

THE next night I was within ten or twelve miles of Austin and on another mountainside. I again built my fire, and as it grew dark I watched for my light again. When it appeared, Columbus, seeing the first gleam of light from out the pathless sea that shone from this, to him, new world, was not and could not have been more rejoiced than I.

For an hour I sat and watched it twinkle, and then I made my own larger and brighter, and then I slept as sound as a babe. The next day I wandered on, over high mountains and deep ravines, until nearly dark, when I came out on top of a bluff overlooking Bartons Creek. The sun was down as I reached this bluff, but from it I could see a house not more than three miles away, and it was from this house the light shone. I descended the bluff, crossed the creek, and came out on the prairie beyond just as night descended.

To understand my position exactly it is necessary for me to remind the reader that I was a stranger to the habits and customs of civilized life. I had been reared, as it were, in a tent on the prairies of Texas, and had made but two short visits to a civilized country, where houses and fences were a part of the surroundings. These were unfamiliar scenes in my Texas home, and were unlooked for, and such a thing as a windowglass I did not dream of.

I took my course across the prairie toward the light, and was compelled to go around thickets and other natural obstructions until at last I came to a high rail fence. I clambered over into an open plowed field. Across it I encountered a high picket fence. The tops

of the pickets were sharpened, and I had considerable
trouble in getting over, but I succeeded at last and
found that I was in a pen of horses and other kinds
of stock.   I crossed the pen and encountered another
picket fence.   This I also climbed, and made straight
for the light, which was some eight feet above the
ground, shining through a narrow door.   As I came
under it I saw that I had to climb up quite a distance,
over logs laid one on the other, to get inside of the
small door.   I took off all of my plunder, set my gun
down, and hung my bow and quiver of arrows upon
it, and climbed straight up to it.

Through the opening I could see my mother sewing
by a table with a candle burning upon it, and in an
adjoining room I could hear the voices of several men
conversing, my father among them.   As I reached the
opening I attempted to enter, and my head and my
face encountered an invisible obstruction which was
shattered into fragments, and made quite a noise as it
rattled on the floor inside of the room.   I attempted
to withdraw my head as my mother raised her eyes.
She uttered a scream, and I dropped to the ground
and heard her shriek, " Indians."   I darted under the
house as I heard the commotion I had been the cause
of, and clambered up on one of the floor sills between
the joists, and lay upon it as still as a squirrel.

Soon lights began to shine in every direction.   They
took charge of my paraphernalia and looked under
the house in every direction.   I heard " Deaf Smith "
say that my outfit was that of a Comanche scout.
When this declaration was made there was a short
consultation among the men, and soon I heard a drum
sounding, and then another and another, and the as-
sembling of men in numbers.   I laid as still and silent
as possible, not daring to move, until I was almost in
a cramp, and I listened until the voices of the men died
away and I could hear no sound of them.

I was wondering if it was not safe for me to get
down and try to make my escape when I heard the
rustle of a dress, and stooping down I peeped out
and saw my mother in the faint light of the young

moon standing just where I struck the ground as I slid from the window. My face had been cut by the shattered glass as I withdrew my head, and I was bleeding a little, a drop here and there. I dropped from my hiding-place and said:

"Ma, it's Lamar."

She recognized my voice and clasped me in her arms. We entered the house, and she stanched the blood and washed my face and hands. As I did not have on any clothing except a small cape made from the soft hide of an unborn buffalo calf, which was simply used to keep the weight of my load from cutting my shoulder, she proceeded to make a long shirt, that reached below my knees, from one of my father's old ones. This she put on me and then took the band of bear claws from my hair. With her shears she clipped my hair short, and combed and washed it and my scalp for some time, until it seemed that she had fully scalped me, and my head was as tender as if it had been skinned. She then washed me over and over and over again, and then put me in her bed. There was a "dry norther" blowing, though not very cold, but when she put me in a featherbed and covered me up my skin felt as if it were on fire, and I was in torture. She talked to me and I understood every word she said, but I could not reply in English, as I had forgotten my native tongue. I would answer in the Indian vernacular.

When my father and the other men who were with him returned, my mother told them who their Indian was. I was brought out, and I thought that they were going to shoot me, so I again said, "Ma, it's Lamar." This was all the English that I could say.

In this crowd of men around me I knew General M. B. Lamar, after whom I was named; also old "Deaf Smith," Captain James G. Swisher, James H. Raymond, "Milt" and Munroe Swisher, and several members of the Texas Congress, which body was at that time in session. Many of these men were boarding at my father's, and it was gratifying to me that I knew them all, but exceedingly awkward that I could not

talk to them. Old "Deaf Smith" could speak Comanche, but could not hear my reply. He said that I
was only an Indian decoy, and sent as a spy among
my own people to murder them, and that I ought to
be taken out and hanged. It made my blood boil to hear
him say this, and I could have shot him with as much
delight as I would have shot a panther or sneaking
coyote.

I told them that I had not seen an Indian for months,
and that I had come from the Rocky Mountains all
by myself, and that not an Indian had come with me.
This they did not believe, as the distance was so great
a child my size could not make the journey alone. Nor
could I convince a single one of them. My father
wanted to whip me until I would tell them the truth,
but General Lamar said it would do no good—that
the best thing to do would be to send out scouts on
my back track, and see if I was alone, and to be prepared for any emergency by keeping the army under
arms and ready. This they did.

I was so uncomfortable in bed with my nightclothes
on that as soon as everything was asleep but the
sentinels out on the prairie, I crept out of bed and
crawled out into the yard, and, throwing my gown
under my head, I lay down between the roots of a
large live-oak tree that grew in the back yard. I was
soon sound asleep and did not wake until nearly sunup,
when I crawled back into the house without making
any disturbance. The soldiers, under the skillful
guidance of Tonkaway and Caddoe Indians, took my
back track and followed it up to and beyond the San
Saba River. They were gone some ten days and returned, reporting that so far no Indian traces were
found, and that I had no companions, and no following
friends; that I was absolutely alone in all my journey
from the San Saba to my home.

During the ten days the soldiers were absent I was
closely watched and my every movement noted. I
kept close to my mother, for I was afraid of old "Deaf
Smith," and thought he would kill me if he got a fair
chance. During those ten days I made considerable

progress in regaining the use of my tongue, by constant practice with my mother, and she learned much of the Comanche language.   I got so I could converse in my native English.

Mother made me new clothes, and fitted them to me, but the torture in having to put them on and wear them was fearful.   As I had not had any on for four long years, every part of my body was as impervious to heat and cold as was my face.   I would wear them while in or about the house, but when I was off from the house, or alone, the first thing that I would do was to disrobe and enjoy the freedom of my limbs, and ease my tortured hide.

My life was not one of pleasure, and I did not enjoy my homecoming as I had expected.   All I said or did was misconstrued.   The children of the neighborhood would make faces at me, and call me " Indian spy," and all sorts of names.   I bore it all with Indian stoicism, and made no reply, but it would not have been healthy for one of them to have met me alone in some out-of-the-way place, for I would not have hesitated to kill him as I would a wolf or panther.   I considered them the worst enemies that I had on earth, having robbed me of my fair name and given me one of derision.   All I said and all the hardships that I had endured were laughed at, and I was considered a menace to the community.   I told my mother my every thought on this line, and asked her if she would be sorry if I went back to the Indians.   She told me not to mind what my persecutors did, that I had performed feats beyond the comprehension of the ordinary mortal, and hence my deeds to them were but lies; that all would come right in the end, when I was better understood.   She gave me all the comfort that lay in her power, but my own heart was sore and I strongly contemplated returning to my little Indian playmates, where at least I was appreciated.

At last it was determined to send me away to some distant school, where my Indian life was not known. When I found this out I felt a great relief, for home was not what I had pictured it on my long and lonesome journey across those wild desert wastes. It was a torture to live in it and I welcomed anything that promised a respite. I was to be sent to Professor Bingham's school in North Carolina, among the hills and mountains of that grand old State, and I felt a secret joy at the coming change.

One morning the carryall was made ready and my father, the negro driver, and I got in. With an extra pair of horses led by another negro we set out on our overland journey to the Old North State.

CHAPTER V

Parting with my mother—Run away from Professor Bingham's school—Home again—Sent to sea—Life on the
Vincens—Return home in December, 1846—Join Perry's
expedition to Japan in 1853—Explorations in the Far
East.

I WILL not recount the incidents of my trip, as they
made but little impression on me at the time. I was
too glad to get away from the home that had been
such a terrible disappointment to me. Strange
thoughts flitted through my brain. I loved my mother
with a passion that was sacred to me, and I would have
given my life willingly to save her even a pang, but I
could not be with her, and life for me was a blank without her.

Those long-ago days now rise before me in all their
vividness. As I pen these lines, nearing the seventy-
seventh milestone in life's rugged pathway, I feel the
loving kiss yet burning on my lips where she pressed it
as she bade me " Good-by." There are some things
in our life that time does not efface, and this is one
of them. They are like the brand of red-hot iron
that sears the tender hide of the bleating calf; once
burned in it lasts as long as life. I can see the last
wave of her hand as she watched us move off across
the prairie, and the picture is branded in my brain.

After about a month or more on the road we reached
Professor Bingham's school. I begged my father not
to enter me under my own name, as there was a chance
of my name having reached there from Texas, through
the newspapers. If it should be recognized, the very
thing that I wanted to avoid would confront me again,
and I would certainly leave the school and return to the
Indians, for I would not undergo in this school the
tortures of suspicion that I had labored under in my
own home. He respected my wishes, and I was enrolled
under a new name.

I was soon a favorite in the mess hall, as well as

campus.   My ball playing was as good as the best, for in the Indian game " shinney " I was an expert, as I had played it for years with my little Indian team on a field many miles in extent, not limited to the narrow lines of our campus.   I was often the first choice in the " toss-up," as we called it, and for two long weeks I was happy as a boy could be in my position. But a cloud hovered over my horizon.   At all schools there are some who are envious of others, and our school was no exception to the rule.   One boy accused me of doing an act of which I was entirely innocent, and, without giving me a chance to disprove the charge, the professor gave me a severe chastisement.   This raised a demon in my heart.   The next day being Saturday, we had a big ball game, in which the professor took a hand.   I was on the opposite side and I laid my plans so as to get near him.   As we both made for the ball I was a little quicker than he, but I waited until he shoved his stick forward and covered the ball, when, without hesitating, I let drive with all my might an upper stroke.   Glancing up his stick, I struck him a fearful blow, unhinging his lower jaw and driving some of his teeth down his throat.   To the outsiders it appeared to be an accident, but I knew that the professor would not so regard it when he recovered.

That night I determined to leave the school and go to some other place, but I wanted to meet the fellow who was the cause of all the trouble.   I met him, and such a drubbing as he got at my hands that night he never forgot.

I took what money I had, and with only the clothing I had on I scaled the college walls and footed it to Newbern, on the coast.   There I crawled aboard a large schooner that was taking on a load of lumber for Galveston, Texas, and for three days I hid in the hold until I could feel the steady swish of the sea and the long swell of the waves.   Then I came on deck and took the crew and officers by surprise.   I told the captain my full story, concealing nothing.   It made the right impression upon him, and he sympathized with me, and made me his friend forever.   He said that he, too, had run away from school and his home for unjust punishment in his early youth, and he knew just how it made me feel.

We were some time at sea, owing to adverse and stormy weather, and I soon became familiar with every part of the ship, and each line and rope. I took delight in climbing to the crow's nest and watching for passing vessels, and the wild freedom of the winds and waves had a fascination for me that I had never felt on the land. During that trip I made up my mind that I would be a sailor and make the sea my home.

We reached Galveston without accident, and I went from there up to Houston by boat. In Houston I met the proprietor of the stage line that ran to Austin, and was given a seat in the coach. I reached home all right, and was clasped in my mother's arms again.

I had been home two days before my father arrived from his long return journey from Bingham's school. He had been delayed by a visit to his own father at Pontotoc as he came back from North Carolina. His surprise was great at seeing me, and my explanations did not seem to satisfy him in all things. He would look at me in such a way that I hated to be alone in his presence. I felt that there was doubt in his mind of every statement I made.

I gave my mother a straight and clear statement of my adventures at the school, and the cause that led to my striking the professor; how I aimed to kill him for the way he had treated me. I told her of the thrashing I gave the boy who had lied to the professor, and caused me to be so unjustly whipped, and I saw her shudder at my words. She told me that I did wrong, and that my father would send me back; that I must apologize to the professor, and to the young man who was the cause of all my trouble at the school. When this plan of going back to school was presented a spirit of unrest took possession of me, and I made up my mind that I would bid adieu to all home ties forever, and go at once to my Indian friends in the far West. I let my old negro nurse into my secret and she informed mother of my intentions.

I made every preparation to leave. When father found
it out, instead of being angry and punishing me, he
said that he had no intention of sending me back to
North Carolina, but that I could stay at home and be
with mother as long as I would behave myself and
be a good boy.

That night I fell asleep in my mother's lap, and the
world had a fairer and broader view for me. I had
a feeling of perfect rest that night such as I have rarely
since felt. My intense love for mother seemed strengthened tenfold, and I never wanted to be out of her sight.
Such feelings and such love can only enter our lives
once in a lifetime. Its memory clings to us sacredly
until we " cross the Great Beyond." I have felt it
on the frozen shore of Greenland, on the burning sands
of Sahara, in the jungle wilds of Asia and Africa, in
the lonely watches of the midnight hour on the trackless sea, and on the snow-capped peaks of the Himalayan and Andean mountain chains. It never dies. It
is a part of the " arcana " instilled into us by the
Hand above. It binds us to the Great I Am, and will
reunite us in the dim hereafter.

I remained at home a few short months or maybe
only weeks, hunting and fishing, generally alone, as
I wanted none of my former playmates about me;
they only reminded me of my first homecoming from
my Indian captivity, and the least word or remark
about my being an Indian decoy or spy would have
given them trouble.

One morning, after a long, hard ride on a bucking
bronco, I was informed that father and I were going
to Pensacola, Florida, to see a kinsman, Lieutenant
M. F. Maury, of the U. S. Navy. In a few days we
bade mother " Good-by," and with a negro boy as my
body servant and " Jake " the carriage driver we drove
to the town of Houston, on Buffalo Bayou. Here
we took a steamboat and went into Galveston. From
there we took passage for New Orleans on the old
Maria Burt, and on reaching that city we took a
steamer for Pensacola by way of the lakes.

One evening we reached Pensacola, and went aboard

a side-wheeled steam gunboat, the *Vincens*. That evening we attended a banquet given by the officers, and about eleven o'clock I crawled into a hammock that was swinging against or near the side of the vessel, and was told by Lieutenant Maury to rest there as long as I wanted to. I was soon asleep, and when I awoke the ship was out of sight of land. My father was not on board, and I was alone on a strange ship among entire strangers. Lieutenant Maury was the only one I had ever seen before. My feelings were strung to the utmost tension. I felt that I had been kidnaped, shanghaied, or stolen. A feeling of resentment arose in my bosom, and I determined to get even some way at the first opportunity and leave them all. I saw there was no way to escape then, as there was no land, and that I would have to wait until we entered some port.

Our vessel I heard from the sailors was bound for the Arctic regions, and that probably our first land would be at the Dutch Cape Farewell on the southern shore of Greenland. This was not very soothing to my pentup feelings, but with Indian stoicism I said nothing. I obeyed every order with alacrity, and in a few days I had made many friends and become a favorite among the men. I loved to climb the ropes, sit far up in the rigging, and feel the sway of the vessel and watch for ships on the horizon. I soon became fond of the sea and my surroundings on the ship, but the reflection that I had been made a prisoner never for a moment left me, and the thought constantly rankled in my breast. I began the study of the higher branches of mathematics under Lieutenant Maury, and was soon familiar with the use of the quadrant, the compass, and the log, and could rattle off the names of the various sails and lines and parts of the ship, and many nautical phrases common to the sailors. I did not grieve over my captivity, but made the best of it.

I learned to love the sea, and to this distant day I am happy when I hear the roar of the breakers and see the long lines of waves as they dash upon the shore and send the spray in clouds far up into the air. To me it is the grandest music that can greet the human ear. I love it in its quiet grandeur; I love it when the " Storm God " heaves its breast and shakes its shores in awful thunder. To me it is like a mirror of eternity, the looking-glass of Nature, and of Nature's God.

We made our first land in Boston harbor, and here many of us went on shore, and I was struck with the wild recklessness of a " Jack Tar " on the land. He is as different a being ashore as it is possible to imagine. He seems to be, and is, as helpless as a child. He needs a guardian here more than anywhere on earth.

At Boston we took on vast stores of all kinds of provisions suitable for an Arctic expedition, and I was soon, I thought, to be a partaker of all the hardships and rigors of a polar exploration. Lieutenant Maury believed that there was an open polar ocean, and we were going to find and prove it. I made up my mind that if I had to go to the North Pole, that it would be on a ship and with a crew of my own choosing; so a few hours before sailing I left the *Vincens*. I met the captain of a whaling vessel and went aboard his ship, thus giving the officers and the crew of the *Vincens* the slip, and a day or so after she sailed we, too, left for a two years' cruise in the far-off frozen zone.

We headed for Greenland, and when off Cape Farewell coasted along the western shore as far as Uppernavik, and then northwest, until we were in latitude 79° 13′ north, and longitude 70° 10′ west. Here we spent the winter, frozen hard and fast. On the 17th of July, 1846, we were anchored in the wake of a grounded iceberg in latitude 74° 48′ north, and longitude 66° 13′ west, cutting up and trying out the fat of several large sperm whales we had in tow.

On the 26th of July the two vessels of Sir John Franklin's expedition, the *Erebus* and *Terror*, stood by, and asked about the channels and islands to the north and west of us. We gave them all the information as far north and west as we had been. We were fully in sight of them for more than twenty-four hours. I believe that we were the last ship and crew that they ever saw.

One winter in this cold, bleak, frozen region was enough for me. I never want to see it again while I live. The eternal silence that reigns fills you with awe and an uncanny dread—a something that you cannot comprehend. Everything is unnatural. The aurora borealis is simply indescribable, and has to be seen to even catch a faint realization of its splendor and grandeur—words cannot paint them. The most wonderful are seen when the thermometer registers ninety degrees below zero. It is the most sublime of all Nature's handiwork. It is the " flaming sword " that God placed in the hands of the cherubim to guard the portals of the Garden of Eden when He drove the man of the living soul from out its walls.

I visited many islands and points of land in the Arctic regions, and was surprised at the vast amount of fossilized remains of animals, birds and beasts, as well as plants, that belong only to a warm tropical climate. In fact they are of larger size, and could only have lived in a hotter country than the tropics now present. I think that this idea will strike almost any observer when he first beholds them. But I will not trouble you with a minute description of these. We were very successful in our voyage, and carried into Boston a full cargo of oil.

In December, 1846, I reached Mobile, Ala., and made a trip to Pontotoc, Miss., where my parents were on a visit to my grandfather.

In January, 1847, I went on board the U. S. frigate *Sabine*, and on the 7th of February we opened fire on the city of Vera Cruz, and continued until that city surrendered. I was with the battery of guns that was sent to the rear of the city, and while on the vessel was at the starboard bow gun, a twenty-pounder, as I remember it now.

After the bombardment and surrender our vessel, as well as the *St. Lawrence*, the *Susquehanna*, the *Mississippi*, and one or two others, was sent to the Far East into the China Sea, and with Bolingbroke we consummated a treaty with China. I marched afoot from T'sin Tsen to Pekin over a marshy, level country, densely populated, and was the first American boy to enter the city. I spent several months in China, and around Hong Kong Island, and went with some natives far up the Yang Tse into the mountains, five hundred miles from the coast. I made many observations for my kinsman, Lieutenant Maury, to aid in his work, " The Physical Geography of the Sea."

In 1853 I joined in Perry's expedition to Japan. Our vessel was dressed as a merchantman, and sent to destroy the pirates off Sasebo. This we did most effectually, not letting a single one reach the land. They thought that we were a merchantman aground, and came in swarms to capture and destroy us, but we were not aground, only ready and waiting for them. As they approached us in their long, low, rakish-looking boats, we could see that their intentions were sinister, and we prepared for them. Our rigging was filled with Chinese sailors, and not an American seaman was visible. When they were within two ship's cables of us the Chinese began to hail them and told them to go back. They paid no attention to their cries, but began shooting at us. It was amusing to see the Chinamen tumble down on deck and scoot for cover. The Japs fired from long single-barreled, match-locked muskets, that took two to fire. One held and sighted the gun and the other touched it off, just as boys now do their brass Fourth of July toy cannons. These " Long Tom " muskets were almost harmless, and their bullets rattled against the sides of the ship like pebbles thrown against the walls of a house, and did as little damage.

We waited until they swarmed around us and threw their grappling hooks up on deck, then we turned our guns, with double charges of canister and grape, upon them, and our marines, with their rifles, sent all of them to " Davy Jones' Locker." I suppose that we destroyed about two thousand in all, and we put a quietus upon these pirates and their descendants forever.

Our ships, that had gone around the eastern shores of the islands, met us in the Japanese Channel, about 150 miles south of Hakodadi; and we took twenty-six of the princes and princesses of Nippon, and brought them to the United States. We kept them here at school for fifteen years, educated and civilized them, and sent them back to their native land. From the seed thus sown in 1853 the present status of the Japanese Empire had its origin.

From the Far East I returned in 1849, and in 1850 I went back and remained in India, China, Persia, Arabia, Egypt, and Syria.

In 1855 I again visited my Texas home. While in the Far East I explored parts of India, and went to the heads of the Indus, the Ganges, the Brahmapootra, the Yang-tse-Kiang, and thence to the Hoang, or great Yellow River in northern China. I followed the Great Wall of China, about fifty miles or more west of where it crosses the Hoang Ho, then turned back east and went on until I reached the great gate lying north of Pekin, some two hundred miles east of the crossing of the Yellow River.

While in the Himalayan Mountains, near Dumjah, I was made a Buddhist priest, and took several orders. This gave me entrance into their secret archives that are hidden alike from Christian or Mohammedan. They are sacredly kept apart from all eyes, save those of the ancient order of the Aryan Sanscrit Priesthood. Only those of the pure white race ever see them. No yellow or black or mixed blooded priest or layman ever lays eyes on these records. In the Vale of Kashmir I found the purest blood of the Aryan people. Here, beyond the Hindoo-Koosh Mountains, they speak of Alexander the Great as if he had only been gone a few short years; all call him uncle, and claim kin with him. These people had never been subdued by the English.

In a series of lectures that follow this biographical sketch I give you some of the things I learned while a sojourner among these brave and true people, the only pure descendants of the ancient founders and civilizers of India, who ages agone migrated westward from the shores of ancient America to this region. There are many traditions among their archives that point to America as the place from whence they migrated, but I will not indulge in speculative thoughts here, as I am only giving you a brief story of my life and wanderings. But before leaving the dreamy land of these Hindoos I cannot help but give you a description of the beautiful temple near Agra, on the banks of the Jumna, a tributary of the holy river of these ancient people. It is called the Taj Mahal, and was erected many hundreds of years ago by Prince Jehan, as a monument to himself and wife. It is impossible to paint it with words or pen, so that you can realize its splendor and its majestic grandeur, as there is no building on earth that can compare with it. When you stand in front and look up at its massive dome, covered with hammered gold, and its pure white Parian marble walls and columns, all rising to a height of 296 feet above you, gleaming in the clear light of a bright, unclouded sun, you seem to feel, as you lift your eyes upward, that you are gazing at the " Great White Throne " of the Living God, and the longer you gaze the more impressive becomes the scene. Go inside and the same feeling of awe comes over you. The massive columns, wreathed in vines of living verdure from whose petals the dew and raindrops seem to glitter and fall and the breezes to fan the clinging ivies that twine around them, are as smooth and cold as polished glass. Place your hand upon these columns and you will find each vine, each petal, each dewdrop a precious stone, inlaid into the cold white marble, without a flaw or blur. Each dewdrop that glistens in the soft subdued light is a pure diamond of the first water, and the colored leaves and vines are of colored quartz an inch and a quarter long, hexagonal in shape and not larger than a cambric needle, fitted so close that it takes a microscope to discern the junction. There are fifty-two of these great columns thus decorated.

Now let us visit the tomb of Jehan and his wife, and

see its wonders.   Here a marble wall, six feet high and
eighteen inches thick, encloses but does not hide it, for
you peer through a real veil of pure marble, so cut
and pierced that it does not obscure the vision.   You
are lost in a maze of wonder.   This solid piece of marble seems in reality but a gauze veil, thin and light,
apparently so fragile that you could lift it with your
breath.   But feel and measure it; it is eighteen inches
thick and six feet high.   At his wife's head there is
a small table, apparently about two feet wide and
three feet long, and seemingly an oil painting of a
beautiful, quiet mountain home scene.   It really is
a mountain home.   You look up at the mountain tops,
and down into the sweet peaceful glens and valleys, in
perspective, such as no artist of modern times has even
attained with pencil or brush.   View it closely with your
microscope, and you will find that it, too, is made of
small needles of various hued pure quartz, no single
stone larger than a cambric needle, but each color
blended one into the other with a master hand, so true
to life that the whole is a living and real picture of the
birthplace and early home of the dead woman.   I asked
my guide if any value had ever been placed upon this
work of art, and he said that several visitors from England and France had offered as high as a hundred and
fifty thousand dollars for it, but that it was in reality
worth several times as much; that there were no artists
in the world that could even polish the delicate stones
into their hexagonal shapes in a lifetime of sixty years,
much less to select the true colors, shades, and the
minutiæ necessary to paint this picture with quartz
needles.   The great Taj Mahal has no equal on this
earth, and many thousands of years of our civilization
will roll away before it can have a duplicate.

I hope the reader will pardon these thoughts that
fill my mind—they are not a part of my life, but the
memory was so strong that I could not help the di-
gression.

One of the best-remembered journeys that I ever
took was from the port of Sallee, on the west coast of
Africa, to the upper regions of the Nile, in the Nubian

Desert. The port of Sallee is about 125 miles south of Tangier, and from there I went almost due east to the city of Fez, the ancient capital of Morocco. Here I fitted out a " desert kit," and in a large caravan, numbering some five thousand or more, I became a unit. I will be as brief as possible in giving you a picture of life on the greatest " sandy sea " on the earth.

The scenery of the first three hundred miles south of Fez is one of real gloomy grandeur. There are some wonderful valleys, rich in the loveliest foliage and verdure. At times we were eleven thousand feet above the level of the sea, and in the clear air the views were grand. After leaving the influence of the wadis, or rivers, leaving all signs of vegetation behind and entering the desert proper, the change was something never to be forgotten. The long line of the caravan, in single file or in groups, would stretch out in an unbroken line for miles. The dust would almost strangle those in the rear on the lee side. At times you could see but a few feet, and the heat was something fearful. I have seen my thermometer register, in the shade of the tent at nine o'clock in the morning, 140 degrees Fahrenheit, and twice during the prevalence of a simoon I have seen it rise to 170 degrees, and at night it would drop to 28 degrees above zero.

At our evening camps thousands of yards of carpeting would be spread on the level sands, and hundreds of the young dancing girls, very scantily clad in soft, clinging, bright-hued garments, would take their places on the carpets, and, to the sound of weird wind and stringed instruments, with drum and tambourine accompaniments, give us varied specimens of their voluptuous " cooche coochie " dance, lasting far into the night. The wonderful fascination that these dark-eyed and dark-hued maidens exercise over these desert-born Bedouins is very remarkable. They hold them with a hypnotic power, and sway them as the winds do the branches and foliage of the trees. Thus to the wanderers of these sandy wastes is life made tolerant. Throughout the long weary day of marching over the black and hot sands they look forward to the night of revelry and dancing, or to the fascination of gambling.

There is no twilight or rosy dawn in the desert. The moment the sun sinks a pall of darkness falls over the earth, just as if the lamp had been extinguished in your chamber. The day bursts upon you like pressing of the electric button. The sun simply flashes out at once without warning, and ushers in the day with all its brilliancy. Not a day passes that you do not see and feel the influence of the magic mirages. They certainly are of hypnotic birth. They hold you with an unseen power, and present to your wondering gaze the most beautiful pictures of lovely scenes, where you lie under the shade of wide-spreading trees, beside the margins of foaming rivers or grand lakes, over whose surfaces the snow-capped waves chase each other and break in sparkling foam at your feet. Or you see the peaceful village of your own nativity, clearly defined against the horizon of the desert. At other times the whole plain will be filled with beautiful groves of trees and green, grassy, cool, shady spots, with here and there a sparkling brooklet, with splashing waterfalls and small placid lakes sleeping in vales between rolling hills, and the camels and horses assume the appearance of houses and towering steepled churches, and the dark boulders of sand-polished stone rise as frowning castles, set upon unapproachable heights, all as real and true to the vision as the reality.

For five months this great caravan was my home. I soon got accustomed to the daily routine, and with the wild roving Bedouins I felt as much at home and at ease as I did on the wild Western plains with my Indian friends in my earlier days. When we reached the valley of the Nile, near the northern boundary of the Nubian Desert, our great caravan divided. Part went south to Khartoum, and I with another part went down the great valley to the city of Cairo. I wandered among the vast piles of ruins from Karnak to the mouth of the Nile, and examined every feature of them in detail as I did the fossilized remains of the flora and fauna of the icy regions of the far north.   The more I studied them, the more thoroughly I became convinced that it was here that ancient civilization ended instead of began.   These works were not those of men who were just learning how to build.   Their teachers and architects had had the experience of countless centuries of time.   It was this idea, conceived on the top of the largest of the pyramids, as I looked down at the other eight of the great structures that form this group, and the lion-man-headed sphynx, a thousand years older than the pyramids themselves, that gave me the impetus to wander the world over, in search of the ancestors and teachers of the builders of these pyramids and ruined cities.   For twenty-seven years I gave my time and money to this endeavor.   I left no stone unturned and braved every danger of land and sea with this end in view.   In my lectures on " America, the Old World," I have given you my conclusions on the subject which are not germane to this biographical sketch.

From Egypt I surveyed the pathway of the Israelites across the Red Sea into the Holy Land.   I camped upon the top of Sinai and listened to the weird sounds that are produced by the sands blown upward upon its summit and then, slowly trickling down its sides over large and small cavities, make mournful sounds.   As the winds blow gentle or strong and shift these musical sands in large or small quantities across these holes, some of which are deep and others shallow, soft, low sweet notes or weird unearthly sounds are produced. To one filled with superstition, and to the ignorant, these sounds have a terrifying effect.   Fear and dread seize upon the poor creatures, and they shake like an aspen leaf.   I bathed in the dense, slimy waters of the Dead Sea, and in the muddy, frothy stream of the Jordan, and in those of Galilee.   I mapped the streets and walls of Jerusalem, stood on Golgotha, and wandered in the garden of Gethsemane.   I ran a line of levels from Joppa through Jerusalem to the Dead Sea, and found that the Dead Sea was 1296 feet below the level of the Mediterranean Sea.

CHAPTER VI

Enlist in Russian army—Siege of Sevastopol—Rewarded
for marksmanship—Back to Austin—Death of my
mother—Explorations in Central and South America—
Enlistment in Confederate Army at Pensacola.

FROM the shores of the Holy Land to the Crimean
coast is not more than a thousand miles, and when the
allied armies of Turkey, France, England, and Sardinia flocked into the Black Sea, through the Dar-
danelles, I, too, went on board one of our vessels, the
Osprey. I landed at Balaklava, and went at once into
the Russian lines, and enlisted in the troop of Kioski
Cossacks that composed the body guard of Prince
Gortschykoff, and took part in the siege of Sevastopol.
This city held out for thirteen long months against
the combined allied armies. The British alone lost
over ninety thousand men; the Turks nearly twice as
many, and I have never heard what the French and
Sardinians lost. This was the greatest and the bloodiest war that had raged since the Napoleonic days of
the French empire. Lord Ragland of the British Army
was the nominal head of the allied armies, but he was
not much of a general. I do not care to go into the
merits or demerits of this war, but shall be brief in
my memoirs of it, although at the time it was a stupendous event in my life, for I was only twenty-five
years old when I entered the employ of the Tsar of
all the Russias.

To give you a clear understanding of the situation,
it will be necessary for me to give you a geographical
description of Sevastopol and its defenses. The Crimean peninsula is about 120 miles long, from its neck
at Perekop, where it is only five miles wide, with the
Black Sea on one side and the Sea of Azov
on the other, the Black Sea lying on the west and the
Sea of Azov on the east. From Perekop on the north
to Balaklava on the south it is 120 miles.

The city of Sevastopol is on an arm of the Black Sea that stretches inland for several miles, and comes to a sharp point where the River Tchernaya flows into it, making a splendid, deep harbor, several miles in extent. From this arm, about a mile east of the junction of the river, another arm of the sea forks, running almost due south for a mile and three-quarters. This also makes a very deep and fine harbor. On both sides of this latter arm, or harbor, and around its southern end sits the city of Sevastopol. The Crimean Peninsula from the city of Sevastopol juts out into the Black Sea almost due west for ten miles, and then turns, curving south and east, to the port of Balaklava, about sixteen miles south of east. This peninsula is indented with deep bays or arms of the sea, making the coast line very irregular, and in outline much like an Indian flint arrow head. The bays are formed by deep ravines entering the sea along the south side of the Sevastopol peninsula. The sea rolls against a rugged, rock-bound shore, overlooked by high bluffs, until you get to the port of Balaklava, where there is a small but safe harbor.

The battlefield of Inkerman is about five miles due east from Sevastopol, and on the banks of the Tchernaya River. The grounds around the city of Sevastopol are a succession of hills and ravines, each having a name. The main works, like the Malakoff, Redan, Mamelon Hill, etc., lie due east of the short arm of the sea, on what is known as the inner harbor. The ship docks, the barracks, and government works all lie on the east side of this inner harbor. Fort Nicholas on the west and Fort Paul on the east guard the mouth of this inner harbor, and all along the outer harbor line for several miles are splendid fortifications. The first bay west of the city of Sevastopol is called Quarantine Bay, and on its eastern point is Fort Quarantine; to the east of it is Fort Alexander. At Fort Alexander begins a series of batteries that extend entirely around Sevastopol, crossing Careenage Ravine, and ending on the shore of the outer harbor at a bluff known as the White Works, so named on account of the color of the soil of which they are constructed. The Malakoff sits between the Dock Ravine on the west and south, and the Careenage Ravine on the east, but much nearer Dock Ravine. The Mamelon Hill lies nearly east of the Malakoff, and the allied armies spread their lines on a great rim outside of all these works.

The Russians were under Prince Gortschakoff, Prince Menschekoff, General Saimonoff, and that great engineer, General Todleben; and the whole army, of course, under Czar Nicholas. It was from the heights of the Malakoff I saw the smoke and heard the guns of the famous charge of the Light Brigade at Balaklava, rendered famous by the poet Tennyson; and it was from this same point of view that I saw a part of the great battle of Inkerman, in which the Russian army of relief was driven back. Every ravine by which the Russians could approach had been doubly fortified, and charge after charge of the most desperate kind was repulsed by the allied forces.

The Malakoff was the key to the inner harbor, and the whole end and aim of the besiegers was to capture or reduce it. Here the bloodiest and most persistent efforts were made by the Turks and French. The Turks were the most reckless and daring of all the nations that opposed us. They are but wild fanatics, and believe that at death they will go straight to the Heaven, to a Paradise where they will have three hundred dishes of angel food served three times a day, on three hundred golden dishes, by a band of three hundred lovely female slaves; and where they will live in eternal bliss without a wish ungratified. This belief renders them fanatics, and induces them to court rather than shun death. It was in this war that the sharp-pointed minie ball was first used. It was hollowed like a lady's sewing thimble, with a solid point; the thin rear end by expansion filled the grooves of the rifle and prevented windage, thus giving the projectile greater force and speed, and reducing the curvature of the course of the bullet to a flatter plane. I had three rifles, one made by Mills of Kentucky, one by Philip Lambert of Galveston, Texas, and one by Schnider of Berlin, Germany. I would sit in a porthole of the Malakoff by the hour, and pick off the sappers and miners of the Turkish army. The Russian officers would watch my expertness through their glasses, and express their wonder in no unmistakable language. My rifle would be loaded by one of the soldiers and handed up to me. I would watch for the appearance of the head of a Turk as he heaved a spade full of earth up, and as it came in view I was ready; my ball would crash into his skull, and the spade would fall to the earth from a graspless hand. At each shot you could tell that my aim was true by the flight of the spade.

The most terrible bombardment that has ever jarred the earth in all history previous to that time took place while I was a defender of the Malakoff. The whole combined forces of England, France, Turkey, and Sardinia concentrated every available gun on both land and sea onto the citadel, and for nine days and nights there was a continuous fire poured into it. When they began to batter its walls with this iron hail it was three stories high; when they prepared to charge it was only a mass of débris, but stronger than ever, for we had strengthened it on the inside, and when they charged they met a terrible fire from under the earth as it were, against which they had no chance. As long as life lingers I can never forget the ceaseless roar and jar of that bombardment. I have seen the blood trickle from the ears of the men, as they slept, from the concussion of the explosion of the shells. Hundreds of these missiles of death were twenty-one inches in diameter, filled with musket balls glued to their inner sides with sulphur. This horrid shell would fill the cavities and bombproofs with a stifling gas that was terrible. We stood this awful thunder and roar without a moment's rest or cessation for nine days and nights. When the awful roar was over it seemed that every faculty that I possessed was numb, or dead, and it was many years after before I was myself again.

For the part I took in the defense of the Malakoff and for my marksmanship I was given the Iron Cross of Peter the Great, by Prince Gortschakoff, by com-

mand of the Czar Nicholas.   It was presented to me
in the presence of the whole Russian army, drawn up
in a hollow square, on the naval parade ground at
Sevastopol.

In leaving the Crimea in a few hours' sail I saw one
of the most sickening scenes of my whole life.   The
sea was covered for miles with the floating carcasses
of dead soldiers, and our paddle wheels would stir them
up like driftwood.   They were soldiers who had died
with the cholera, and had been weighted and thrown
into the sea.   The weights had became detached, the
swollen, bloated bodies had risen to the surface, and
the whole sea was a reeking mass of rotting carcasses
of human beings.   It was reported at the time that
the British alone lost ninety thousand men from the
cholera.

When I look back at those long-past days and think
of the awful scenes that I beheld in and around Sevastopol, a shudder creeps over me and I try to forget
it all, but memory is too strong.   At some unwonted
noise in the silence of the night, when roused from a
sound sleep, I hear that awful bombardment of the
Malakoff and feel the deafening roar.   It is only for
a moment, yet it leaves its impress on my brain.

On the trip home I was like one freed from a terrible bondage.   The soft, still beauty of the shores of
the Mediterranean Sea, as we steamed by them, seemed
a land of enchantment.   For hours I would sit alone on
the deck, and in a dreamy way throw the horrors of
Sevastopol behind me.   When we reached New York
I hastened aboard a vessel for New Orleans, and, on
reaching that port, I was soon on board a coaster for
Galveston.   I reached Austin, Texas, in the latter part
of May, and, after resting up a few days, I went with
my mother, who was in the last stages of consumption,
up to the Lampasas Springs, about sixty miles from
Austin, to try the effect of the water and outdoor life
upon her.   But it was of no avail, and at the end of a
month we returned.   On the 13th of July her pure
spirit winged its flight back to the God who gave it.
In the lonely watch, by the side of her inanimate dust,

I sat the livelong night, and reviewed every event of my whole life. When they laid her to rest in the village cemetery I felt as one deserted upon a barren isle in a trackless sea.

I left at once for the wilds of Central and South America. Until December 21, 1860, I was an explorer and civil engineer in some part of that region of the earth. Under Henry Meigs, who had a contract under Totten and Trautwine, I aided in building a railway across the Isthmus of Panama, and for a while in 1858 I acted as private secretary to General M. B. Lamar (after whom I was named), while he was minister from the United States to Nicaragua. In the latter part of October, 1859, I came back to Texas with him, and on the 19th of November, about ten o'clock in the morning, he passed away from an apoplectic stroke. I returned at once to Managua, and thence to Lake Titicaca, and began a long journey up the ancient macadam road that was built by the first civilized people of earth. I followed this road, with all its meanderings, for fifteen hundred miles; past the ruins of hundreds of cities, and through vast forests of petrified trees, whose trunks have lain for countless centuries; across the ruined walls and sculptured statuary of many ancient cities that were in ruins and deserted ages before the pyramids of Egypt or the foundation stones of Baalbec or Palmyra were dreamed of.

In the last days of December, 1860, I reached the mouth of the Ulna River in Honduras, and learning from a small fruit steamer just out of New Orleans that Abraham Lincoln, one of the old abolitionists and one of the worst enemies of my sunny Southland, had been elected President, I gave up my work and went at once to the United States. Finding that South Carolina had already withdrawn from the Union, I went with a party to Pensacola, Florida, and aided in the capture of Forts McCrea, Barancas, the Redoubt, and the Navy Yard. I insisted that we should above all others take Fort Pickens, and send Lieutenant Slimmer home, but I was not in command and was overruled.

I stayed in and around the port of Pensacola, doing guard, and other duties, until some time in the month of March, 1861, when I went up to Jackson, Miss., to see my father, whom I had not seen since the death of my mother. He had married again, and was living about fifteen miles from Jackson. Here I spent a few days, and hearing that a company was being organized at Jackson to go to the front, or seat of war, wherever that might be, I at once joined this company; it was called the Mississippi Rifles, and the original company was at one time commanded by Jeff Davis, and was a part of the regiment he commanded at the battle of Buena Vista in the war with Mexico. For the first time in my life I enrolled under my own name. We went at once to Pensacola, and on the 13th of April, 1861, we were regularly mustered into service. We elected Moses Phillips, of the Yazoo County company, our colonel.

On signing the muster roll each man put down after his name the term of days, months, or years he would serve in the army. When I signed I wrote in a clear and distinct hand, " Forty years, or the war." I was then in my thirty-second year, and I thought that by the time I was seventy-two my life's race would be run, and I could retire with an honorable record, spend the remainder of my life in some pleasant, quiet spot, and dream of the past. Many of my comrades, to whom I was an entire stranger——I had never met a single one of them before I became a member of the company ——exclaimed at my foolishness in writing such a long term of enlistment after my name. I cited the civil wars of the Romans, and the thirty years' war of the Spaniards, and the war of the Roses in England, and said that I thought that we could fight as long as any people on earth, and that the Yankees would do the same; that they had all the ships and could hire all the foreigners, and bring as many as they wished from every clime under the sun. I said that we would have to fight our battles alone without any aid from abroad, as we did not have a friend among all the nations of the globe. They laughed and made fun at my predictions, and said that the war would be over and all of them except me be at home before Christmas. I was guyed at every point by the boys as one who "knew it all." I had been a hermit apart from my fellow-man so long that their jibes fell on dull and unheeding ears, and I kept on the even tenor of my way. In later years my old comrades have made amends and ap-plauded my acts in those long-ago days, and profited by the example I set.

My recollections of those early days of the beginning of the great Confederate war are growing dim, as the years go by, but there are some things that cannot be forgotten, and several are indelibly impressed on memory's tablet.

Once we were issued rations of condemned salt-bar-reled beef. The boys resented this and we dumped each man's share on a great improvised litter, and, with our muskets draped with strips of black cloth tied to each bayonet, with fife and drum muffled, we marched around the entire encampment, then behind the com-missary's tent, where we dug a deep hole and deposited the salt junk, popped three caps each in military style, and set up a headboard with this inscription in white chalk: "Here lies old Ned, strong in life, in death still stronger."

We suffered from various kinds of insects, especially flies and mosquitos. The latter were very annoying, but fleas were the most tormenting. They seemed to be the product of the sand of the beach—they were all over the face of the earth and clung to you like leeches. I hung my hammock as high as I could reach between two small pine trees. Before going to rest I would strip on the ground, hang my clothing on an adjoining limb of a tree, and, with a brush, dust myself from head to foot. Then I would break as hard and fast as I could run, and leap up to my hammock, and wipe the sand and fleas that might have clung to me as I ran. Thus I would be able to avoid many of these vicious, blood-thirsty pests, otherwise they would keep me in a constant torment during the night. When we bathed, many of the boys were speckled with their bites, until they looked as if they had measles, or some skin disease.

My friend, Sergeant Louis Burt, was taken with typhoid fever and I went to the hospital to assist in nursing him. At this time the measles broke out in camp, and many of the men were very ill. The first death in our ranks was our colonel, Moses Phillips.

On the 20th of June I was transferred from Company A, of the 10th Mississippi, to Company K, the Burt Rifles, of the 18th Mississippi Regiment. My father was captain of the company, and Sergeant Louis Burt's father was colonel of the regiment. It was stationed at Manassas, in Virginia. I left Pensacola on the evening of the 20th of June, and on the 25th I reached Camp Walker at Manassas, and reported for duty. I received a letter from Sergeant Burt, thanking me for my kindness in nursing him through his long spell of illness, and Colonel Burt also received one from Colonel Robert A. Smith, of the 10th, my former captain, calling his attention to my kind ministrations to his son. These letters were very gratifying to me, as I was an entire stranger to every man in the 18th Regiment at that time, except, of course, my father.

CHAPTER VII

Life in camp—Opening guns of the war—The first battle—
My father's bravery—Intense thirst saves me from an
untimely grave—In the hospital—On guard.

LIFE in camp was very dull, and on the 17th of July,
in company with a few of the boys, we went on a
scout hunting for fruits and vegetables, chickens, or
any edibles to add to our camp fare. Many of the
citizens around Manassas were truck farmers, and had
been in the habit of supplying the markets of Washington City with supplies. Many of them were full-
blooded Yankee South-haters, and strong Unionists,
acting as spies for the Yankee army during the movements of our troops in and around Manassas.

The morning we went on our scout we came to a
peach orchard on the east side of the pike that led to
Washington. Several of the boys were up in the trees
gathering peaches, when a Yankee cavalryman came
down the pike from the direction of Washington, and
ordered them out of the grounds. I was on the outside of the orchard farthest from the pike, and had a
good view of all the surroundings. When I saw that
it was a Yankee soldier that had given the order to
get out, I turned to Hal McGee of my company and
said that we had as much or more right to gather
peaches there than that Yankee had, as we were on
our own Southern soil, and that we should not obey
him or any other Northerner. Hal agreed with me.
The boys were leaving the orchard and climbing over
the back fence, when I got up on the fence, and in a
loud tone told the Yankee that if he did not leave and
mind his own business I would send a bullet after him.
He rode right up to the fence from the pike, stuck
his horse's head above the rails, and said:

" What did you say? "

I repeated my order, and he threw open his breast with both hands and said:

" Shoot, you d—— Rebel ! "

I did not hesitate. The white face of his horse and the white front of his open breast was a fine target. I raised my old Savage pistol and fired. My bullet sped true to the mark, and he tumbled from his horse without a sound. His horse whirled off up the pike toward Fairfax Court House. I went over to where he lay on the edge of the pike, and most of the boys followed me. We held a consultation and concluded that we had better bury him where he lay. We sent one of our negroes to the nearest house to borrow spades and picks, and on his return we dug a grave and laid the Yankee in and covered him up. I took a part of a plank from the fence and with a knife and pencil I wrote upon it this obituary :

> " *A Yankee host, a mighty band,*
> *Came down to take our Southern land,*
> *But this low barren spot*
> *Was all that this d——d Yankee got."*

Some of the boys were indignant at the want of feeling I displayed in the matter, and made bold to say so, reproving me openly and in no uncertain ways. I told them that they would in the end be more callous and used to death; that I had not a particle of feeling in the matter; that I was only a soldier, and that it was my duty to kill an enemy and defend my country. It was for this purpose that I had enlisted, and I would so continue until a bullet from an enemy sent me to join the great band that had gone before to the shores of eternity. The killing of this one soldier was the first death that many of them had ever witnessed, and I was often asked if it did not make me feel bad, to which I replied that I had no feeling in the matter.

The advance of Scott's great army of invasion began on the 18th of July, and our pickets and the Yanks had their first skirmish. We were held in readiness all day to move at a moment's warning, and listened to the irregular firing. At about daylight on Sunday morning, the 21st, we heard the opening guns of the first great battle of the Confederate war. Every man was ready and anxious to meet the advancing Yankees, and to test the prowess of the Southern arms against the North. The firing was steadily approaching and we felt and knew that our forces were being driven back by the Yankees. I saw many a lip pale as the sound of the cannon grew louder and nearer. Suddenly a shell flew over our heads, and every man at once assumed the position of a soldier. A courier dashed up and handed a dispatch to General D. R. Jones, our commander, and in a few moments came the sharp command:

"Forward, double-quick, march."

We trotted in the direction of the roll of musketry and the quick, heavy crack of the rifled Parrott guns. After about a mile and a half of double-quicking, with here and there the hiss of a deadly minie, the shriek of a shell, or the hum of a solid shot above our heads, we halted. We could hear the yells of the Confederates and the huzzahs of the Yanks; louder and nearer they came. The excitement was intense, and we wondered why they would not let us go on. Several of our officers and a few men went forward to the top of a hill that was in front of us, and were gone some time. In the meantime the roll of musketry was increasing, and we were standing stock-still in an open field, but near the skirts of a small belt of timber.

For a while the incessant roar of the musketry increased, and the huzzahs of the Yankees seemed to grow fainter, and we saw our officers returning. Again a courier galloped up and gave our general another dispatch. We were about-faced, and in a double-quick, hurried back past our starting point, and on down in the direction of Union Mills, far on our extreme right, some five miles from the fight at the Henry house. We crossed Bull Run and stopped under a hill, and were ordered to rest in line. Many of the men looked pale and exhausted, and fell down from the long run of five miles. I leaned on my musket and retained my position in the ranks. My father rested against one of the small saplings close by. Presently an old gentleman of General D. R. Jones' staff, Colonel J. J. B. White, came dashing up from our rear and rode to the front. Orders were given to "fall in," and the lines were instantly formed. Shells began to burst around us in close proximity. I saw one cover Colonel White and his horse with smoke and dust, but it did not injure him.

We were moved forward in the direction of the cannonading, and crossed over a hill into a small valley, through which flowed a small branch, and in a crooked road, with our left in the front, we marched alongside of this branch. Its banks were about eight feet high above the water and almost perpendicular, with blackberry vines between us and the branch.

While in this narrow valley we came in sight of the Yankees posted on a hill, directly in our front, and with a line of skirmishers to the right and left of us on high hills. I could look right into the mouth of a ten-gun battery, and could see a brigade of regulars of the old United States Army on the brow of the hill below it. We heard a voice sing out in a clear, sharp tone:

"Are you friends?"

Not a sound was uttered by us, but our hands were raised for silence, and the signal passed down the line. Our colors were rolled up in an oilcloth cover, and never unfurled during the day that I am aware of. We marched straight ahead and kept our eyes on the Yankees in our front. Again came the voice from the Yanks, but we paid not the slightest attention to it, and marched on toward them. They ordered us to halt, but we did not obey. Then came the command, "Ready," and involuntarily each of us cocked his gun, but did not halt. We heard the command given by the Yanks, "Aim," and saw every one of their guns come into position, like clockwork. Before the word "Fire" rang out, every man of us, with the exception of a dozen or more, jumped through the blackberry thicket into the bottom of the branch, and the two volleys of the Yanks were poured into vacant space, and we felt the wind of the bullets as they passed over our heads.

Some of the guns of the boys were discharged as they reached the bottom of the branch. Cass Oltenberg's gun jarred me as it went off not more than a foot from my head. Just after the Yankees gave us their volleys from the front, rear and side, someone gave the order for us to charge. Up we rose out of the branch, and, with a loud yell, rushed straight at the nearest body of Yanks As we mounted the top of the steep bank and went toward the hill on which the Yanks were, we came to the top of a steep bluff that we could not get down. There they poured a galling fire into us which we returned, but it was foolish for us to stand exposed to the fire of a whole brigade of infantry and ten rifled Parrott guns. Father at once ordered us to follow him, and led us by the right flank into the rear of their line. Every man who was in the sound of his voice followed him. I was shot just as we reached the top of the bluff, and lay there until ten o'clock that night. I heard the first volley our boys poured into the brigade from their rear, and heard the awful roar of the retreating Yanks as the volley, delivered in their rear, surprised them. They thought that they were surrounded and cut off from their line of retreat.

For his daring act my father was complimented by General Beauregard in his official report of the battle. I have tried to give you a brief description of the part I took in this great battle, which should have been one of the most decisive of the whole war, for we had the Yankees at our mercy, and could have entered their capital. This was the desire of Generals Joseph E. Johnston, E. Kirby Smith, Stonewall Jackson, and Beauregard, but President Davis ordered otherwise, and prevented us, thus turning our great and glorious victory into nothingness.

I can never forget those long hours I lay, on that July Sunday, in the blazing sun after I fell on the top of the bluff. The roar of the cannon was around me, and the incessant hiss of the deadly minies, as they threw the dust into my eyes and ears, was fearful. I could not move hand or foot. We sometimes live a whole lifetime in a few short minutes, but here I had hours, and they were fearfully long ones at that. I was not in any very great pain, as I was completely paralyzed. My neck was twisted, and my chin rested against my backbone; I was doubled up into a short space, and wedged in a small gully.

Toward night everything grew dim and confused, and the silence of death fell on the field. Close by me a little drummer boy was lying, cut nearly in two by a cannon ball. His blood and entrails had been scattered over me until I, too, looked as if torn to pieces. Near my feet lay Captain McWillie, a son of Governor McWillie of Mississippi. I saw my father, as he passed, raise his arm to his eyes to hide my body from his view, and pass on with his men to the front. It was not long before my eyes began to grow dim; everything had put on a lurid glare, then it faded to a yellow tinge, then to a dark blue, and finally to a black; I tried to speak, but my tongue and throat, like the rest of my body, were numb, and would give no response to my efforts. My brain and thoughts alone were active. I felt no pain, only a tingling sensation, just as you feel when any of your limbs are asleep.

Some time in the night I heard the approach of voices and the tramp of men. Soon I heard the sound of picks and spades and caught the gleam of lanterns, and knew a burial party was on the field, and that surgeons, with their attendants, had come to pick up and care for the wounded. Again and again I tried to speak, but no sound came. Presently I felt the jar of the picks and spades as they dug a grave by my side, and then I felt a strong hand grasp my head and another my feet, and lift me clear of the ground. There was a sharp click, and then a loud buzzing sound in my ears, and my whole body was in an agony of pain. A fearful thirst tortured me. I spoke, and my friends let me drop suddenly to the ground. The jar awoke every faculty to life. I asked for water, and at once a strong light was flashed in my face, a rubber canteen applied to my lips, and I felt a life-giving stream of cold, refreshing water flow down my swollen throat, and seemingly into every part of my frame. I was carefully lifted from the ground and placed upon a caisson box of a captured cannon. I saw them lay the mangled form of the drummer boy in the grave which they were preparing for me.

I was carried to a large house, across Bull Run, several miles from our part of the battlefield, and laid on a mattress on the floor in a large room with folding doors. There were some nine or ten other wounded men in the room, and all were South Carolinians, as I soon learned from their conversation, and belonged to the 5th Regiment, which was a part of our brigade.

Soon after the South Carolina burial party had removed me from the field, my father, with another party of our own regiment, passed over the ground, and seeing the grave of the little drummer boy, took it for mine. Upon returning to camp my father ordered a casket from Richmond to send my body home in.

About five days after the battle we were moved from the house and placed in comfortable cots in hospital tents, and every care given us possible under the circumstances. On the day that we were moved into the open air, my negro boy George was passing by and I hailed him. My neck was swollen fearfully, my thigh was black up to my waist, and I was in some pain. My negro recognized my voice, and came at once to where I was lying. The look on his face made me smile. Knowing the superstition of the negro, I asked him if my father had escaped unhurt in the battle? He stammered for a while before he could reply, and said:

"De bullets just raised two big welks, one under Old Massa's left arm and one clean across his back, like you hit him wid a club; and I done patched up de holes de bullets make."

I told him to go and tell father where I was, and to come and take me to our own hospital. He said:

"Lord, Mas Lamar, Old Massa done saunt to Richmond for your coffin, and gwine to send you back home in it."

As soon as he delivered this information, he broke off in a trot for our camp, and in an exceedingly short time I saw my father and Dr. Holloway, our surgeon, with George and Eli, my father's body-servant, come in sight, and I felt that all was well. I was moved to our own regimental hospital, and under skillful nursing was able to get up and move around, but Drs. Isom and Holloway both said that I would never again be fitted for infantry service. My casket came, and the remains of Captain McWillie were sent home in it. I read a very flattering obituary of myself in the Richmond papers, and learned of the details of the great battle, in which I took so small a part.

I could relate many incidents that are yet fresh in my memory of that, our first encounter with the Yanks, but it would make this volume too large and tiresome.

We were joined by the 13th Mississippi and the 8th Virginia, and sent to Leesburg, soon after the men were rested up. Our brigade was then composed of the 13th, 17th, and 18th Mississippi Regiments, and the 8th Virginia, all under General Nathanael Greene Evans of South Carolina. Toward the last of July we went into camp near the town, and pickets were placed along the banks of the Potomac. Captain Duff's company, of the 17th Mississippi, was at a large spring above Leesburg, and our Company K, of the 18th Mississippi, near Goose Creek, below Leesburg.

Instead of being discharged, I took a transfer to Company I, Captain John D. Alexander's company, the Campbell Rangers, from Lynchburg, of the 2d Virginia Cavalry, commanded at the time by a Colonel Radford, and afterward by Colonel T. T. Munford. Our company was attached to Evans' brigade, and we had to do picket duty from above Point of Rocks, down to near Dranesville, only a short way out from Washington City.

In the cavalry company to which I had been transferred I was an absolute stranger, not even having a single personal acquaintance. Among the men was a young married man, William Moore by name, who was also a stranger in the company. I think he was from

Botetourt County, near the line of Bedford County, just under the Peaks of Otter. Young Moore and I soon formed a close friendship that was cemented and strengthened in a common cause, and we loved with a love as close as that which brothers feel. We were as inseparable as twins. We ate and slept together. On picket and guard duties we were always together, and we had little pocket editions of our favorite poets, his being Burns, and mine Byron. Together we would sit under the shade of overhanging rocks or trees while on the lonely picket posts, and read poems from our favorites to each other.

On a certain day, the 6th of August, we were together below Goose Creek and not a great way from Dranesville, when we received a large bundle of delayed mail matter, the mails having been cut off by the movements of the army before the late battle of Manassas. In that mail was a long and patriotic letter from Moore's wife, and in it a ferrotype of his two little babes. He read me parts of this letter, and while we were reading the papers and commenting on the battle there came a hail from a Yankee picket across the Potomac opposite us. He asked if we would exchange papers with him, if we had any late ones. We at once answered that we would. He asked us to meet him in the middle of the river. I arose and walked down to the water's edge, divested myself of clothing, and, taking several copies of the Richmond papers in my hand, I waded out and met my Yankee friend, and made the exchange. For a while we stood and conversed about the great battle, and he kindly invited me to cross to his side of the river and take dinner with him, as it was about dinner time. I accepted his invitation, and together we went into his camp where there were about thirty Yankees, under command of a lieutenant. I put on a Yankee overcoat, and sat and conversed with these men for some half hour or so, and told them of the part I took in the battle. Now and then we could hear the crack of a rifle, up or down the river as the pickets would fire at each other, and the lieutenant said that if we would stop this firing at our post, he would. I at once agreed to this, and he drew up an agreement in duplicate, and we both signed it. At this moment dinner was served, and I ate a hearty meal, better than I had had since the battle.

After dinner they brought clay pipes with short stems, made of chalk or some such substance, and a lot of tobacco stems, cut up into fine and coarse strips. I lit one and the taste and smell was not at all like tobacco. I asked if they could give me a chew, and they gave me a short, narrow plug of a very dark-looking substance that did not at all taste or resemble tobacco. I turned to the lieutenant and asked if this was the kind of tobacco they used all the time, and he replied that it was what the commissary issued to them, and that they had no other. I then told him to let my friend of the morning return with me and I would send them some real old Virginia chewing and smoking tobacco. He agreed, and the Yank and I returned to our side of the river. I gave Moore a description of my trip, and told him for what purpose the Yank had returned my visit. We gave him several plugs of fine Lynchburg chewing, and half a dozen twists of the very best smoking tobacco. I took pains to tie them all to a stout pole, long enough to feel his way while crossing the river, for any deep holes that he might stumble into. After he returned, we saw a good many of them come down to the river, and strip and take a swim. They thanked us for the tobacco, as they swam halfway across, and said that they were glad that they could take a bath without having to dodge bullets, and that they hoped the war would soon be over and we could all go home. Moore and I sat on the bank in full view, watched their sports, and read the Northern version of the great battle, and the various causes of their defeat. The principal excuse was our use of masked batteries and our overwhelming numbers.

When night came I went on guard duty at six o'clock, and Moore made down our pallet in a small shady place, sheltered by a dense foliage, just back of the spot that overlooked the river, and just under where we had sat and read the papers. A small ravine led into the river, and a wet weather spring trickled down from near our sheltered camp. Moore used both our blankets, and a lot of pine straw and brush made a nice soft bed, and he retired to dream of home and his loved ones. I walked my beat in silence and kept a watchful eye upon the river, listening to the bugles of the Yankees and the sounds from their camps. An occasional song would swell upon the air until the tattoo would sound, then all sank into silence, except the cry of the sentinels, such as:

" Post No. 9, ten o'clock, and all's well."

Just before the midnight hour arrived, it became a little chilly, and I went up near the spot where we had read the papers, and gathered a lot of dry pine limbs and brush, and built up a bright, blazing fire. I could see several such, far up and down the river on the opposite side.

CHAPTER VIII

Comrade Moore shot on relieving me of picket duty—My vow of vengeance—Writing the poem, " All Quiet Along the Potomac "—Stricken with measles—" The massacre at Ball's Bluff "—Our life at winter quarters near Leesburg.

WHEN my fire was at its brightest, I stepped down to where Moore was in a deep sleep, and roused him to take my place on guard. He rose at once and made his way to the fire. I knelt down and was smoothing out the wrinkles in our bed, sheltered from the direct rays of the firelight, when I saw a flash on the walls of the ravine and heard the thud of a bullet. I rose and saw Moore, with his gun resting on the ground and his arms stretched out, sink to the earth. I ran at once to him, saw a gush of blood pour from his skull, and his brains scattered over the pile of papers on which he had fallen. In large bold type were the headlines staring me in the face, " All quiet along the Potomac to-night." I could see nothing further—the words burned in my brain and obscured everything else.

I dragged his body away from the fire, and for a while was dazed. At last reason asserted itself. I felt that I was a murderer—that I had, without provocation, murdered my dearest and best friend in cold blood. I trembled like an aspen leaf, as I gazed upon his cold, bloody, inanimate form, and thought of his wife and orphaned babes in their far-off mountain cot. I felt that I had kindled that fire, and invited him to his death.

I gathered his things together, and made a bundle of them for the express. I took my place on the picket line, and, no matter where I turned my gaze, I could only see his blood and brains scattered on that paper, and hear the thud of the bullet that had sent him into eternity. While in this state of mind, I wondered why I had kindled that fire and sent my comrade to his long home? When I remembered the compact I had

that day made on the opposite shore of the river with
the Yankee officer, and remembered the crowd that had
gone in swimming in full reach of my rifle, it all became plain, and I had a breath of reason for the kin-
dling of that blaze. I did not feel that I was a
murderer any longer, but that I had trusted too much
in the honor of a treacherous foe, and was only guilty
to that extent. I breathed a sigh of relief, and watched
the opposite shore with a vengeful eye.

Toward the breaking of the day I again looked upon
the form of my friend, and above his dead body I registered a solemn vow to high Heaven that I would
avenge his death, and during the continuance of the
war would never again trust to the promises of any
Yankee, under any consideration. How well I kept my
oath of vengeance, I let the annals of my country tell.
Sufficient to say that when I glanced along the barrel
of my rifle and touched the trigger, it was with a
prayer, and the bullet winged its flight to the heart of
my enemy with the thought of my dead comrade to
guide it. Never did I let an opportunity to send one
to his long home escape me. I felt a fiendish delight
in shooting them.

It was while in this frame of mind that I penned
these verses to the memory of my murdered friend, who
sleeps in a lonely grave, far from the home of his loved
ones.

" All quiet along the Potomac," they say,
　Except here and there a stray picket
Is shot, as he walks on his beat to and fro,
　By a rifleman hid in a thicket.

It's nothing; a private or two now and then
　Will not count in the news of the battle,
Not an officer lost; only one of the men
　Moaning out all alone the death rattle.

All quiet along the Potomac to-night,
　Where the soldiers lie peacefully dreaming;
Their tents in the rays of the clear autumn moon
　Or in the light of their camp-fires gleaming.

A tremulous sigh, as a gentle night wind
　Through the forest leaves softly is creeping,
While the stars up above, with their glittering eyes,
　Keep guard o'er that army while sleeping.

There's only the sound of the lone sentry's tread
  As he tramps from the rock to the fountain,
And thinks of the two on the low trundlebed
  Far away in the cot on the mountain.

His musket falls slack and his face dark and grim
  Grows gentle with memories tender,
As he mutters a prayer for the children asleep—
  For their mother, may heaven defend her.

The moon seems to shine as brightly as then,
  That night when the love yet unspoken
Leaped up to his lips and when low murmured vows
  Were pledged to be ever unbroken.

Then drawing his sleeve roughly over his eyes
  He dashes off tears that are welling,
And gathers his gun close up to its place
  As if to keep down the heart's swelling.

He passes the fountain, the blasted pine tree,
  The footsteps are lagging and weary,
Yet onward he goes through the broad belt of light,
  Toward the shades of the forest so dreary.

Hark! Was it the night wind rustled the leaves?
  Was it moonlight so wondrously flashing?
It looked like a rifle; Ah, Mary, good-bye,
  And the life blood is ebbing and splashing.

All quiet along the Potomac to-night;
  No sound save the rush of the river;
While soft falls the dew on the face of the dead,
  That picket's "off duty" forever.

I did not write this in a day, but from the 6th until the 9th of August I strove to make it in accord with my feelings. On the 9th it was complete as above, and I gave it to my comrades. Hundreds of copies were sent out by the boys of our brigade to friends, sweethearts, wives, and sisters, as well as mothers and fathers. I gave autograph copies to several ladies of Leesburg, among them Miss Eva Lee, the sister-in-law of the mayor of the town; also to the Misses Hempstone. The latter set it to music and used to sing it to the boys to some familiar air. So many of the men wanted copies that I took a copy to the editor of the county paper, and had a thousand printed on small strips of paper. These I gave to whoever asked me for a copy. I think that all the members of my own and Captain Duff's company, of the 17th Mississippi Regiment, were given copies. Mr. J. H. Hewitt, a bandmaster, asked for a copy, and I gave him an autograph copy, and a written permission for him to set it to music. I think that at least five thousand copies went out to the public from Leesburg, a month before the battle of Leesburg, or Ball's Bluff, as the Yankees called it. Early in September, several members of the 20th Massachusetts Regiment, U. S. A., in camp near Poolesville, Md., opposite Leesburg, were in possession of it and sent it home to their friends in the North at that time. On the 19th of August, 1861, I sent President Davis an engrossed copy, with my compliments, and received a nice letter in reply, which I took great pride in showing to the boys of my company. Mr. Hewitt set it to the air that soon became familiar to every soldier in our army, and Mr. Julian A. Selby, of Columbia, S. C., published, and copyrighted it in the Confederate States, before it was published in the North. The first printed copy I saw of Selby's music was at Richmond, in the first days of November, 1861. I sent it to my father at Jackson, Miss.

I tried to throw into this poem the ardor of my inmost soul, so that to the soldiers that were along the Potomac in those wild heroic days of our great struggle, it would breathe the true animus of their souls. And I am satisfied that when a true soldier, be he of the Gray or Blue, reads that poem, he can see the stars shining through the tree tops that waved above his head in the silent watches on the lonely picket lines. He can hear the thud of a bullet as it strikes a tree or comrade; he can hear the clear notes of the bugle as it sounds taps and lights out; the far-off neigh of a horse, and the distant boom of a gun. It is replete with life, love, memory, and death; and it will live as long as the memory of that great Confederate war. It came straight from the heart of a soldier who was an active participant in that stupendous struggle, that never before had its counterpart on the face of the globe. It is a monument of word painting that will endure as long as the civilized white man exists on earth. Time and the plural actions of the elements of nature disintegrate the carved granite, and crumble into dust the brazen images made by the hand of man, but the thoughts are a part of deity, and can never perish. When given out to the world they go on the wings of the wind, sounding down the dim aisles of the temple of eternity, imperishable forever.

It is with pride that I now look back through the lapse of forty-five years at those long passed days, and I need no more lasting monument or mead of wealth to leave as a legacy to my children and grandchildren, than that poem, " All quiet along the Potomac."

The routine of camp life and picket guard, with an occasional skirmish here and there along our lines, kept us from the terrible ennui that the soldier feels, but here and there nostalgia would assert its baleful influence on some poor soldier. In September the camp measles became an epidemic, and we lost many noble men. I was stricken and carried to the hospitable home of the Rev. Mr. Nourse, a Presbyterian minister, where I was kindly cared for, and, on the 19th of October, I resumed my place in the company and answered to roll call.

On the morning of the 21st, as I was relieved from picket duty, just below Point of Rocks near the old Mason plantation, above Leesburg on the Potomac, I heard considerable skirmish firing below Conrad's Ferry, at Big Spring, where Captain Duff's company of the 17th Mississippi, was on duty. I put my horse into a gallop and was soon opposite them, on the river road, and could see that the Yankees had crossed the river and that our boys were giving them the best that they were able, under the circumstances. The company was retreating toward Leesburg, not all together, but in squads, each squad loading and firing as it fell back, but not seeming to be in a hurry or much excited. I kept abreast and a little in the rear, watching for the enemy, who was invisible to me. As I passed the west end of the old Ball field, I looked in the direction of

Leesburg and saw the Confederates on the move. I could see a color or two flying, and could see handkerchiefs and small flags waving from some of the upper windows of the houses in the town. Suddenly, as I glanced my eyes across a field of shocked corn in the direction of the river, I saw a Yankee come out of the woods nearly opposite me, get up on the back fence, and look, with his glasses, toward the town. I jumped from my horse, and, with the reins over my arm, I sent a rifle ball through him. He hung halfway across the fence, and there he was two days after the battle was over. I remounted my horse, after loading my rifle, and galloped into Leesburg, just as the 18th Mississippi was hurrying through. I joined them, as my own command was absent, and with my father's old company I went into the battle.

For long years afterward this battle was called, in the Yankee histories, " The Massacre at Ball's Bluff." In reality it was a terrible slaughter of the lager beer Dutch from Philadelphia, under command of Colonel Baker. Our company was thrown forward as skirmishers as soon as we crossed the corn field and entered the woods. We descended a gentle slope and suddenly came right upon a Yankee regiment only a few feet off. We called for their surrender, and our guns were leveled directly in their faces. Instantly they reversed their arms and went through the motion of surrendering. Just at this moment another Yankee regiment obliquely to our right poured a volley toward us, and we turned and fired at them. Just as our front rank delivered their volley, the surrendered regiment poured a deadly volley into us at close range, and here we lost some of our best men, among them John Pettus, a son of our Governor. I had not fired and instantly sent a shot into the brain of the nearest Yankee, and like demons we drove our bayonets and clubbed guns into their treacherous ranks, sparing none.

We dropped into a small ravine that ran parallel to the river. Our regiment was on the slope of a hill behind us and many feet above us. In our front was a thicket, very dense, of mountain laurel, and I could see nothing. To me it was like looking for a bear in a Mississippi canebrake, where the dogs are baying around you, and the animal not in sight. The little drain that I was in was about three feet deep, and a sapling about eight inches in diameter was just in front of me, not more than a foot from my head. I at once saw the great advantage and protection I had, if we could only hold our position. Soon the rattle of the musketry began, and the bullets flew high above our heads. The smoke rose in dense columns out of the laurel thicket, and the roar was deafening. We shot volley after volley into this obstruction that hid our view, and soon the thicket seemed to melt, and disappear. Here and there a glimpse of a Yankee could be caught, and our fire from the skirmish line began to increase. Before an hour had elapsed the laurel thicket had been mowed down, and our field was clear. I then began to single out my Yank, and with a steady, deadly aim I hunted a belt buckle as my target. Every time I touched the trigger I thought of my murdered comrade, Moore, of the lonely picket line, and of the morning treachery when John Pettus was sacrificed.

Our ammunition was getting low, and the enemy in front of us some ten lines deep, seemed to increase in numbers, as the places of their dead were instantly filled. I was afraid that we would have to fall back from our chosen ground, but my fears were unfounded, for I saw the " powder monkey," in the shape of a member of our regiment, making his way up our ravine with an ample supply. My cartridge box and pockets were soon overflowing. I shot coolly and deliberately, as if firing at an ordinary target for a prize. I did not want a shot to go astray; and I don't believe that a single one did. Night had fallen and the flash of the Yankee muskets threw sparks almost into our faces, we were so close to them. The fire seemed to be on the increase. I had torn most of the front of my shirt away, and used it on the end of my ramrod to keep my gun clean and unchoked, and, as I had to wet it each time by holding it a moment in my mouth, before wiping the rifle out, of course I was as black and powder stained as I could well be. My hair and eyebrows were singed from the escaping flashes of my open gun tube on which the cap rested.

About sundown, as the twilight began to grow dim, there came a clear and very distinct command to us from the rear:

" Drive them into the Potomac, or into h——! G—— d—— 'em ! "

With a loud and fiendish yell we arose as a single man, and, with our bayonets fixed, we made a quick dash at them. They broke, and yelling like fiends incarnate we pursued, each man doing his best to catch and bayonet a Yank. I singled out a big Dutchman who weighed about 250 pounds, but, do all I could, I could not gain much upon him. When close enough to hurl my rifle spear fashion at him, I did so, and as the sharp saber bayonet struck him full in the back he disappeared as if the earth had swallowed him, just at the edge of what I thought was a thicket of underbrush. I halted at the very edge of it, and as I halted I heard the thud of a heavy body falling far under me. My Dutchman had dropped over a bluff onto the solid rock, fifty-two feet below us, and I had come very nearly following him. The discovery made me feel nervous for a moment, as I paused on the brink of the abyss. But I did not stop long. I heard the voice of my captain cry out, " Burt Rifles, rally on me ! " I snatched up a deserted musket, examined it as I ran, and gathering up a cartridge box and belt, I reached the captain, as he stood on the top of the bluff looking down into the river. He said:

" Do you boys see that boat load of Yanks out there trying to get away? Give them a volley, and don't let one escape you. They may be a part of those scoundrels that slaughtered us this morning. Ready, aim, fire ! "

We poured a deadly volley into them, as they were huddled like turtles upon a log on a genial summer's day. We emptied the rear of the boat of its human freight, and the front end, which was overcrowded, went to the bottom, I suppose. Soon the water was covered with a mass of men struggling and making for the opposite shore—but none of that boat load ever reached it. We stood and loaded and shot at every head, or wave, or riffle of water that appeared on the surface.

When all was still I sank like a rock, exhausted and utterly worn out, right upon the top of the bluff where I had fired my last shot. When I awoke, a fine misty rain was falling, and I was wet and stiff. I could see men raising up from all around me with sunken, haggard looks and powder-blackened faces. The sun was high up in the heavens, as we began to look around us and ask for our commands. All were in the same boat, and no one knew who we were, except that we were on the banks of a river, and on the edge of the battlefield. That was all. We did not know the result of the battle—whether we or the Yanks had been victorious. We only knew that we had driven those in front of us into the river, and killed all we saw.

Slowly each one of us got up and rubbed his eyes and looked at the comrade nearest him. Then we began asking each other what we had best do. I said, "Let's go back to Leesburg and find out where our men are." I was asked if I knew the direction to go. I said I did, and we all set out under my guidance and were soon in sight of the town.

I am not writing a history of the great Confederate war—only the part that I took in it—and, as more than forty years have elapsed since its close, of course my memory is all that I have to depend upon. Yet that memory is indelible with many scenes and incidents that will never be erased until I cross into the "Great Beyond."

For a few days after the massacre at Ball's Bluff we were moved about to various points, just to keep up our spirits, and not let us stiffen our joints by too much sleep and camp ennui. Daily guard duty, a few drills, and changing of camping places for our health was the order of the day. Soon came the question,

where were we going to build our winter quarters?
Where was the whole army going to spend the winter?
This and other questions kept us with something to
talk about.   Our cavalry company began building log
huts, with canvas tops and stone chimneys, on a slop-
ing hill, facing the north and the river, just opposite
the battlefield, and above Leesburg, and south of the
road leading from Conrad's Ferry, and in full view of
the Yankee encampment at Poolesville, in Maryland.
With a good glass they were plainly visible from my
shanty, and were not more than four miles away.

During some of the bright, clear days in November,
the Yankee batteries would occasionally throw a few
shells at our shanties, and every man in camp would
turn out to watch these iron Yankee visiting cards
come over the river to call on us, and it got so that
we felt something was missing if they failed to come.

I loved the picket line, and would take the place of
any of the men, in preference to the routine of camp
life.   I wanted to be actively at the front all the time,
any many a bluecoat, from above Lovettsville on the
river front, down to a point just above the head of
Seneca Island, felt my bullet slip through his anatomy—I never let a single chance escape me.   I was
frequently in the guard house or under arrest for
picket shooting.   Of course my shots would disturb
the picket next to me, and he would fire his gun in
the air, and thus the firing would go down the line
until it reached the camp guard.   The long roll would
rattle, the men fly to arms, and form in line ready for
an attack.   In a few minutes would come the word:

" It's nothing but that fool Fontaine.   He's up to
some of his pranks just to disturb the camp."

I can truthfully say that I rarely fired my gun at
a bluecoat that he did not fall.   I can't say that I
killed every one I shot at, but I shot only to kill.

Our pickets had a very narrow escape one morning
at Lovettsville.   We were in the habit of entering the
village every morning just at daylight, or a little before, and on this particular morning it was a little
before day that we approached it.   When about a half

mile from the town, we saw, in an upper window of a house, a hand waving a white flag at us, with a quick motion to go back. We returned the signal, but kept on. I was in front, and, as I rode into the village with Corporal John Moon, he asked what I thought about that waving from the window? I said that I thought it a warning of danger, and that we had better keep a sharp lookout. There were about twenty of us in the picket squad from our camp, and we generally patroled the river from Buzzard Roost down to Leesburg. I had ridden nearly to the upper end of the town when I saw that the street in front of me was barricaded. I rode up to the obstruction, and said:

" Look there, John."

Instantly there was a flash and a roar of musketry all along the street, from one end to the other. I did not hesitate, but dashed straight at the barricade in front of me, and spurred my horse upon it. She went over like a cat, and not a shot hurt us. Corporal Moon also escaped, and we only lost two men. This ambush taught us a lesson that we never forgot. We set a secret watch after that, and I picked up the traitors and we gave them short shrift. After escaping, I rode up to the house, where the signal of warning had been given us as we were going into Lovettsville, and met a young girl not more than twelve years of age. She asked me why we did not go back when she told us to. She said that she saw the Yankees when they were at work setting the trap for us, and that she had been up all night waiting to tell us about it. I thanked her very kindly, and reported her conduct to General Evans, and he complimented her very highly, and he and his staff paid her a special compliment by bringing her to a grand reception in her honor at headquarters in Leesburg.

CHAPTER IX

Hair-breadth escapes—Am appointed scout to General
Jackson—My appreciation of General Jackson—The
Romney Expedition—Jackson's splendid generalship and
military genius—My personal experiences in Jackson's
campaigns.

At our picket post just opposite Point of Rocks,
one chilly day in early November, I was sitting on my
horse watching the signal flag of the Yanks about a
mile away, as it waved from right to left and up and
down and sidewise. I was trying to catch their signs,
when I saw a Yank kneel by the side of a rock and bring
a rifle to bear on me. The distance was so great that
I sat still and watched him. I saw the smoke curl
up and suddenly the ball struck me just above my
ankle in the fleshy part of the calf of my leg, grazing
the large bone. My leg was lying across the neck
of my horse in front of the saddle, and but for this my
wound would probably have been fatal, as the shot
would have entered my bowels instead of my leg. The
ball lodged in the fleshy part of the calf, only bulging
the skin on the opposite side. It was as fine a shot
as I had ever seen in my life, and I waved my hat
at the Yank, as I rode off to have my wound attended to. Dr. Holloway removed the bullet and bound
up the wound, and in a few days I was all right.

I met with a hair-breadth escape from the Yankees
at a point opposite Lovettsville early one morning. I
had spent the greater part of the night on the Maryland side of the river, and had two Yankee prisoners
in charge. I was just getting them into my boat to
cross over, when I saw a woman on our side wave a
light several times in a circle around her head; two
other lanterns just below me on the Maryland shore
answered her. I hurried my prisoners into the boat and
shoved off from the bank. As I did so a bullet whistled
close over my head, and another and another, and I
saw that I was discovered. My two prisoners became

obstreperous, and ordered me to surrender; they both rose in the boat and started toward me.   I did not hesitate a moment, but drew my pistol, dropped them both into the river, and, putting all the strength I had into my paddle, I struck out for the opposite shore. It was too dark for accurate shooting, but the Yankees made the water bubble up around my boat, and I could see them below me on the river in boats, trying to reach the opposite shore ahead of me.   However, I beat them and landed first, but such a landing place I had not anticipated.   It was an almost inaccessible bluff of smooth rock, but I caught on and lifted myself clear of the boat, and began a hard climb up its steep, almost perpendicular sides. Reaching a shelf some three feet wide I ran along its sides until I found a place I could ascend to a higher point. Up this I went as fast as possible, clinging to a projecting rock here and there.   I climbed up for more than a hundred feet before I found a level foothold on another shelf.   I ran along this shelf, which had an upward tendency, for a hundred yards or so, when I again began to climb. I reached another shelf that I thought would take me to the top, but it did not, and I had to stop to rest, as this running and climbing was too much of a strain. The Yanks, in the meantime, were not idle, as the zip of a bullet here and there plainly told me.   I felt that if I did not have help from my own men I would meet my fate.   I remembered that two chambers of one of my pistols were empty, and I at once reloaded them, and as I pressed the last bullet home I determined not to be taken alive.   I knew that the overhanging rocks prevented them from seeing me from above, and that I was protected from the river, as I could not see the water from where I sat; also that no overwhelming numbers could charge me along the narrow ledge that I had just passed over.

All the thoughts flashed with rapidity through my brain as I sat in silence awaiting developments.   There was an occasional shot, and now and then a mumble of voices above me, and I heard a woman's voice, clear and distinct, say:

"You can't get down that way."

The sound came from directly over my head, and apparently not more than a hundred feet away. I looked up, but the hanging rocks hid everything from view. Several stones were loosened, and came rolling down the bluff into the river below. I heard a Yank say to another:

"Where was he when you saw him last?"

I could not catch the answer. I kept my eye on the track I had come over, and presently I caught a glimpse of a bluecoat cautiously creeping along the bluff, his gun in one hand, and clinging to the rocks with the other. As he came into plain view, not more than forty feet away, I sent a bullet crashing into his brain, and he dropped into the river more than a hundred feet below. In a moment there was a shower of lead spattering around above me and fragments of rock rolled down the mountainside.

Again and again some foolhardy Yank would try to approach over the route that I had come, and he would meet the fate of his predecessor. In a little while they changed their tactics. Sharpshooters began to send their bullets from the opposite side of the river, and they would spat the rocks uncomfortably near. But I could not see the shooters, and I knew that I was invisible. The sun rose and I knew that it would not be long before I would hear from my own men, as the news would not be long in reaching Leesburg. I suppose that an hour or more must have elapsed after I fired my last shot, when I heard that same woman say:

"The Rebs are coming, a whole world of them."

I did not dare to move or expose myself, but sat and waited. I heard the bluecoats taking to their boats, and the short commands of their officers as they passed off from above and around me. Ere long I heard a volley fired down the river, and another and another, until it sounded like a sharp skirmish. I then rose cautiously, and, clinging close to the rock, so as to expose as little of my person as possible, I took a good look down the river, and could see a perfect fleet of boats pulling rapidly for the Maryland shore, and those landing were running for cover.

It was not long before I heard the voice of Corporal Moon say that they did not come any higher up than there. I sang out:

"John, is that you?"

And he answered:

"Hello, are you hurt?"

I said no, but I had had a close call. I soon found a place to climb up the mountain, and while our men of the Washington Artillery were shelling the Yanks in Point of Rocks I reached the command and went back safe to our winter quarters.

A few days after this adventure I was sent by Lieutenant Colonel Jennifer with a dispatch to General Stonewall Jackson at Winchester, in the valley of Virginia. I reached Jackson's headquarters about the last day of November, 1861, and from that day until the 3d of May, 1863, I was his scout, under orders only from him. I was sent on many secret expeditions of great import to our common cause, having been highly recommended to General Jackson by Lieutenant Matthew Fontaine Maury, and our Secretary of War, Seddon, both of whom were kinsmen of mine. My life in the camp of Jackson was not one of roses, as I was a complete stranger and made but few acquaintances. Of course I was known by sight to most of the men, but no familiarity existed between us. My duties required silence, and I practiced it to the letter of my commander, and had communion with no one.

I am satisfied that no greater commander ever lived than Stonewall Jackson. No army was ever too large for him. Among the English speaking people of this earth there never were but five real generals, in the full sense and meaning of the word. They were Marlborough, Wellington, Washington, Lee, and Stonewall Jackson, and, but for seniority, I think that Jackson ought to head the list. I saw him in every phase of a general's life. In victory and defeat he was the same. He had a master mind, one that at a glance could take in the whole detail of a subject. His resources were unbounded.   He was as gentle as a woman in manner, pure as a vestal virgin in thought and act in his every-day life, and as stern in duty as a Roman Senator, and obedient to law and its commands as a Spartan soldier on the picket line.   His counterpart has never before appeared in the annals of history in any age or clime.

I rode in his rear, that beautiful bright New Year's Day, out of Winchester on his disastrous Romney ex-pedition, when we were not allowed to take an overcoat or blanket on our horses, but had to deposit them in our baggage wagons that were to keep up with us (said wagons to this distant day have never yet over-taken us).

In that awful campaign I saw the weary men, like horses, pulling the heavy guns into position; saw them fall and slip on the ice-sheeted mountainsides, bruise and shatter their limbs.   With him I have lain against a log at night, and, with a blanket of snow for a cover-ing and the frozen earth for a mattress, await the coming of the day.   Without fire or food of any kind, save a few grains of raw Indian corn saved from that wasted by our horses, to satisfy the awful cravings of hunger.   I have listened to the loud and deep curses of the half-frozen men, as they trod the frosty ground, with the piercing north wind chilling their very marrow, the thermometer registering ten degrees below zero.   And after the fierce fight at Kernstown, where he held his own against ten times his numerical strength, and compelled the Yankees to cease their advance, and again at McDowell, he circumvented Milroy and his cohorts, and practically destroyed his army.   Then he swung down the valley of the Shenandoah, and, at the head of his corps, rode into Front Royal, and galloped across the two burning bridges with but a handful of scattering cavalry.   On the pike leading from Front Royal to Winchester, with but sixty-eight men, he compelled the retreating forces to halt until his re-serves could come up and capture the major part of them.   Then, in a rush, he cut off and destroyed the wagon trains and ammunition, and, in a word, crushed the corps of Banks and freed the valley of Virginia of every Yankee.

Again, when the armies of Fremont and of Shields were doubled and concentrated upon him, and the great army of McClellan was about to invest Richmond, he sent dispatches to Davis and Seddon by couriers, with the request that they send him fifty thousand men and he would relieve the siege of Richmond, capture Washington, and dictate terms of peace in Philadelphia or New York. This seemed like a pipe dream, when he had only fifteen thousand men, and in his front two army corps of twenty-five thousand each confronted him, only a few miles apart and each determined to capture and destroy him. And how he paralyzed Fremont's twenty-five thousand one day and scattered his hosts to the four winds, and then turned the next day and annihilated Shields, and, without a pause, swept across the State and fell with overwhelming force on the rear of McClellan's great army around Richmond, driving him into the sea!

Thus he showed the power he had, and made himself the idol of all the South. Thus he gave to the world a new record of generalship that had no place before in the annals of history. And what was more he led and was followed by the same soldiers who had cursed and condemned him on that fearful expedition to Romney, but a few days or weeks, I may say, before. There hatred was turned to idolatrous love, and, with the confidence he inspired, his men would have stormed any works on the face of the earth. Nothing could shake their confidence in him.

I am satisfied at this distant day, and so is every man who served with Jackson, that if Davis and Seddon had sent him the fifty thousand men he asked for at that time in the valley of Virginia, he would have fulfilled his promise to them.

But the past is in the eternal past, and there is no recall. When the military student comes to survey the genius and generalship of Stonewall Jackson he will have to lift his eyes to a towering height, far above the plain of ordinary humanity, and it will be a snow-shrouded and cloud-dimmed peak that will greet him. Centuries will roll away before his equal will again tread the fields of martial glory. If I could only soar to that blue vault that arches o'er this sunny southern clime of ours, I would dip a fiery pen into the stardust that sparkles along the pathway of the angels, and write his name in letters of living light upon the dome of heaven, there to shine until earth shall pass away. His spirit is immortal, and his example is ours, and our children's children through all eternity. I hope the gentle reader will pardon me for this tribute to my great commander, for I felt it a duty that I, as one of his men, owed him and his memory.

In the stupendous movements of Jackson in his campaigns I will give some of my individual adventures.

Just before driving Banks out of the valley, I was sent down ahead of the movement to look over the situation, and to note the movements of the Yankees. I was in Page Valley, near Luray, when I saw a squad of bluecoats around Kite's distillery, not far from Marshhead Mountain. I led my horse into a small grove, and, leaving my pistols and belt on my saddle, I climbed up a pine tree to get a clear view of the surrounding country, and especially the party around the distillery. I was fully sixty feet from the ground when three bluecoats rode up and ordered me to descend. I came down rapidly, as they leveled their carbines at me, and as I reached the ground I twisted around the tree, and put it between me and them. I pulled a small Smith & Wesson pistol from my pocket and shot the Yank that had my horse, and put a second shot into the brain of the next nearest. As the third fired at me, I shot at him just as he whirled. I struck him, as we learned afterward, through the bowels.

My horse stood still, as she had been trained, and I mounted and caught the other two, and put out up the winding road that led to the top of the mountain where we had a heavy picket. I was going as fast as I could make the horses travel, when I looked back and saw about thirty bluecoats coming as fast as they could travel. They were gaining on me rapidly. I made one of the turns in the winding pike up the mountain, when the bullets of my pursuers began to whistle around and kick up the dust uncomfortably near. I had to turn my led horses loose and put mine at full speed, as I had to pass again in close range, on account of the windings of the road up the mountain. Some of them had dismounted and were coming straight up the mountain to cut me off. My little mare seemed to realize the danger, and of her own accord increased her speed. As we crossed the danger line the bullets whistled uncomfortably near.

As we again came around the screw-shaped incline, I slackened my speed, for coming down to meet me was a squad of our men, and I knew that I was not going to be captured. I dismounted and put my horse out of danger, in the small spot outside of the pike and next to the mountain. I laid flat on the ground and peeped down the ascent that my pursuers were climbing. The first fellow that came fully in view I tumbled down the bluff, and at the same time those who were on horseback following were met by a withering fire from the boys who were coming to my rescue. This put a new phase on the proceedings and the pursued became the pursuers. We killed several of them before they got out of range.

I spent the night on Marshhead, and the next morning there were no bluecoats visible about Kite's distillery. Half a dozen men rode with me that far. I rode down in the direction of Front Royal, but, seeing a well-beaten path of infantry, cavalry, and artillery going in the direction of Flint Hill, I followed them, and was soon in view of their rear guard. I turned off at right angles, and rode about a mile down a neighborhood road at full speed, and then turned and paralleled their line of march. I was going at full speed so as to get in advance of this brigade or division, and find out whose it was, when I was suddenly halted by a squadron of my own regiment. I reported the object of my movements and Captain Alexander sent Corporal Moon and ten men with me. We ap-

proached Flint Hill just as the Yanks were entering
it. I told Moon to halt and conceal the men, and that
I would ride down as close as I could and try to ascertain what troops they were. I rode almost into the
town, in fact so near that I could distinguish the color
of the men's hair, for I felt that the nearer I was the
less notice they would take of me, thinking that I
was one of their own men.

I was in quite a deep cut, with a high fence and
hedgerow on my right and a steep incline and a stone
fence on my left. I was counting the files as they
passed, and noting the numbers of the regiments, and
looking for the corps badge, when I heard a bugle
sound a short distance behind me. I glanced quickly
back and saw a whole company of Yankee horsemen
coming directly toward me from my rear. I did not
hesitate, but rode up the embankment to my left, stuck
the spurs into my horse, and made straight for the
stone fence, which was about four feet high, and I
cleared it like a bird.

There were several companies of bluecoats, and they
were on the north and east side of the little field that
I was in. They all set out to kill or capture me.
Several rode up to where I had jumped the fence,
spurred their horses, and tried to make them jump
it as mine had, but they failed. In the meantime I
had turned a little southwest, diagonally across the
field, and as I reached the south side of it they sent a
shower of bullets after me. This woke the whole marching army to my right, and many horsemen and some
infantry tried to cut me off. My little mare out-dis-
tanced every pursuer, and across fields and pastures
I sped like a fox hunter, with possibly two hundred
soldiers doing their best to overtake me, and a constant rain of lead flying around me.

I gradually inclined my course toward where a part
of my regiment was on duty. Presently I saw about
a hundred of them hid in a hedgerow within twenty
feet of me, and I was ordered not to check up. I
understood the meaning of the move instantly, merely
leaned forward, and increased my speed. I glanced

back and saw that the head of the pursuing cavalry had just about passed our ambuscade, when there was a sharp, rattling volley poured into them, and the road was instantly full of fallen men and horses. I turned and met a lieutenant of the 12th New York Cavalry and a sergeant. They surrendered at once, and I rode back to where the dead and dying, some thirty odd, lay.

I, of course, succeeded in accomplishing my mission, and reported by courier to General Jackson all that he wished to know. I rode leisurely back up the valley, and when but ten miles above Front Royal I stopped for the night, inside the advancing lines of our army. By midnight we were on the move, and at daylight our advance guard struck the enemy and drove him out of Front Royal. They retreated in the direction of Winchester, setting fire to both the bridges that span the Shenandoah at this point. Our advance guard was close up to the retreating Yanks, and a squad of us dashed across the burning bridges, with Stonewall at our head.

We left the river in a gallop. I saw Stonewall drop slightly behind, and a Major Davis, quartermaster of Wheat's Battalion, of the Tiger Rifles from New Orleans, went to the head of the column. The dust was so thick that I could scarcely see my file leader at times.

In an hour or less we rose a hill, and I could see down the pike for half a mile or more. Before us, from near the foot of the opposite hill, was a brigade of bluecoats, formed in line of battle. A battery of six guns overlooked the incline, with a regiment of cavalry in the rear. In front of the guns were three regiments of infantry, one above the other, on both sides of the pike. Below them, in the form of a " V," was a skirmish line of about three hundred men. The wings of the " V " opened toward us, and the nucleus of the line rested in the pike. To the left of us was an apple orchard and to our right a beautiful grove of large trees, and a residence of no mean proportions. The left wing of their skirmish line was directly in front

of the residence.   A stone carriage house jutted out
on a slight elevation over the pike on my right.   I took
this scene all in at a glance.   I was about the twentieth
man from the front, and we were in a column by eights,
which covered the whole width of the road, and I could
not see across it for the dust.

As we came in sight of the Yankees, there was a
slacking up of our speed, and the order was quickly
given, "Forward the cavalry," and we dashed on.   I
never expected to see the sun of that day go down.
I knew that a withering fire would greet us at the
foot of that hill, and I said a mental prayer and com-
mended my soul to the God who gave it.   Just beyond
the carriage house that jutted over the road was a
spring branch, and when I was within fifty yards of
it there came a clear, ringing voice from the front,
"Charge!"   I drove the spurs deep into my horse's
flank, and she quivered and closed on my file leader
at once.   Then there was a crash of musketry, and the
road was full of dead men and horses, rolling over each
other.   I saw Stonewall under the protection of the
stone carriage house, waving his cap, and saying in
clear tones: "Forward, the cavalry!"

My horse's hoofs touched the skull of a fallen comrade, and I felt her ease up for a second, and then
gather herself together and dash on.   I had my saber
drawn, but as I rose the hill I saw a solid wall of bayonets in front, three lines deep.   I held my saber in one
hand and drew my pistol, and leaning forward concentrated my fire at one spot.   From being the twentieth
man, I was now the first, and when my pistol was
emptied I threw it into the line of bayonets.   As my
horse reached the line she reared and plunged, and
struck out with her feet.   For a moment I had all I
could do to keep my seat.   I struck right and left
with all the power I possessed at the seething mass of
bluecoats that now filled the pike, like men at an
auction, in no order, but densely crowded together and
in each other's way.   I could feel the jar of my sword
as it struck a bayonet or man, and I kept it rising and
descending with all the power that I could concentrate.

I was completely surrounded as far as I could see with Yankees crowding over each other, in the cut in which we were densely packed. I could see them hurrying up the steep sides of the road, jerking each other down and trampling on the fallen, in their frantic efforts to get out of the road into the open wheat-fields on either side. I was like one in a trance. The excitement was far beyond any that I had formerly experienced, and I was striking with a forced power that was beyond my control. The pike gradually emptied, and I could hear the shouts of men, the rapid crackling of small arms, and the ping of pistol balls all around me. I was very near the top of the hill on a level spot.

When I recovered my senses from the intense excitement, I was in a tremor, head to foot, and my little mare was holding her head down and panting rapidly, as from a long race. My arm was hanging down and felt as if a heavy weight was attached to it. I raised it and found that my saber was fastened as if by compression to my hand; the guard of the hilt was forced down against my fingers, and so bent that I could not remove it. I sat quietly for a moment or two and heard a voice near me say:

"Fontaine, are you hurt?"

I turned half round, and saw Moon approaching. He dismounted and came up to me, and I got off of my horse and staggered and fell. The jar of falling seemed to revive me, and I rose at once. He asked why I did not let go my saber, and on examination he took a bayonet from a musket and pried the guard of the saber from my hand, and I felt relieved. He said that he and I were the only ones left that were in the original column that made the charge.

After resting a few minutes, listening to the irregular popping of the pistols in various directions of the pursuing cavalry, I remounted, and we turned off to the right of the pike and rode across an open wheat field. We picked up several prisoners who had hidden in the growing grain. We had some eight or ten, when Moon proposed that he would take them back to the provost guard. He did so and I rode up near a hedgerow that ran at right angles to the pike, and suddenly came upon a very tall Yankee, apparently dead, lying in a sink. I halted and looked at him and saw that he was breathing very slowly. Cautiously, I rode just over him and said:

" Are you hurt? "

He did not move, and I said:

" Poor fellow, he is badly hurt, I had better put him out of his misery."

I cocked my pistol, and he roused at once and said he was not hurt, but would surrender. I saw he was a member of the 8th Virginia, U. S. V., as his cap was so marked. I told him to get up, and he arose at once. We were about a hundred yards from the hedgerow, and I noticed that he often looked that way. I asked him if any of his friends were hidden there. He said that he did not know. I turned that way, and when only a few feet from it I saw the red fez cap of a Zouave under it. I leaned over some distance, peeping under as far as I could, and ordered the Zouave to come out and give himself up, or I would send a bullet after him.

As I was intently watching to see him crawl out, the tall Yank picked up a musket that had been dropped by some of his fleeing friends, and tried to bayonet and shoot me at the same time. He made a failure, as his bayonet struck the pommel of the saddle, and the ball went wide of the mark. I turned with my coat on fire from the explosion of the powder and sent a bullet into his skull, and as he dropped I continued to give him two or three more, until his head was a jelly. My red fez fellow dropped on the ground and begged piteously for his life. I looked into his fair, young, terrified face and I pitied him, and asked him if he was a married man. He said he was not, but that he had a mother. I turned with him toward the pike, and when about a hundred yards from a squad of our men I heard the crack of a rifle behind me. I turned and saw the smoke rising from a spot in the wheat field. I asked one of the boys to take charge of the prisoner, and I rode directly to the place from which I saw the smoke rise. I saw two bluecoats close together in a tall clump of wheat not more than fifteen feet away. I rode directly over them and saw that they were shamming. I sent a ball into the brain of one, and as the other started to rise I cut his spinal cord in two. I rode all around over that field up to the hedgerow, and picked up three fellows who had not been hurt and carried them in. The last two fellows that I shot belonged to the 8th Virginia Renegade Regiment, U. S. V., as did the one who tried treacherously to assassinate me after he had surrendered. If these last two had not been cowards, they could have escaped by keeping quiet until dark.

That night Moon and I were together under the same blanket on the inside of the field near the pike. We discussed the events of the day. I found that my little mare had a flesh wound from a bayonet or bullet in her thigh, but it was bleeding but little, and scarcely discernible unless particular attention was called to it. My arm was very sore and stiff, and I had a powder blister as large as the palm of my hand where the renegade Virginian tried to shoot me, otherwise all was well with me.

The next morning we were roused up by the bugle call of a camp not far off. As we got into our saddles I was quite stiff, and did not feel as if I had had a night's rest. We rode down the pike in the direction of Winchester, and as we passed the first house General Jackson rode into the pike ahead of us. He remarked:

" You boys were in the charge on the pike yesterday? "

We answered, " Yes, sir."

He told us that we need not perform any duties of any kind until we received orders from him, and that Corporal Moon need not answer to roll call, but to scout with me and keep in touch with the army, and that the best thing for us to do was to go somewhere and get breakfast.

CHAPTER X

It was not long before we came to a nice looking
residence, about a mile to the right of the pike, and
about five miles from the battlefield of the day before. Here were two or three ladies, an old gentleman, and a deformed boy. We asked if we could get
a glass of milk and some bread, and we were told to
come in. They were just about going in to breakfast
when we rode up, and, as we got down and hitched
our horses, they asked us if we were in the fight they
had heard the day before. We were asked if we had
ever seen Jeff Davis or General Beauregard, and if
we had ever heard of Stonewall Jackson. We answered
yes to every question, and told them that we belonged
to Jackson's army, and if they would go to Winchester within the next week or so they could see him.
We had a nice country breakfast, such as we had not
tasted for many a long day.

We turned in the direction of Winchester, but kept
a mile or so away from the pike. As we reached a point
near an old water mill we passed an old farmer, with his
two horses geared to a plow. He told us the
"Rebs" had been driven back, but were near by. We
heard the crack of a ten-pound Parrott gun not very
far away. We started at once for the scene of action, and as we rose a hill overlooking the surrounding country, we were greeted by the rattle of musketry
and the sharp crack of a Parrott gun and heard the
explosion of a shell not more than a quarter of a mile
away. We could see a large body of two or more
companies of our cavalry retreating toward Front
Royal. We thought that the Yanks were advancing
to meet Jackson, so we kept ourselves and horses con-

cealed. I dismounted and got into a position where
I could see down the pike beyond where the firing came
from, and I was surprised to see a company of Yankee
infantry, on the double quick, making in the direction
of Winchester, followed by a squad of their own cavalry in a trot. I could see about a dozen bluecoats
near the south bank of the creek, seemingly on picket
duty. I came back and told Moon of the situation,
and that it was not an advance but a retreat of the
Yanks.

We rode down the creek to within two hundred yards
of where the pike crossed it, and when we entered the
pike we turned in the direction of Winchester. As
we turned a sharp elbow in the pike, we were greeted
with the crack of the Parrott gun, and a shell just
missed my head and exploded in our rear. I whirled
instantly, and going about a hundred yards dismounted
and told Moon to hold my horse, and I would take
one more view of the situation. I climbed the hill that
overlooked the scene, and could see nine cavalrymen
only. One of them was pulling a charge of ammunition out of his saddle pocket, and handing it to one of
the men at the gun. I saw at once the condition of
affairs. The gun was one that had been abandoned
the evening before in the retreat, from our charge. It
having become unlimbered, they did not stop to relimber
it, as they were in too much of a hurry. I crept back
and told Moon this, and that I believed that we could
capture the gun if we made a bold dash. He agreed.
I was to charge around the bend down the pike, and as
they fired at me, I was to yell:

" Charge them, boys! We have got them! "

He was to follow, saying:

" Come on, boys! We've got them! "

We carried out the program, and sure enough they
broke as soon as the gun was fired.

We pursued, and killed two and captured one. We
brought our prisoner back to the gun, and I stood
guard while Moon rode back to where the old farmer
was plowing with his team. We compelled him to
come with a doubletree and chain and hitch to the

trailpin. We started back down the pike in the direction of our advancing columns. I made our prisoner straddle the gun, and in a sharp trot we passed along the pike. In passing the first house there were several ladies on the gallery, and as we came directly opposite they rushed to the gate and greeted us with shouts and waving handkerchiefs. The yard was full of beautiful red peonies. I stopped and asked for one, and several were handed me, and one of the ladies gave me a miniature Confederate flag. I thanked her and galloped on and overtook Moon and our gun. I stuck one of the peonies in the touchhole of the gun, and the flag in the cap of our prisoner, who was having a rough ride on his iron horse.

We soon came in sight of our advance guard, drawn up in line of battle, with guns unlimbered, ready to pour a volley into us. I halted the gun, and raising a white flag galloped across the bridge to where I saw a group of officers, and saluting, I informed them that we had captured the cannon and were bringing it in. I waved to Moon and on he came with the gun.

The whole division gave us a cheer, and when they saw the Yank riding on the gun there was a perfect storm of cheers. General Ewell rode up, and I reported all the circumstances of the capture, and that evening at parade we were read out in general orders, and in the presence of the division each of us was presented with a handsome saber. Now, forty-four years after, that saber hangs on the sitting-room wall of my cottage in the peaceful valley of the great Mississippi River at Lyon; a sacred memento of those stirring times.

Moon and I reached the outskirts of Winchester, and in the direction of Kernstown we could hear the roar of Jackson's guns. He had struck the advance of Banks' retreating army, and we could see a long dense cloud of smoke, seemingly miles long. We could see a crowd of cavalry and disordered masses of infantry scattered all along the roads leading in and out of Winchester. We rode as near as possible to observe their movements. It was not more than an hour before we saw the approach of our pursuing cavalry, under that great leader, Turner Ashby. No bolder, braver, knightlier leader than he ever strode across the plains of death, in any clime or century of the world's history. Moon and I entered the city close up to the rear of the retreating Yanks, ahead of any of our cavalry. Our pistols were soon popping, and dropping a straggler here and there, as I was opposed to taking foreign hireling stragglers prisoners, or showing them the honors and courtesies of war.

A dense smoke was rising, in the direction of the railroad depot, and I dashed down in that direction. As I came in sight, I saw several bluecoats dart around the far corner of the burning building. I galloped diagonally across the opening, and Moon took another way of approach. I was close to the building and the sparks were beginning to rise, when I happened to glance down, and saw the ground covered with cartridges, shells, and open kegs of powder, scattered over fully an acre of ground. I had entered the grounds in considerable of a hurry, but I can assure you that my hurried entrance could not compare with the speed of my exit.

As I whirled and tore down a side street, and put a square or two of buildings between me and the expected explosion at the depot, I saw a bluecoat several squares away making good speed, but trying to enter any door that seemed to offer him a refuge. I saw several ladies out on the upper porticoes of buildings as I passed, and just as I was getting close enough to halt my fleeing Yank, I saw a lady in a small balcony looking at me and the bluecoat. She seemed to be very much excited at the race. The Yankee was making directly for her door, and I had my pistol ready to stop him at any moment, when, as he was passing her, she pointed a small derringer downward, turned her head and fired. She did not even see the Yank when she pulled the trigger, for I was watching her every motion, but her shot went true, and the Yank tumbled to the pavement, as dead as if struck with a sledge hammer.

I reined up my horse and congratulated her on her deadly marksmanship.   A pallor spread over her face as she exclaimed:

"Oh, I did not kill him, did I?"

I replied, "You certainly did, madam; and I must say you made a fine shot, in fact as good as any soldier could have made."

She then begged me to say that she had not killed him, but that I did.   I told her that I did not care to rob her of the honor, and rode off.

Our army entered in time to save the depot, and strange to say not a spark fell on the scattered powder, and the greater part of it was saved.

In and around Winchester I made many warm friends, and for several days life passed like a dream.   The citizens were as warmhearted, true, and generous as anywhere in all our sunny southland.

At headquarters, from General Jackson's own lips, I heard the particulars of that "gallop of death" on the pike from Front Royal toward Winchester, and the losses we sustained.   We only had sixty-eight men in the charge, and at the first fire thirty-eight went down to rise no more.   Out of the whole number, Moon and I were the only survivors who ever again answered to roll call.   The General said that when the little squad passed him, as he stood in the shelter of the stone carriage house, he never had such feelings in his life, and that not for his life would he experience them again. He thought his whole cavalry force was closed up and together with him, as they were all at the bridges when he galloped across to join the advance.   But, after we crossed, the column had halted and put the fires out, and then followed.   This caused a delay of some five or ten minutes, and in the meantime we had dashed into the heart of the dense line of bluecoats, and been wiped from off the earth.   But we had broken their lines and routed them, as our reinforcements reached us.   He said that he saw the hand of Providence in it all, and that it was for the best, and that if the whole of our men had been together our loss would have been several times greater.   He said that he saw me stoop and enter their lines like a meteor, and saw my horse rear and plunge in the smoke and dust, and could see the flash of my saber. I can never forget his expression, while relating these incidents, while the dim candle light sputtered in the soft May night not far from Charlestown, on the pike leading to Harper's Ferry, in 1862, now more than forty-four years ago.

Slowly and reluctantly Jackson retreated up the valley of Virginia, before the concentrating armies of Banks, Fremont, and Shields, growling and showing his teeth at every step, and striking stinging, paralyzing blows whenever he was crowded by his pursuers. At Harrodsburg, on the evening of the 6th of June, we lost our great cavalryman, Turner Ashby. And that bright Sunday morning, the 8th of June, we let Fremont catch up with us, and have his cohorts scattered to the breezes, and a large portion of his men left to fertilize the farm land around Cross Keys. Monday morning, Shields felt the grip of Jackson around his throat, and he was choked into insensibility, and shaken by him as a hound would shake a summer coon.

Before the echo of Jackson's guns had ceased to reverberate around the plains of Port Republic, he had planted his bayonets in the rear of McClellan's army, on the opposite side of the State, and compelled that doughty warrior to " change his base," and take to his gunboats and the sea to escape his grasp.

When Jackson went to Richmond to help in the seven days' battles around the city, he left the cavalry in the Shenandoah Valley, with strict orders to keep in daily contact with the Yankee army, and to harass them at every point, as if he was near by with his corps. This was to keep them from sending out scouts to ascertain his movements.

I remained in the valley to watch every movement, and, should there be any change, I was to at once give warning. I had been given very strict and precise orders, verbally, by General Jackson, before he left for Richmond, and they were constantly ringing in my ears. I was anxious to go with him to engage in the great struggle around our chief city, but he said I would be of more use in the valley.

At the fire of the first gun at Cross Keys I was on a slight eminence, watching the advance of Fremont. I took in the situation, and galloped up to the little church, where Jackson was attending the services. As I dismounted and was about to enter the door, a shell came hissing over the church, and burst a short way beyond. The congregation was not long in dispersing, as they were principally soldiers. I made a hasty report to the general, and he told me to watch their movements and report their progress.

I left at once for the front and made a short detour to the right of where I last saw the columns advancing. While riding rapidly through a forest of scattering trees, I found that a brigade of our men were marching at right angles and to the westward of the approaching Yanks. I whirled and came up to their left wing, and seeing the colonel I hailed him and told him the enemy was on his left flank, and would soon have him cut off from the rest of our army. He instantly reformed his line to face in the direction indicated by me. I learned from him that he was Colonel Posey, and that his regiment was the 16th Mississippi. Just as his regiment swung into line and formed, a voice behind us asked:

"What is the meaning of this move?"

I turned and saw a small man with a naked sword in his hand, no belt or scabbard, and no insignia of rank. Not even a coat did he wear, but was in his shirt sleeves. I started to disregard him altogether, when Coloney Posey answered:

"This gentleman says that the enemy is on our left flank and will soon be between us and our army, General Trimble."

"And who the hell is this gentleman?"

I replied that I was a courier from General Jackson.

"Well, sir, show us where they are and take the lead at once, for we are anxious to meet them."

As I turned my horse, I said:

" Follow me and I'll show them to you."

Thus that Sunday morning, the 8th day of June, 1862, at Cross Keys, I had the honor of leading into its first baptism of fire and blood, the 16th Mississippi Regiment, commanded by Colonel Carnot Posey.

At the first volley from the enemy, I lost my horse; several balls penetrated her vitals, but I was only scratched. I took a musket from a wounded man, and joined in the melee, as an infantryman of the 16th Mississippi, and went through the battle.

After the battle of the next day, at Port Republic, Moon and I went down the valley in the charge after the fleeing and disordered remnants of the troops of Shields.

Our men took but few prisoners, for General Butler's orders about the ladies of New Orleans, and General Beauregard's accompanying orders had been read to us at dress parade the evening before, and our soldiers were burning to avenge the insults offered by " Beast Butler."

Our cavalry shot the hirelings as they would mad dogs, as ninety per cent. of them could not speak or understand English.

About ten miles below the battlefield, as Moon and I were returning from the chase, and were following a dim road near the foothills, we saw a smoke up a small cove or valley. We halted, and I got off my horse to reconnoiter. I saw a company of Yanks who had halted, and seemed to be preparing to go into camp. I saw them putting their campkettles on the fire, and could see several of our own men sitting off to one side, with bluecoat guards watching over them. I saw the exact conditions surrounding them, and that we could get very near them on both sides. A thicket of mountain laurel came down, within a few yards of them, just opposite where we then were. I told Moon to creep up to where I had been, and take a good look at the ground and see how they were camped, and then to come back, and we would see if we could not recapture our men. After he returned I proposed that he ride round, dismount, and crawl into the laurel thicket, just as close as possible to them. I would wait until I saw his signal, then I would mount my horse, and ride boldly down into their midst, and demand their surrender, declaring that I had them surrounded, and that I would annihilate the last one of them, if they hesitated even for a minute. As I raised my arm he was to demand in stern tones:

" Captain, shall I fire into them? "

Coming so near and from their rear, I knew this would have the desired effect. When I saw Moon in his place, I mounted and rode right down within a few yards of them, and with my pistol in hand commanded them to surrender, as I had them surrounded. As I had expected, every one sprang for his musket in the stacks.

Just then, Moon, from in their rear, said, " Captain, shall we fire into them? "

They came to a sudden halt, and I commanded each man to file by and pile his pistol or any side arms he had onto the stacked muskets; this they quickly did, and I asked the prisoners to come up and let me see who they were, and at the same time, turning in the direction of Moon, I said in a clear voice:

" Lieutenant, let your men keep these fellows covered, and shoot any man that disobeys any order I may give."

Moon instantly gave the order, " Ready! " and a dense silence ensued.

One of the prisoners was a lieutenant of the 1st Maryland, and had a slight wound in his head. I said:

" Lieutenant, take charge of these muskets and arm every one of your fellow prisoners. March these Yankees out to the valley pike, and if they become the least disobedient do not fail to shoot to kill. I will be near with my company to enforce any of your orders."

I formed the Yanks in line and gave them marching orders, and as they moved off I beckoned to Moon, and we bent and destroyed the guns left behind. We rode on each side of the road that they were on, until we reached the open fields, then we came up from opposite directions, and I rode up and told the lieutenant that

I would keep my men in the woods, but near enough to aid him in case of need.   I said this in a clear, distinct voice so that each captive could hear it, and I again told him to shoot any man who did not respond at once to any of his orders.

I left Moon on the flank next to the woods, and I galloped on in the direction of our army.   Within a mile I overtook about twenty of our boys and told them the fix we were in.   They stopped, and as the prisoners came abreast, we rode up and formed on each side of them, and I relieved the lieutenant, and let him ride a led horse one of the boys had captured.

There were thirty-six of the Yankees, and they never knew the ruse I had played on them until they heard my report to the provost marshal in charge.   Our prisoners were a part of the provost guard of Shields' army, and had marched away to the rear before they knew the result of the battle.   I received a certificate from our provost, which I sent to our Secretary of War, and I received a very complimentary letter from him in regard to the strategy Moon and I used in the capture of this company, and I gave the letter to Moon and told him to send it to his mother to be kept as an heirloom in the family.

From the day of the battle of Port Republic until the 20th of June, I was constantly in the saddle, keeping up with the cavalry on the south side of the Shenandoah, and riding near the pickets of the Yanks, picking off one here and there as I had an opportunity, and harassing in every way their retreat.

A mile or so east of Strasburg Colonel Jennifer called for four hundred volunteers to go into the town if possible, and reconnoiter the position of the enemy. I spurred to the front at once and took my place at the head of the column, and in a few seconds our complement of men was full.   When within a mile of the town, we saw a battery of two guns unlimber in our front, and without a moment's hesitation Colonel Jennifer ordered us to charge them.   We started forward at a quick trot.   I was riding a large, heavy captured horse, and was at the head of the column, and the shells began to whistle and hum uncomfortably near, but passing directly over my head. The nearer we got the nearer they came, and as we descended a small depression they began to explode in our ranks. We were in a column of eights, and in close order, and I said that I thought we had better scatter, so they would not have such a good target to shoot at, but no attention was paid to my suggestion. When we rose the top of a slight elevation, not more than three hundred yards from the battery, the order came:

" Draw sabers! Charge!"

We obeyed to the letter. I stuck my spurs deep into my horse's flank, and fixing my eyes on the guns I rode straight for them. When within about three hundred feet of the battery a shell struck my horse square in the head, and burst at his shoulders. I was thrown far off into the pike, my right thigh fractured, my right collarbone broken, and my whole body paralyzed. Two of the men, whose horses had been killed, lifted me from the pike, and laid me on the bank. Just as they did so, another shell exploded, and blew one of them to pieces and stunned the other, and gave me another wound that nearly crushed my right side in. I lay in a stupor for some time, and saw our men retreat by me, and the Yanks pursuing. Then the Yanks came back on a run, and our men followed. The Yankee infantry came up right over me, and for a while a hard skirmish took place all about me. I was shot again in the back of the neck, and a ball shattered the pelvic bone. A dead Yank lay within three or four feet of me, with the cap of his skull torn away.

The Yankees fell back and our men did not come up to where I was lying. I had spit up a great deal of blood and seemed to be swelling up inside, but the ball in the back of my neck and the one that shattered my pelvic bone seemed to relieve the pressure on my lungs, and I breathed freer. I tried to move, but was unable, and I spoke several times, but no one answered. I watched the sun go down and prayed for water. Some time in the night I felt that if I could get my head on an elevation I would find some relief. My eyes fell on the body of the dead Yankee, and I began at once to make an effort to reach him, but the progress was exceedingly painful and slow, as my lower limbs were useless, and I was only able to use my left hand and arm to propel the whole body, and as I moved my belt would press heavily on my breathing apparatus, and I would have to stop. I tried to take the belt off, but this required two hands, and I could only use one. I suffered untold agonies from thirst, and here nature came to my aid by sending a cooling rain, and I caught the wet tail of my coat and began to suck it, but it was soaked in my blood and it almost nauseated me. I held my left elbow against my lips, let the water accumulate in the hollow thus made, and got some relief.

I continued the struggle to reach the dead Yankee and rest my head on him, and some time during the night I succeeded. I must say that the relief I felt compensated for all my struggles. Toward daylight the heat of that June night became great, and I suppose that I grew feverish. The Yankee now began to swell, which caused his limbs to draw up and clasp me too caressingly for comfort; the swelling of his body had a tendency to bend my neck and force my chin down onto my breast, thus interfering with my breathing. I tried to move away from him, but I was too stiff and weak to do so. Toward the coming of the day the green flies began to come in swarms all over me, and I was kept busy keeping them out of my mouth and nose. By sun-up I was pretty well exhausted.

My dead pillow grew larger and I saw that if I did not get relief I would be smothered. My knife was in my right pocket and I made desperate efforts to get it out, and at last succeeded. I knew that if I could open a cavity in my dead pillow the gas would escape, and I would thus get relief. I tried to stick the blade into his cavity, a good distance from my nose, but I could not do so, and at last I forced it in within a few inches of my nostrils, and the fumes that escaped almost stifled me. The swarms of flies increased, and the unclouded June sun, on that longest day in the year, blazed with fearful intensity upon my hatless and unsheltered head, until it seemed to burn my very brain; and the scent of my pillow did not tend to better my case.

About ten o'clock in the morning I heard the voices of men, and some of our pickets passed and gave me water, and aided me in keeping the flies off, moving me to a shade, while they sent for the ambulance and a surgeon. I heard the rattle of the ambulance and felt the surgeon's touch, and the arms of strong men lift me on to a swinging stretcher. The will power that had sustained me through those long hours seemed to vanish, and a strong feeling of faith in the surgeon's help took its place. I sank into insensibility and was free from pain.

I was carried to Port Republic, to the residence of Mrs. General Lewis, and placed in a beautiful room in an upper story, with a window that permitted a lovely view of the Blue Ridge Mountains. A snow-white canopy and a soft curtain of netting, walls of purest white, and a gentle, almost imperceptible breeze, like the flutter of a bird's wing, and a sweet perfume of violets greeted me as I opened my eyes.

For several moments I lay still and tried to gather my wandering thoughts; I could not move, but out of one corner of my eye I caught the dim blue haze of a mountain top, and out of the other side I could see the forehead and outlines of an angel face; could feel the fanning of her wings on my brow, and the sweet perfume of her breath gave life to my soul. I remembered the terrible night on the pike. The scenes were flitting vividly through my clouded brain. I lay in a trance, half dreaming, while these visions would come and go. I could feel a gentle breeze fan my brow, and I thought that my soul had left the body and winged its flight to the gates of the bright upper world, and that I had entered Paradise. I broke the silence by asking my angel companion if I was in Heaven? She said that I must not speak, but lay quiet, and not make the least exertion. I tried to turn my head so as to get a view of her, but it seemed as if every part of my body was dead. My angel got up and left me. I saw that I was bandaged from head to foot, and only my left arm free.

While I lay in this half-dreamy condition, there came into the room one of the sweetest, most motherly faced women I ever saw.   Her hair was as soft and white as snow, and her face seemed to shine with a radiance not of this earth, and I was more certain that I was in Heaven.   I asked her also if this was not Heaven?

" No," she replied, " you are at the house of Mrs. General Lewis.   I am Mrs. Lewis, and you must lie perfectly still, and not try to move a muscle, as you have been terribly wounded.   It is as much as we can do to nurse you, and you must help us all you can."

Her voice was as pure and angelic as she seemed, and it quieted me as the voice of a mother does an infant in her arms.   She gave me something to eat, feeding me with a spoon with her own hands, while a negro girl stood by holding a waiter.

When I again was roused I was in an ambulance, going down a mountainside, and by my side sat a surgeon and a nurse.   At the next gleam of consciousness I was in a large building, with whitewashed walls, my body in an iron frame, swung to a pulley fastened to the ceiling, and my negro boy George sitting by my side fanning me.   Thus almost unconscious I had been transported by ambulance from near Strasburg, in the valley of Virginia, across the Blue Ridge Mountains to the hospital at Charlottesville in Albemarle County.

For twenty-one days I laid in this iron frame, swung to the ceiling and closely compressed in bandages.   I could only move my left arm.   Once every twelve hours the bandages were changed, and I made George soak both lint and bandages in strong tar and camphor water, before I would allow them to be replaced.   And it was due to this mode of treatment, and my healthy physical condition and the watchful care and skillful attentions of Drs. Cabell and Davis that I recovered. I emphasize Dr. Davis' name, for it is to him that I owe my life.

The seven days' fight at Richmond was a thing of the past many days before I heard of it; and in the hospitals at Charlottesville were the major portion of the sick and the wounded from Jackson's Valley Campaign. More than three thousand were cared for here at this time.

Nearly every preacher and chaplain in the corps were here, and daily and hourly they sang and exhorted, and kept up a constant excitement among the sick and wounded. My window at the head of the cot, from which I was raised and lowered, permitted a good view of the road to the burial grounds, and hourly the carts would pass, with gun boxes in which the dead bodies were encased. I noticed that after each long continued shouting at these revivals, as they were called, from twenty to twenty-five extra carts passed, loaded with the remains of a dead soldier. So I requested our surgeon to forbid the practice, as the intense excitement of these daily meetings had a tendency to unbalance the already fever-weakened soldiers, and cause their death. I especially requested that they be forbidden to come into our ward, and he granted the request.

Our ward had about sixty men in it, all desperately, and supposedly mortally, wounded. Just to the right of the door, as you entered, was a Tennessee captain, with most of one side of the right frontal bone of his skull removed, but he was able to leave his cot and walk about. Up each side of the ward were pale, emaciated men, with different kinds of fearful, ugly wounds. Small curtains were dropped by the surgeons to hide the patients when they were dressing their wounds.

My bunk or cot was at the extreme end in the southwest corner, next to the street leading up to the University buildings, and the corner rested on the ground. Persons passing could look right into my window, and down onto me. A few minutes after I received the promise that there would be no campmeeting proceedings held in our ward, I asked George if he knew where the pistol that I had captured from the lieutenant of the 12th New York Regiment was. He said it was in my knapsack, and he got it out and handed it to me.

It was of peculiar make, and shot twelve times. It had a double cylinder and two hammers, and the charges had been rendered waterproof with a coating of sperm. As I took it I cocked and revolved the cylinder, and found it in first-class order. I laid it under the sheet by my side, and was resting from the exertion, when a preacher, with whom I was familiar, stepped in the front door. He stopped at the cot of the Tennessee captain, sat down on the side of it, and commenced conversing in a low mumbling tone. In a few moments I saw the captain's face flush, and the tears gather in his eyes, and his frame shake, and he turned and hid his face. The preacher rose, dropped the curtain and left him, and came on to the next in line, the same scene being enacted in each case. I could not hear his words, but the nearer he got to me the madder I became at the farce perpetrated upon these poor, wounded, helpless men, by a mistaken fanatic. Before he was within three cots of me I caught the formula of his proceedings and prepared my own plan.

He reached my cot, and in a very cool, sanctimonious manner came around the foot and up near my head. He was drawing his coat tails to one side, preparing to take his seat, when I sang out:

" Don't you sit down on my cot, d—— you. Don't you see that I am in a frame and don't want to be jarred? George, get up and give that fool that stool."

His face flushed, and he said:

" Oh, you are very wicked."

I told him I knew that, as we were all born in wickedness. That God made us so and that I could not help it."

" Oh," he says, " you have not found Jesus."

" No," I said, " I did not know that he was lost, and have not been hunting for him."

" Oh, you are so wicked."

" I know that," I replied. " I was born so, and it is not my fault, I cannot help it, and there is no use of your telling me the same thing over again."

" Oh, my dear young friend, you should make your peace with God."

I replied, " You are a d——— crazy fool. I never was at war with him, never fired a gun at him in my life, and I never expect to as long as I can get a Yankee to shoot at."

" Oh, my dear friend, you should find Jesus."

" I am not able to get up and hunt for him now. Have you any idea where he got lost; in what neighborhood? I will send George to help you hunt him."

" Oh, my friend, you are very low, and in an awful condition to talk so."

" Yes, my cot and this end of the ward are not very high, but you are mistaken when you say that I am in a terrible condition, for I am able to eat everything they bring me, and the doctors all say that they never saw anyone in a better condition. Either you or they have lied to me, and from the way I feel I think that it is you who have lied."

His face flushed, and he said:

" My dear sir, you are not prepared to die; you are not fit to face your God."

I replied: " You don't know what you are talking about when you say that I am not prepared to die.   I certainly make a poor soldier, and so do all these men in here, from your standpoint.   They certainly have been very near death from their wounds, and a man not prepared to die makes a mighty poor soldier. These are Jackson's men and they say that he has the best soldiers in the Virginia army, so I think that you have made another misstatement, and if you keep on these boys will soon think that all you have said is false."

" Oh, I am so sorry that you are not prepared to meet your great Creator."

I asked him if he felt that he was ready to meet his.

He lifted his eyes and hands in very dramatic style, and said:

" O Lord, I hope so."

I brought the pistol quickly in front of his eyes, and said:

" Now's a good time to die."

At the crack of the gun, no startled animal ever

made a quicker bound, or better time than did the parson from that building, and he shattered a panel of the light door as he made his exit.   I sent the bullet up through the roof so no damage was done, and such a roar of laughter as followed that preacher out of the ward was never heard in the confines of a hospital before.   Every curtain he had lowered was lifted and thrown high, and bright smiling faces were on all sides, and " Hurrah for Fontaine! " came from every quarter.

We had no more attempts to hold a campmeeting in our ward, and it was said that I was crazy and ought to be put in a straitjacket. After I had lain for three weeks in my iron frame without moving, I was slowly relieved of the binding pressure by Dr. Davis, and the week after the removal of my body from its frame, I was carried out to the hospitable home of Dr. Carr, at Bentovar.   There, under the kind ministrations of Mrs. Carr and her two daughters, I was soon myself again.

CHAPTER XI

Back to camp—At Cedar Mountain—Receive my discharge
from the army—Remain in camp at request of General
Jackson—Exhibit my marksmanship to General Lee at
his request—I report to General J. E. B. Stuart—The
" Second Manassas " battle.

EARLY in August I got a hospital leave, and while
yet on my crutches I went back to camp to resume
my duties at headquarters. Many of those I had known
in the valley campaign were asleep on the fields of
glory around Richmond, and there were many vacancies
in the ranks. But the morale of the army was un-
surpassed.

I took eleven sharpshooters and crossed the Rapidan
River, about four miles above where the railroad crosses
it between Gordonsville and Manassas, and circled in
toward the rear of Pope's army, while it was encamped
near Cedar Mountain.

As I was looking over the valley from the top of
a hill, in the direction of the enemy, I saw a squad of
thirty odd Yanks in the front yard of the residence of
a Mrs. Taliaferro, about a mile from my point of observation. I saw that I could approach very near them
without being seen, and concluded to reconnoiter their
position and ascertain their mission in that region.

We rode close up and hid our horses behind some
straw stacks, nearly in front of the house, and then
crept up to the hedgerow and peeped over. Two men
were on duty with the horses, and the balance were ran-
sacking the interior. I saw a young lady with a handkerchief to her eyes pacing back and forth in an upper
room, seemingly very much excited. I could hear the
hoarse oaths of these Yankee brutes, who were merely
carrying out the orders of the braggart Pope. We
could hear the voice of an elderly lady remonstrating
with these fiends, and it made my blood boil.

While we were lying behind the hedgerow, the raiders

came out on the front gallery, each with a bundle in his hands. I heard one say:

"We will eat out here where we can look around."

Following the soldiers, carrying a folding table, were several negro servants of the household, and they seemed to enjoy the discomfiture of "Old Miss." One bright mulatto was all smiles, and she announced to the officer in command that she was going to the camp with him.

The table was set and chairs placed for the crowd, and laughing and swearing, using the most horrible language, they took their seats at the bountifully loaded table.

Little did those beings dream that the angel of death had his wings spread over that feast.

I had my men count from one to twelve, as we lay concealed, so that no two would shoot at the same man. The Yank, as he sat at the festal board, corresponded with his number, and at the first fire we would rush through the hedge with our pistols and make a clean sweep of them; not one of them must escape alive. I issued these orders in a whisper, and they were obeyed to the letter. As our rifles cracked, some had two in range and made double killings, and before those left from our first fire knew or realized what had happened they felt the shock of burning bullets in their vitals. I got the two who were guarding the horses, as I left the cover of the hedge.

The lieutenant in command escaped the first and second fires, and, jumping from the gallery, broke for the rear of the house, but it was of no use. When he was brought back he was confronted by Mrs. Taliaferro and her granddaughter, and his doom was sealed. I ordered the men to put a halter around his neck and to hang him to the arch of the front gate, as a warning to any of Pope's future trespassers.

The bundles that these villains had made up consisted of all the silverware, jewels, and heirlooms of the family, and many old fashioned garments of costly fabrics of a bygone age. The lieutenant had stripped Mrs. Taliaferro's wedding ring from her finger, and with fearful oaths compelled her to open secret drawers and hiding places, under the fear of death with which he constantly threatened her.   She told me with tears in her eyes, while I was making the negroes remove the dead bodies from about the table and scour the fresh blood from the gallery floor, that when they were in the house, she asked the lieutenant if he was not afraid that God would strike him dead for the fearful language he and his men were using.

He replied with a sneer, " God, who is he?   He's played out long ago."

As I returned her ring, she threw her arms around my neck, saying, " Heaven will bless you for this day's work, you and your brave men."

I advised her to get into her carriage, and take all her valuables, and with her granddaughter to go at once to some friend inside our lines and there remain until a day of safety came.   These raids were liable to occur at any time, day or night, and she might not have a defender near at hand as I had been, as it was a mere accident that I happened to be in reach.   She took my advice, and the next day she went to a friend's place near Charlottesville.

The check Jackson gave Pope at Cedar Mountain opened his eyes, as he there saw the front of his enemy, instead of his back, and, if General Lee had acquiesced to Jackson's plan before Pope turned tail for Culpeper, Pope and his army would never have reached Washington City again.   But I pass that by, for bygones are bygones.

I was given a final discharge from the army by the surgeons of the hospital at Charlottesville, while I was with the army near Clark's Mountain, opposite Pope's camp.   This discharge recited that I would never again be fit for any kind of service.   It said that my wounds were such that it was impossible for me ever to regain my strength, and it then recited the kind and nature of eleven of them.   In great distress I showed this to General Jackson, and he said: " Remain in camp and let me see what you can do."

I   did   so,   and,   although   encumbered   with   my

crutches, and at times not able to mount my horse without help, I continued to do every duty he asked. My eyes were as keen and every faculty as alert as it ever had been, and my aim and marksmanship as deadly and unimpaired. I rode with Stuart around Pope's army, and through it at Catlett's Station, shared all the hardships of that maneuver, and again reported to Jackson a full description of all our adventures, and asked him if I was not fit to take my place again with any of them? He said to wait a while.

When we were in Pope's rear at Waterloo Bridge in Fauquier County, in the latter part of August, just before the second battle of Manassas, I crossed the river, about three-quarters of a mile above the bridge, one morning about half an hour before day, with the intention of getting in the rear of the forces opposing us, and ascertaining how many, and to what commands they belonged.

As I was riding slowly through a dense pine thicket, I heard voices just ahead. I halted, and crept forward to reconnoiter. I found a small opening of not more than half an acre in extent, with a single-roomed cabin in the center. This I saw at once was inhabited, apparently, by a negro family, and as I listened I could hear the peculiar intonation of a Yankee voice. Soon two of them came out, and with them a Confederate soldier with a rope around his wrists, his hands bound behind him, and one of the Yanks holding him. The Yank who had hold of the rope had his company and regimental numbers on the front of his cap, Company D, 111th Pennsylvania. The other belonged to Purnell's Maryland Legion, and the Confederate captive was a member of the 1st Maryland Regiment, C. S. A. They were a part of a provost guard of the U. S. A., and members of the corps of the Yankee army in our front. They stopped at the cabin all night, as it was deserted, and were just starting with their prisoner for their encampment, when I came upon them.

I was almost directly in their line of march, and

I crept as close as possible to the path they were in. As they came directly against me I arose, with a pistol in each hand leveled at each, and demanded their surrender. They dropped their muskets at once, and did not hesitate. I made them back off, and I took charge of their guns, and compelled them to untie the hands of the prisoner. I handed him a gun, and told him to shoot the first one of them that made the least noise, or that made any attempt to escape. I marched them to where I had left my horse, mounted, put my prisoners in front, let my Confederate boy mount up behind me, and rode back to the river. One Yank could not swim, and I made him catch my horse by the tail and hold on, and I plunged my horse in and was soon on the opposite shore.

I carried my prisoners up to General Jackson, and from them he obtained the information we wished.

Soon afterward, as we attempted to advance toward the bridge across the Rapidan, we were met by a sharp fire from the skirmish line of the enemy, who were stationed at Warrenton, and Fauquier Springs, and their reinforcements began to pour in from every way on the opposite side of the river. Our men held their place in the cellar of a large frame house near Waterloo Bridge, and the musket fire soon became general all along our lines. We were in a valley, and the Yankees occupied the hills overlooking the valley, which were crescent shaped. They had all the advantage of position, and could concentrate their fire upon us.

Jackson's headquarters were on an eminence, nearly opposite the left wing of the Yankee line of battle, and just about on the same plane of elevation as they were. We could look down on the whole valley in which our men were, and watch the progress of the fight.

There was an old burnt brick mansion at our point of view, with several fallen columns, and on one of these Jackson was seated, with his staff near him. A Federal battery of ten guns unlimbered just in front of us, and began to shell the valley. I was leaning against a part of a column base, about a foot higher than my head, and I had a fine view of every gun in this battery, from five to six hundred yards away. I asked the General for permission to open fire on them with my rifle, and he granted my request. I rested the rifle on the shoulders of my crutches, as they leaned against the brick column, adjusted my sights for the distance, and taking the gunners in rotation I opened fire, and every shot went true to its mark. After I had fired twenty shots General R. E. Lee rode up with a portion of his staff, pulling out his watch as he dismounted, and shook hands with General Jackson. As Lee raised his glasses to scan the situation, General Jackson remarked that they had just been watching the deadly fire of my rifle, and the wonderful marksmanship I displayed. General Lee asked me to continue my exhibition, and I did so, directing his attention to No. 1, Gun No. 1, calling out at each shot a victim, and for forty shots not failing to drop the man selected. At the fortieth shot witnessed by General Lee, and the sixtieth I had fired from my position, my ammunition gave out, and I so announced. The General glanced at his watch again, and said:

" You say you have fired sixty shots from your Whitworth rifle, without a miss? "

I replied, " Yes, sir."

" Why, you have not been an hour at it." Looking straight into my eyes, he asked, " Young man, don't your conscience hurt you? "

" For what, General? " I asked.

He replied, " For shooting so many of those people."

I asked him if he had ever shot a *rattlesnake?* He replied that he had. I asked him if his conscience hurt him for it?

" No," he said. Then I said:

" General, I shoot these people for the same reason that you do a rattlesnake, and I have no conscience in the matter. They are here to kill me and my companions, and to destroy and desolate our land, and it is a duty I owe my country, and what I enlisted in our army for. I thank my Creator that I am able to perform the duty imposed upon me so well as to meet the approval of my commander and my comrades, and all those who are near and dear to me."

There was a silence at the end of my reply, and General Lee drew his dispatch book from his pocket, and wrote for a minute or two, tore the leaf out, and, without folding, handed it to me.

As I took it from his hand, I asked:

"Who must I hand it to, General?"

With a gentle smile on his face, he said: "Show it to posterity."

I turned away and read it with a full heart. It was a certificate from him testifying to the fact that he had witnessed my deadly marksmanship at Waterloo Bridge, on that August day in 1862, where sixty men fell before my single rifle in less than sixty minutes of time. I thanked him for his great kindness, and handed the dispatch to General Jackson, who remarked to General Lee that in every engagement in which he had watched me shoot, he was satisfied that I had destroyed more of the enemy single-handed than had any company in his command. He said that he had time and again witnessed my shooting and that he had never seen me make a miss, and that he was satisfied that I was the best shot in his corps. This, of course, was a record I was proud to have my great commander relate to General Lee, and a legacy to my little ones in the future.

Shortly after this I was sent with a dispatch to General J. E. B. Stuart, and upon handing it to him he said that I would remain with him. The cavalry crossed over the river, and we moved toward Manassas Junction, and in the rear of Pope's army. The main body of the cavalry moved toward Thoroughfare Gap, and I, with two men, went on a scout as far as Bristow Station.

I struck the Gordonsville & Manassas, or what is known as the Orange Railroad, where the Warrenton Junction enters it. I reached Bristow Station one dark night, and rode right into a large body of Yanks. No pickets halted us, not even a camp guard, and we were in among the sleeping men and stacked muskets before we were aware of it. We did not disturb them. I rode pretty fast, after passing through them, in a northwest direction, and at about daylight we were halted by our own men. I immediately reported to Stuart the forces I had discovered, and their position.

We marched at once on to Manassas, and found Jackson's infantry awaiting our arrival, only about a mile from the Junction. We took the place with only a slight battle, and about four hundred of us galloped on to Centerville, where we were met by a brigade of bluecoats and driven back. We decoyed this brigade into the arms of A. P. Hill's corps, and they surrendered. We then went down to the railroad crossing, on Bull Run, and took possession of the bridge and its guard. We lay in ambush here, awaiting events that might transpire.

Jackson was in communication with the Federal Quartermaster-General at Washington, and was ordering vast quantities of ammunition and supplies, in the name of Pope, for his own use and that of General Lee. Soon we could hear the rumble and shrieks of the engines, and heavily loaded trains, as they sped toward us from the city of Washington. We let several trains pass our ambush, and when we could hear no more approaching from Washington we removed several rails from the bridge and set them so as to throw an engine against the opposite bank of Bull Run. We noticed as the last train passed that an extra engine was pushing it in the rear, where the caboose generally is, and that this engine was full of Yankee officers of various rank, all scanning the country with their field glasses as they passed. Some ten minutes had elapsed after we had finished tearing up and fixing the bridge, when we heard a train coming back from the front at a fearful speed. A glance up the track revealed the engine containing the officers who had just passed. A volley did not halt them, and they dashed upon the bridge at a speed of a mile a minute. Leaping into the chasm, the engine struck the opposite bluff, about thirty or forty feet below the level of the bridge, with a deafening crash and explosion that shook the surrounding country like an earthquake. The engine and its occupants were crushed into a bloody mass, the steam obscuring everything, and the waters of Bull Run hissing and foaming as the coal fires and heated iron dropped into it. It was a sight I can never forget, and I can shut my eyes and catch the vision to this distant day.

We returned to Manassas, and such a sight as greeted my eyes I never could have imagined. Jackson's men had marched from the Rappahannock, a five days' journey, without an ounce of cooked food, as fires were not allowed. They had subsisted the entire way on green apples and raw roasting ears, culled from the fields on the line of march. Here at Manassas they were in the midst of plenty, more food in sight than they had ever before seen. Great piles of meat, smoked and splendidly cured—yes, a hundred tons or more in a pile, and sutler's stores of every kind of canned goods and delicacies, from rum to sparkling champagne and Rhine wine. Cakes and candies of all sorts, and a whole army's supply of the best boots and shoes and underclothing, far superior to anything in " Dixie." Bolt after bolt of calico and blue cloth were stretched between the rails of the railroad, an impromptu table, on which was spread a feast fit for the gods' banquet. The ragged and tattered men of Jackson's corps at this table were enjoying the bounties so plentifully supplied by the Yankees from the rich store houses of the North. It was a scene never to be forgotten. Such toasts as were drank to wives, sweethearts, and mothers, by these men, would fill a volume. And what is more it was a picnic on a field of death, for before the feast was over the legions of Pope began to assemble on the distant plains, and the " Second Manassas," that awful carnival of death, began.

That evening, with Stuart's chief scout, Farley, I left Manassas and scouted as far north along the pike as Fairfax Court House. We captured a lieutenant and a wagonmaster, and turned them over to the provost guard of General Fitzhugh Lee. We could hear the boom of Jackson's guns, as Pope's army attacked him, and we recrossed Bull Run, and rode straight to Jackson's headquarters. We reported that there were no troops in sight, coming from the direction of Washington, and that we had captured the only two Yanks we had seen between Centerville and Fairfax.

I took my place not far from headquarters, on A. P. Hill's right flank, and soon entered into the conflict that was raging along the old railroad cut. Here I witnessed some of the most desperate fighting of the whole war, and here we encountered real American soldiers, not foreign hirelings.

I had a good position, at short range, overlooking the field, with plenty of ammunition for my Whitworth rifle, and for about three hours I did my best. I paid little attention to the privates, and had the satisfaction of seeing every officer fall upon whom I " drew a bead."

There was one officer, I well remember, mounted on a dark-roan horse, just in the skirt of woods beyond the railroad cut from me. He was as calm and cool as any man I ever saw, and I hesitated about shooting him, but I soon saw that his presence and example were an inspiration to his men wherever he turned. As reinforcements came up, they would cheer, and he would show them where to go. I saw it was best to dismount and send him to his rest in the " Great Beyond." As I fired he rolled from his horse, and the horse wheeled and galloped down the line toward our left, but only a short distance from where his master lay he stopped, and started to return, when he, too, fell, and, with scarce a struggle, he, too, was dead.

A few minutes after this officer fell, the Blue line began to waver, and I only got in three more shots before they were in the woods, and out of my sight, but they continued to fire as they retreated. Our men crossed the railroad bed, and I saw many of them filling their cartridge boxes from those left behind by the retreating enemy, on the bodies of the dead, as well as on the wounded.

Our troops were soon closing in a compact mass against the retreating Yankees in the woods. I came down from my hiding place, and again reached Jackson's headquarters. Our men kept up the chase for possibly a mile, and as night came on they fell back to where the fight began, leaving the dead and wounded in their front.

I sank to sleep soon after the fight was over, and early the next morning I was aroused by the roar of the cannon, the bursting of the shells, and the rattle of the musketry. At the beginning the battle promised to be a fiercer one than that of the day before. Far away, in the direction of Bull Run, I could see long lines of bluecoats, and could hear in the distance the whistle of engines and the rattle of musketry. Long lines of glittering bayonets gleamed in the rising sun, and it was a magnificent array, such as I had never had the opportunity of seeing before.

The crash of the picket firing kept drawing nearer, as the sun rose higher.

I was sent with a dispatch to General A. P. Hill, and as the Yankee columns advanced I looked toward Thoroughfare Gap, and saw the men of Longstreet's corps coming at a quickstep. As they neared the hill on which I sat, I saw them halt and deposit their blankets and knapsacks in long rows in regimental order, and place guards over them, then they filed past me to the front in line of battle. Soon the real din of battle began on my right, at the foot of Groveton Heights, in the same spot the Yankees first occupied in the first great battle of the 21st of July, of the year before. We occupied the exact grounds the Yankees then held.

I was sent with a dispatch to a long line of batteries on our right wing, mostly North Carolinians, and had to ride nearly the whole length of our line. As I rose to the crest of the hill where the guns were belching forth their thunders, the sight was the grandest that I had ever witnessed. For four miles I could see the bluecoats, seemingly covering the whole earth, in long unbroken lines, their bayonets glittering in the morning sun like sheen on the wind-stirred waters on some placid lake, before the breaking of a storm. Soon the landscape was darkened by clouds of sulphurous smoke that rose from every point. The very earth trembled, and the green leaves of the trees fell in showers, as if from an autumnal blast, when the frost king had breathed upon them. The hum of the solid shot, the scream of the shells and hiss of the deadly minies, and the shriek and crash of the screaming bombs, made a din almost unbearable.

As I gained the crest of the hill, just in the rear of a ten-gun battery, and in advance of the regiment supporting it, a shell entered my horse just in front of my left knee; the wind of the shot sucked my knee inward toward the track of it, and we were hurled some ten feet or more, nearly into the line of men lying below us. I was shaken and jarred, but not hurt to amount to anything. I arose at once, delivered my dispatch to this battery, and, mounting an artillery horse, I galloped just under the crest of the hill to the next battery. As I again rose the hill another solid shot played the same trick, and I again rolled to the earth, my horse dead, and I stunned and as bloody as if terribly wounded. But I was not hurt, only bloody from contact with my horse. I secured another horse, finished my errand, and reported back in safety.

The din of the battle far surpassed any that I had ever before experienced, save that at the seige of Sevastopol, in the Malakoff. I saw the exhausted gunners of Longstreet's corps as soon as they were relieved drop down almost under their guns, and in a moment be sound asleep; yes, sleep as sound as babes in their mothers' laps, amid this awful din, and with the blood trickling from their ears and noses.

I dismounted, fastened my horse near our headquarters, and crawled to the top of the hill to watch the progress of the battle. As I was looking, I saw Hood's Texans march by just under me, going into the fight at a double quick, and their coming was greeted by tremendous bursts of cheers on every side. I fell into ranks with them. We marched over the crest of the hill and down a declivity, and took position in the edge of a small skirt of timber, with an open wheat field in our front. A gentle slope led to the top of the hill before us, and we were fully concealed by a fence overgrown with vines and bushes. We pulled down the rail fence and built a temporary, concealed breastwork of the rails. Behind this we lay as still as death.

Soon down the slope came a magnificent line of Zouaves, in gay uniforms that lent a bright hue of variegated color to the green of the wheat field. These were the flower of the Yankee army. I never saw a prettier line of men, or a more perfect formation on a dress parade, than they presented as they approached us. A whispered count of men came down our line from our right wing; I was number 305, and the man to my left was 306, and then, when the count was over, we were ordered to count the Zouaves, and each man to fire at his number in their ranks. We waited until we could see them wink their eyes, each man selected his target, and a deadly aim was taken. At the signal every rifle in our front rank cracked, and I don't suppose that so deadly a fire was ever before so coolly and deliberately delivered on any battlefield. The Zouaves went down in a perfect line, as wheat before the scythe. In an instant those left were mowed down by the rear rank, before their comrades had hardly fallen, as they were hardly forty yards away.

As the smoke died away, the Zouaves were a thing of the past. Only a handful were left, and a drummer boy stepped to the front and demanded the surrender of the remnant. Without the fire of a single gun, they laid down their arms, and were marched to the rear.

As soon as I found that we had annihilated the enemy in our front, I went back to headquarters, and watched the progress of the battle. George, my negro boy, was at the wagon train with an extra horse, and finding where we were, he came up and I was soon in my saddle again, ready for duty.

I mounted my little roan filly and rode to where our cavalry was held in reserve. About the time I reached them, the 2d Virginia, my old regiment, was ordered to the front, and we moved off. On reaching an eminence, we could see the whole Yankee army in disorderly retreat, and our artillery limbering to the front, and pursuing them like cavalry in close order, pouring grape and canister into their disordered ranks.

We were ordered forward at a trot, and as we crossed Bull Run, near the stone bridge, and rose the bank on the opposite side, we were met by the 4th New Jersey, the 4th Michigan, and the 12th New York in succession; and here we had a terrible hand to hand saber fight. It took all my knowledge of saber and broadsword exercise and practice that I had ever been taught to keep my head on my shoulders. I only got in three fair licks during the melee, and if one of them had missed my horse would have received the full force of the blow. I saw Colonel T. T. Mumford assailed by four Yanks, and fought my way to his side and got in two of my blows, thus giving him a chance.

The dust was fearful and the heat intense; we were surrounded by overwhelming numbers, and almost exhausted, when I heard the bugles of the 12th Virginia, coming to our assistance. I glanced back, and saw the men of the 12th, with their double-barreled shot guns at a level, coming at a full charge into our midst, and I was afraid that, in the excitement, they would not distinguish friend from foe. But they did, and when they were in our midst they sent a volley into the bluecoated legions, and eighty men of the Yankee host rolled from their saddles to rise no more. This gave us a chance to draw our pistols, sheath our sabers, and draw a breath of relief from the long strain, and the Yanks went down before our fire, like autumn leaves before a wintry blast. My saber guard was driven down upon my fingers and clamped, so that a comrade had to aid me in prying it off.

I joined in the pursuit, and before reaching the woods east of Centerville, we were scattered over a goodly scope of country, picking up a great many straggling bluecoats: I was closing on a fine looking Yank, riding a magnificent dapple-gray horse. When within about twenty paces I ordered him to surrender. He paid no attention to my demand, but spurred his horse and did not look back. I sent a pistol ball into his back, and saw the dust fly from his jacket, at the impact of the bullet. He did not turn, and I sent another ball into him, and still he paid no attention to me. I fired a third, fourth, fifth, and sixth shot at him, and saw each take effect. At the sixth shot he fell back on his horse, and as his head struck the crupper his carbine, which was grasped tightly in his hands, exploded, and the ball grazed the top of my skull and knocked me senseless from my horse.

How long I lay on the ground I have no idea. When I came to, some of the men of my old company had my horse near me, and were removing my dead Yank from his mount. He was so firmly fastened to his saddle that it was impossible for him to get off, until the straps that bound him were released. He had on a steel jacket that came more than halfway round him, and covered the whole front of his body, and the balls I had fired at him were all lodged against the back of this breastplate. After falling backward with his spine cut in two, his saddle had turned, and his face was very much disfigured from the bruises he received from his horse's feet, while being dragged.

The shot in the top of my head gave me a fearful headache. I took a drink of water from my canteen, and got the boys to wash the blood out of my hair, and examine the wound. They said it was only a scalp wound, and had done no harm. They cut some of the hair from around it, and bound it up with a handkerchief. I got on my horse, and, leaving Centerville to my right, a mile or so beyond, far out to the left, I overtook Cozzens, General Lee's chief scout. Together we rode in the direction, but to the left of Fairfax Court House. The whole country for miles was covered with scared, fleeing Yankees, not one carrying a gun, pistol, or baggage of any kind. I never saw such a complete disorganization or rout of an army or body of men before. Cozzens and I could have taken one thousand men without a struggle, as they were completely demoralized and without arms. We only shot a few hirelings, who could not speak a word of English, and were in small groups of three or four and some distance from their friends.

We were three or four miles northwest of Fairfax Court House, and just outside of a stream of fugitives. Even here the ground was covered with the debris of fleeing bluecoats. Guns, blankets, overcoats, and knapsacks were strewn everywhere. We kept close enough to the stream of retreat to see the columns not yet in disorder, and could see their flags and bayonets. Seeing two men on an eminence to our left, we thought that they were Farley, Stuart's scout, and some comrade. We decided to join them, but as we got nearer we saw that they were Yankee officers. We rode up slowly, and when within a few yards we drew our pistols and demanded a surrender, which they at once obeyed with alacrity. One was a lieutenant of the 2d Dragoons, and the other a captain in the 4th New Jersey. They were riding splendid horses. Cozzens took their arms, while I held them covered with mine. They were very much surprised to see us, as they thought we were some of their own command, or they would have given us a fight or a good chase. We were sorry that they were Americans, as it necessitated our return sooner than we anticipated, for we did not kill real American soldiers in cold blood, as we did the hirelings of foreign countries. Had they been foreigners, we would not have taken them prisoners, only shot them as we rode up.

We turned them back and met the advance of Fitzhugh Lee's men. I saw Cozzens ride up to the New Jersey man and demand something from him, and the fellow put his hand in his breast, and drew out a beautiful revolver, and handed it to him. After we had left the prisoners in the hands of the provost guard, and had turned back on our scouting expedition, Cozzens said that while disarming them, he thought he saw the gleam of a pistol in the New Jersey's man's breast pocket, but he was not certain, and he determined to keep an eye on him ; so when we turned him over to the provost he demanded it, with the above result.

We rode that day almost in sight of Alexandria, and the nearer we got the greater the stampede of the retreating Yanks, and the more disorder was apparent. We stopped and fed our horses at a farm house about a mile west of the line of retreat, and got an elegant meal.

As night closed in, a few reinforcements met the retreating army, and they began trying to halt and form something like order in their ranks. Squad after squad would halt, and as our men were not making a very vigorous forward move, they would listen to the efforts of the Yankee officers, in all kinds of tongues, trying to bring their men to their senses. They seemed to have a holy horror of the " rebel legions " that nothing could overcome, but they made preparations as best they could to stay the advance of our army.

When it was very dark, I dismounted. I hitched my horse in a small thicket of dense pines near the pike, and Cozzens left me. I crawled down a slope to the edge of the bluff over the pike, and found it full of Yankee infantry, with regiment after regiment in columns of fours. It began to rain, and every now and then in the distance, in the direction of Centerville, I could hear the rattle of musketry, drawing very near, and getting more distinct and more frequent. Now and then the shells would explode in sight and a minie ball hiss over my head. Suddenly there was a heavy crash of musketry close by, and dense masses of infantry on the retreat scurried by, and the bullets began flying in every direction. At the same time the rain poured in torrents, and the roar of the guns, the flashes of lightning, and peals of thunder added a terror to the scene. As the lightning flashed I would glance up the pike and not a bluecoat was visible, but I could hear the rattle of their canteens and the tramp of their feet in the brush on the opposite side of the road.

As I entered the pike, an officer in a raincoat rode right up to me and said:

"What regiment do you belong to, and why are you not with your company?"

As soon as he opened his mouth, I knew he was a Yank, and as a vivid flash of lightning blazed out I ordered him to surrender. He wheeled his horse, lay almost flat upon him, and started back into the thicket on the opposite side of the pike. I fired at close range, not more than ten feet, and almost lifted him from his saddle with the force of the bullet. He rolled off into the middle of the pike, and his horse darted into the pines on the opposite side.

I ran at once to where he had fallen, and as I reached him a shower of bullets rattled around me from up the pike. I halted and started back to my horse, but no more shots were fired, and I returned to the body and took off his waterproof coat. As I turned him over I saw he had but one arm, the other had been cut off above the elbow. I took his watch, overcoat, knife and pocketbook, and the papers he had in his possession. He had a small goatee and mustache, and the epaulets of a general. I left him where he was lying, climbed the bank, and waited developments. The next day his body was removed from the pike, and recognized by General Fitzhugh Lee as that of General Phil Kearny, of the Federal army. He lost an arm in the Mexican War. I turned over his watch, knife and purse to General Fitzhugh Lee, and they were sent through the Federal lines with the body the next day. I kept the raincoat and wore it through the Maryland campaign.

In the examination of the body I found my bullet had entered his left side, just under the belt, near the hip, ranged upward and come out near the collar bone, on the right shoulder, having passed through almost the entire length of his body. His death was instantaneous. He was a noble looking man, with his gray hair, mustache, and goatee, and one arm, and even in death he had a military, gentlemanly bearing.

CHAPTER XII

At Frederick City—With Jackson at Harper's Ferry—Re-Sharpsburg—With Jackson at Fredericksburg—Ad-ceive letter of dismissal from my sweetheart—Battle of vance of Hooker's Army—Bravery of dying Confederate soldiers.

THE rain was pouring in torrents when I remounted my horse, and I turned away from the pike and rode for a half mile or more at right angles to it. Then I halted a while, put on the raincoat, readjusted my saddle, and put on the general's spurs, and set forward on a line parallel with that the retreating army was following. I rode at a walk, almost feeling my way in the dark, and taking advantage of the flashes of lightning. The rain at times was blinding and I would have to stoop to hide my face from the gusts.

After following the angle of the pike for a mile or two, I turned again toward and entered it at an angle. Our men were marching almost side by side with the Yankees, and I passed a squadron of Fitzhugh Lee's cavalry just before I rode into the pike. They were standing still. Just about half a mile beyond them, and just where the road from Dranesville enters the Chantilly pike, I rode right into the midst of a company of the 2d Dragoons of the Yankee army before I found out who they were. I quickened my pace and was riding past them when an officer spurred out in front of me, and said:

"Halt! Where are you going?"

For my reply I put my pistol almost against his side and fired, and then drove the spurs into my horse's flank and dashed right past the company. There was a rattling fire of pistols, but not a bullet came near me. The cut in the pike at this place was not deep, and in a few seconds I was out of it and safe in the brush on the west side. I dismounted, and, hiding in a pine thicket, was soon asleep. At daybreak I was

140

again in the saddle, and riding in the direction of
Leesburg.

Our fight at Ox Hill gave the enemy a new impetus
in their movement toward Washington. The Warrenton pike was almost paved with their dead for miles,
and the earth was covered with the debris of their
routed army. As I rose to mount my horse the Yankee camp fires could be seen for miles in the direction
of Washington. I stopped at a farm house, about
three miles from the pike, and fed my horse and got
a very good breakfast. After breakfast I sat in the
parlor and conversed with ladies of the house for a
few moments and then went fast asleep. They did
not disturb me, but kept everything quiet, darkened
the room, and put my horse out of sight. When I
awoke it was quite dark, and the family was going in
to supper. My hand and head ached fearfully, and I
felt feverish and exhausted, but after drinking a strong
cup of real coffee I felt considerably better, mounted
my horse and bade farewell to my kind friends. They
informed me that they had fed a number of our men
that day. I saw camp fires in almost every direction,
and could hear the bugles and see the men moving
about around them. I dismounted and got the ladies
to wet a new bandage, and bathe my head in tar and
camphor water and turpentine, and I bathed my hand
in a saucer of whisky, or rather brandy. I then remounted and rode off toward the farthest light, in
the direction of Leesburg. I found the camp of the
18th Mississippi Regiment by a lucky chance, and
spent the balance of the night with them.

Early the next morning I rode into Leesburg, and
shook hands with Captain Ball, John M. Orr, and
several others, and met Miss Eva Lee, who expressed
a great desire to meet General Lee. I told her that
he would soon be along, and she could have that pleasure. I called on the Misses Hempstone, and they gave
me a letter of introduction to their cousins, who lived
in Maryland, near Poolesville, and I presumed to call
on them as soon as I crossed the Potomac. I rode up
the river to just above Conrad's Ferry, where about

thirty of us crossed. As we rose the bank, we were fired on by a squad of Yankee home guards. We returned the fire, and they fled at the first volley, and disappeared.

After putting out a picket, we sat on the bank and watched Stuart's whole cavalry corps cross the river. For more than an hour we gazed at the long lines of infantry, under the immortal Jackson, fording the river. The sight can never be forgotten. As the straggling line would reach our side, the bands would strike up " Maryland, My Maryland," and each man in that great concourse would yell, and ten thousand voices in chorus join in the song. From miles around citizens came crowding, and in a short while every eminence and point of view had a crowd of living, sight-seeing men, women, and children upon it, and our men marched by, as if on dress parade.

Moon and I rode away from the river, and, learning from a citizen where the Hempstones lived, we rode up to the house. I gave them my letter of introduction, and we spent a very pleasant hour with them. We then rode down the pike in the direction of Washington, and soon came in sight of the fortifications that surrounded the city. We spent that night within ten miles of the dome of the Capitol, and the next morning started back toward Frederick City, making a detour, of some four or five miles only, in the direction of Gettysburg, and keeping a lookout in the direction of Washington.

About seven o'clock we saw a couple of mounted men in front and to our left; we circled and came up in their rear. When within fifty yards of them, we drew our pistols, Moon taking the one on our left and I the right; we approached the top of the hill on which they were standing, and as they halted us we shot them both, and made a dash for their horses. But before we got to them about thirty bluecoats hove in sight, not more than a quarter of a mile in our rear, and they commenced making the bullets hum around us. We began a masterly retreat, and for four or five miles we put our horses at full speed.

At a sharp bend in the pike, in a beautiful clump of timber, we met a large body of our cavalry, and our pursuers rode right into their arms and surrendered. Our cavalry did not fire a gun at them, as the surprise was complete.

We rode into Frederick City and watched our army file through the place. Many laughable incidents occurred in the town. All over the place the Union flags were flying, and not one was molested. Many of the women wore dresses with the blue field of stars on their breasts, and the red and white stripes of the Yankee flags forming the skirt. Many wore the Yankee flag pinned to their breasts, and as our boys would march by they would tap the colors on their breasts and say:

"Here's the flag, boys, to fight under."

In fact I did not see any but Union sentiments expressed in the place.

At one street corner there were six or eight young ladies, all clad in Union colors, with a superabundance of small Yankee flags which they waved in our faces as we passed. One young lady, with a large flag in her hand and a small one pinned to her breast, leaned on the gate, and with flushed face waved the colors almost in the face of one of the men, saying:

"Close up, you ragged Rebs."

One tall Texan halted right in front of her and said: "You had better take down your flag, for the Texans are h—— for charging breastworks where Yankee flags are flying!"

The next day Moon and I recrossed the Potomac and joined Jackson as he was crossing the Shenandoah on his way to Harper's Ferry, where were some ten thousand Yankees under Colonel Dixon S. Miles. I passed the 13th, 17th, and 18th Mississippi Regiments on this march, and shook hands with many of the boys whom I had not seen for months.

Our forces were soon hotly engaged with the enemy on the heights in and around Harper's Ferry. I got a good position above the south end of the bridge, and was soon sending my missiles of death into the ranks of the Yankees, picking off the most conspicuous officers.   I saw the 18th Mississippi scale the nearly perpendicular walls of this almost impregnable fortification, gain the plains above, and silence the fire of their guns.   As the crest was carried by other regiments the Yanks put up the white flag, and Harper's Ferry was ours with but a trifling loss to Jackson.

As soon as we captured the works, we put out at a forced march to meet or overtake the army of Lee. As we advanced at a quick step, we could hear the guns at Sharpsburg, and we knew that Lee had his hands full if Meade had overtaken him.   This knowledge gave strength to the " foot cavalry " of Stonewall, and you could see every man quicken his step as the guns sounded nearer.

I was overtaken by a member of the Albemarle Light Horse, of my old regiment, the 2d Virginia Cavalry, and he gave me several letters, as he had the mail for the whole regiment.

My letters were anything but pleasant, as one was a dismissal from my sweetheart and contained my ring of betrothal and my photograph or ambrotype.   Others told of her marriage, and how she was dressed, and all about the wedding.   That night I composed the following letter to her, and as I wrote by light of our camp fires I could hear the boom of Lee's guns on South Mountain, the prelude to the battle of Sharpsburg or Antietam.

OENONE, THE FAITHLESS ONE

I sit by the door of my tent to-night,
  Watching the drifting clouds,
With which the moon, like a trained coquette,
  The light of her beauty shrouds.

A starry-crossed banner floats over my head
  With a listless, rustling sound,
And distinctly I hear the sentinels tread,
  In a silence that reigns around.

I've been dreaming, my pride, of when last we met,
  Of that long-remembered night,
When the pale stars shone on an upturned face,
  So tearfully sad and white.

You were wretched that night, my peerless one,
  Or at least you told me so
As I kissed the dew from your silken hair,
  And you wept that I had to go.

Remember, love, how we stood that night,
  In the old oak colonade,
In a little spot where the moon looked through
  The canopied arch of shade.

How your queenly head on my breast was bowed,
  And your hands in mine were clasped,
And the words you murmured were low and sweet
  As a summer's wind that passed.

How we spoke of the time we learned to love;
  The long, long summer hours,
Of our whispered vows, our tender trust,
  Ah, ne'er was love like ours.

How the waning night sped swiftly by,
  Bringing the hateful day,
Till I breathed my soul in one lingering kiss,
  And wretchedly rode away.

The moon seems to shine as brightly now
  As it did that summer's night,
And 'neath the gloom of the forest trees
  Makes patches of silver light.

I have thought of the past, of our early love,
  Till even the crisp night air
Is filled with the scent of the orange bloom
  That was twined in your braided hair.

And again do I hear, Oenone dear,
  In the swell of the forest trees,
The grand old hymn of ancestral oaks
  As they rock to the passing breeze.

Again do I feel your soft hand's clasp,
  And your proud head on my breast,
As we stood together that summer night,
  And your lips to mine were pressed.

But it is over now; that dream is gone,
  For you are another's bride;
And to talk of love were wretched sin,
  A shock to a young wife's pride.

The few cold words you sent me once
  Are all that I have to tell
Why you broke the faith of a plighted love;
  Yet I have learned that lesson well.

They tell me you looked like a queen that night,
   As you murmured the marriage vow;
That the orange bloom of your bridal wreath
   Looked sullied beside your brow.

They tell me your laughter was blythe and gay,
   That your step was light and proud;
That you lavished the smiles, that once were mine,
   On a senseless, flattering crowd.

Did you think of the blossoms, O faithless one,
   That you used to wear for me,
When your heart was as pure as that bridal wreath,
   As it never again can be?

Did you think of the vows that your lips once framed,
   That syllabled wealth of love?
Did you deem the maid with a perjured heart
   As a wife could faithful prove?

Did you think of the tears that dim'd your smile
   When your scarf for my sword you gave,
And I swore it should lead in the battle shock,
   The bravest of all the brave?

That scarf is steeped in my own red blood,
   Yet I laugh with a bitter scorn
To think how false is that beautiful one
   By whom it once was worn.

You have taught me the worth of a woman's word,
   The faith of a woman's heart;
The tenderest tear that ever was shed
   Is a triumph of woman's art.

Pass on in your beauty, but yet the thought
   Of our last, our first caress,
Shall dim the light of your sunniest smile
   With a shadow of wretchedness.

To-morrow, Oenone, the gray pale morn
   Will dawn on a field of death,
And the *starry cross,* that is drooping now,
   Will flap in the battle's breath:

My brave men will fight for their homes, their loves;
   But I, with a grim despair;
For all that is left me, left of the past,
   Is this lock of a false woman's hair.

I made a neat copy of this and sent it to her, without name or date. As I am not writing a love story, but only a few of the most important events of my life, I here dismiss the subject. But I was low spirited, and felt that one I had loved and cherished most on earth had proven false. It left me with a very bad case of "the blues," something I was not usually subject to. Life seemed to have lost its charm, and I determined to give my Yankee foes a clear chance at me the next morning, as I felt that I would rather go to that bivouac beyond the stars.

The next morning I was in the saddle at the first dawn of day, and galloped off in the direction of Sharpsburg. As I approached the field, the roar of the guns and the crash of musketry was deafening, equaling that at Groveton Heights at Second Manassas. Longstreet had his hands full, and Jackson was being attacked by Hooker with something like forty thousand men. Glancing over the field, I saw Hood's old brigade of Texans lying down, and exposed to a fearful fire from some thirty pieces of artillery, posted on a commanding height, and from a long line of infantry. I saw the flag of the brigade go down several times in the open wheat field, and at last it fell, and there seemed to be not a hand to raise it. The boys who bore that flag were from the home of my birth and the State of my infancy, and lived in sight of the resting place of my sainted mother; all were personal friends and acquaintances.

Burning with the memory of my faithless Oenone, and with a cool determination to die, I dismounted, put my horse in a sheltered spot, and made straight for the fallen colors of the brigade. Amid the awful storm of shot and shell I raised them above my head, and stood like a statue. The shaft of the flag was cut in two several times, and the flag riddled with bullets. They hissed and spat all around me like mad hornets; the canister and grape combed the very earth from under and around my feet; the shells and solid shot almost swept the colors from my grasp as they winged by, and my clothing was often torn as they sang around me. It seemed that an unseen hand warded them off; that a special guardian angel watched over me, and despite my wish to fall on that field of glory, it was denied me. I did not once turn

my head, but kept my eyes steadily to the front.   As
the staff would be cut by a bullet I would steady it,
and wave it above my head.   This awful strain continued for two long hours, and when the "dance of
death" was over, the enemy was driven from our front,
and the day was ours.   I was not even bruised by a
bullet, shot or shell, but was so weak I had to lie
down, and my pulse and heart throbbed with a high
fever.   As I mounted my horse, I could hardly balance
myself.

I crossed the Potomac the next day, and soon our
whole army was over.   The Maryland campaign was
a past history, and the battle of Sharpsburg, or Antietam as the Yankees call it, took its place in the
annals of the war.

We camped some time in the beautiful region around
Martinsburg, Virginia.   I continued to have a severe
pain in my head from the shot I received from the
Yankee at Manassas, and it would at times almost blind
me.   I would often ride down to the river and have
some fun with my Yankee friends, and they soon
learned to distinguish the crack of my rifle and the
sing of my bullet from others.

Finding that my headache was not going to cease
troubling me, I left with my horses and negroes for
my kinsman, Colonel Edmund Fontaine, at Beaver Dam
Station, in Hanover County, on the Virginia Central.
Here I was kindly nursed by the members of the household.   My skull was trepanned by Dr. John Fontaine,
and a small particle of bone that was pressing directly
upon the brain was removed.   With my cousins, Kate
and Mollie, to minister to my every wish, I was soon
myself again.

While convalescing, I hunted with Cousin Alexander, an uncle of the young ladies of the family, and
a bachelor brother of Edmund Fontaine, the president
of the Virginia Central Railroad.   It was not a great
distance to Cousin Alexander's or to Mr. Pollard's,
and we would frequently ramble that far, and spend
pleasant hours with him and his household.

Thus I pased some three weeks very pleasantly

among friends and kinsmen in and around this neighborhood. Cousin Ellen Pollard was especially kind and considerate, and she has to this day a kind memory in my heart. Colonel Philip Aylette's old homestead was another rendezvous for us in our hunting expeditions. Colonel Aylette was a son-in-law of Patrick Henry, and his wife was a younger sister of my great-grandmother.

Amid these surroundings, I rapidly recuperated, but the wound I had received from Oenone rankled deep in my heart, and I was desperate at times. The world looked dark and the future gloomy to my inner soul. About a month was spent in this neighborhood before I felt that I was ready for duty, and prepared for the arduous duties of my calling.

Early in November I reported for duty to General Jackson, near Fredericksburg. Along the Rappahannock I was ever on the lines, and for a few days before the battle of Fredericksburg I had a splendid position down near the river, in front of Barksdale's brigade. I had two barrels of sand and an old mattress stuffed with cotton, and from behind this, through a peep-hole, I had a splendid view of the river and the heights beyond. Here, daily, I would spend hours with my rifle, dealing death to any Yank who came in range. It was from this point I fired the last shot on the morning we were driven out of the town, when the Yanks were within a few yards of us. The fog was so thick and the weather so cold that we were almost numb.

We retreated to Marye's Heights, and behind a small stone fence we awaited the charge of the Irish Brigade of the gallant Meagher. They came up to our lines with a gallantry seldom equaled by any troops, and I kept my rifle as busy as possible, picking off an officer at each shot. When they were only a few yards off, the men of Barksdale's Brigade poured such a withering fire into their ranks that but a remnant, shattered and broken, were left to beat a retreat. We were careful to let as few as possible get back to their lines.

After the awful slaughter I aided in getting the women and children, who had been driven out of Fredericksburg, places of shelter from the inclemency of the awful sleet and snow. We housed as many as possible, temporarily, in our vacant winter huts. The intense cold caused much suffering before we could get them away from this region. I did not do much duty, outside of the camp, but I aided all I could in the care of the sick, wounded, and helpless.

On the evening after the battle, when the Yanks had been driven back across the river, and quiet reigned on every line, a band on the opposite side began to play, softly and sweetly, the old Scotch air, " Bonnie Annie Laurie." One after another of our bands responded, and for a full hour or so soft, sweet music filled the whole cold, bleak atmosphere with a weird warmth, that only music can convey to the inner fiber of the soul. Just before " taps " every band, on both sides, sent the strains of that immortal song, " Home, Sweet Home," in soul-stirring notes out on the wings of the night, quivering and reverberating, with endless echoes from hill, dale, and valley—and answered by a thousand brass instruments, bass and kettle drums, and more than a hundred thousand living throats. It was a time and scene never to be forgotten, for in that hour Yank and Reb were kin, and the horrors of war, the groans of the dead and dying upon the bleak, wind-swept field of death at our very feet were forgotten, and the whole armies of the Gray and Blue were wafted back to the quiet firesides of mother and father, wife and babes, far, far from the bloody, corpse-strewn plain beneath us.

The God of Battles looked down upon Fredericksburg that cold December night, and wrapped a mantle of snow over the crimson-dyed field, hiding every vestige of man's inhumanity to man, and each soldier not on the picket line sank to a peaceful rest, dreamed of home and its soft mystic ties, and heeded not the howls of the chilling north wind's blast.

The scenes and incidents of that December night are a bright spot, I know, in the memory of any sol-

dier who had a spark of sentiment or love in his
soul, and that memory will at times awaken those
scenes to his mental vision, as the years take their
places in the cycle of time.

In my long life of three-quarters of a century I
have witnessed many scenes and incidents in the various regions of earth, and through the varied incidents
of three wars through which I have passed, none made
such an impression upon me.   I have witnessed the
death-bed scenes of soldiers of every race of man on
this globe, but I must say that the dying Confederate
soldier had no counterpart.   The savage red man,
the bronzed Turk, the dark-hued Bedouin of the desert,
the rugged Russian, the fair-haired Irish or British
soldier, the stolid German, and the nervous, high-
strung Frenchman all have their peculiarities when
they come to face the "Great Reaper."   The soldier
of fortune, who fights for the emoluments of office, or
for the glitter of gold, has his mode of meeting death
upon the field of battle, and the agony at times is fearful to behold—but the Confederate soldier has no
counterpart on earth.

I have seen all classes in the throes of dissolution,
on the bloody fields of carnage, on many hundreds
of red fields with their bloody corpses strewn, but the
Confederate soldier has no equal.   I have taken the
dying messages of these brave men, while their life
blood ebbed away, to mother, father, wife, sister, child,
friend, or to dearest, sweetest, and most sacred of
all, the betrothed!   Her name was never spoken save
in a whisper and with a sacred tone, and I would have
to bend my head and stoop low to catch the cadence
of that whispered name, and the address.   Tears would
well up as her name would sound faint and soft.   These
men were not afraid to meet their God, nor to cross
the dark and silent river of death.   They only thought
of the loved ones at home, and the distress that death
would bring to those dear absent ones in the far-off
circle, where the oranges bloomed and the soft sea
breezes sang æolian anthems among the ancestral oaks
of the old "homestead."   No loud or pent-up groans

of pain greeted your ear as you took their cold, stiffening hands in yours, but a slight quiver, and then a smile would sweep over the clammy face, as the death damps would gather, and that message or token was intrusted to you.   No thought of self, only of those they were leaving behind; and when those last words were intrusted to your care and the last duty performed, they would sink into the eternal sleep, with a smile as soft and sweet as that of a babe upon its mother's arm.

This is not an isolated picture I have given you, but, as a thousand surgeons of the Confederate army can testify, it is the universal picture presented by all those falling under their observation.   Every soldier who has lifted the head of a dying comrade from the red sands of the battlefield, or borne a message or a token to the loved ones left behind in the sunny southern home, can confirm it.

Peace to your ashes, O Confederate soldier, where e'er you sleep!   Be it in sunshine or shadow, among friends or in an unknown grave among strangers, from the shores of Lake Erie to the sun-kissed plains of Rio Grande.

Pardon me, gentle reader, if I let my feelings get the better of me, but memory rises in her might, and the strong current sweeps me from my moorings.   Let us turn back to the shores of the Rappahannock, and those stirring times that followed as the winter broke. My scouting duties increased, and no idle moments were spent in camp, but we kept a watchful eye along the river, and on the 29th of April Hooker's great army began its advance.   They held every crossing from Raccoon Ford to the mouth of the river, and all was activity on both sides.   I may say that it was one continuous battle or skirmish from the 29th of April, until the 6th of May, when the last remnant of that mighty Northern army, shattered and broken, found safety on the opposite shores of the river.

During the night of the 2d of May, I rode through the lines of Sickles, and along the whole rear of Howard's corps, and saw the unsoldierly situation of the latter, composed mostly of foreign hirelings. I captured a Dutch lieutenant and three men, one a sergeant, in a small sink, while they were enjoying a game of poker. Making a detour around Howard's right wing, which was stretched out in a long line without any guard or support, in front of a dense and tangled wilderness, making an ideal place for us to creep up and attack without being seen or heard, I hastened my prisoners along as fast as they could travel, making them break the way through the brush for my horse. When in a small road, the lieutenant made a break for liberty and I disposed of him and his comrades in a short, sharp moment of time. Being unencumbered, I soon reached the extreme end of the Yankee line, and turning in front of and about half a mile from it I rode inside of Stuart's pickets, who were keeping the enemy busily engaged in their immediate front. I took a survey of the surroundings, and found a dirt road that led directly in front of and parallel to Hooker's line of fortifications. This I followed until I came to a cross road that gave me a chance to reach our lines in front of Sickles' corps.

As I was galloping along, I was halted by a " vidette," who said that I could not pass that spot, as Generals Lee and Jackson were alone there on the bridge, holding a consultation, and no one could approach. I told them that they were waiting for me, as I had important information for General Jackson. He called the officer in charge, and I was at once passed through the guard into the presence of the two great commanders. I dismounted, and going straight up to General Jackson, saluted, and told him the situation as I had found it only a few hours before. General Lee questioned me very closely, and I drew with a stick, on the floor of the bridge, the exact position of Howard's and Sickles' corps. Jackson sat like a statue while I made my report, and as I finished he asked:

" Is there any road or beaten paths that I can get the men along the route you came? "

I replied that I could lead an army, if necessary,

along the front and in the rear of Howard's line of fortifications.

Jackson immediately got up and said: "General, I will move at once into their rear."

In an hour the whole of Jackson's corps was passing in front, and out of sight of the skirmish and guard line of Howard's corps.

As we came to the old plank road leading from Orange Court House to Chancellorsville, Rodes' division was thrown across it, screening the rest of the corps from the Yankee pickets. Stuart's men began a feint on Howard's front, and we slipped by in double file, and entered the bushes some half mile in Howard's rear. We stole along on this parallel line until we passed the spot where I had found the Yankee lieutenant at his card game. Here we halted, the men swiftly formed in line, and with a cautionary signal of silence we crept up in the rear. Several deer, rabbits, and foxes were scared from their cover and dashed ahead of us into the Yankee lines, and such yelling as they kept up, as we approached in deathly silence, can hardly be imagined.

When the fun was at its height, and the Yanks were chasing the deer and other animals, we came out into the opening, not more than fifty yards away, each man crawling like a panther, ready to spring upon his unsuspecting victim. With deadly aim at this short range, we poured our first line of fire into their midst. Pen nor pencil can picture the effect of these first two volleys. Their surprise was beyond conception, and they went down before our guns like wheat before the reaper's keen blade. Such abject terror as each face depicted is past description. They fled over their works into the arms of Stuart's men, and in droves toward Sickles' corps. We pursued and poured volley after volley into their disordered ranks, until the men tired of the slaughter.

As we marched along the inside of those almost impregnable, scientifically built breastworks, and drove Sickles' men out of their position from the rear, the poor Dutchmen had no rear. With a squad of our best men and scouts, I kept them on the go until nearly midnight, when we reached Hunting Run. We killed them in scores, as we could not take care of prisoners, for we frequently had as many as two to one in our front. Not one of them could speak a word of English, and they had only been in the army a few weeks at the most, and in America not exceeding two months. They were only foreign hirelings, and were here to kill us merely for the greenbacks and gold they received. Therefore, we had no scruples of conscience in disposing of them to the best advantage. Suffice to say I did my level best, and sent as many out of our way as my physical endurance permitted. I have nothing further to say, and no apologies to make for my acts.

CHAPTER XIII

Ordered to General Joseph E. Johnston's headquarters at Jackson—Am sent with supplies and dispatches to General John C. Pemberton—My most perilous undertaking—" Whistling Dick "—Adventures at Vicksburg.

THE death of Jackson, and three wounds, again sent me to the hospital at Richmond. An order from the War Department forwarded me to General Joseph E. Johnston's headquarters at Jackson, Mississippi.

As our train left Meridian, a small embryo city, about a hundred miles east of Jackson, the conductor gave Lieutenant Williamson, of the 17th Mississippi Regiment, and myself a double seat on the north side of the coach, as we were both wounded and on crutches. Just as we were whistling for Chunkey Bridge Station, about twelve miles west of Meridian, Williamson got up and went to the tank at the rear of the coach, and I moved into the seat which he had occupied, placed my crutches with the shoulders just under me, and the legs resting on the top of the seat in front, and stretched my legs out upon them. I had hardly completed the operation and settled myself when there came a jar and crash, and I was thrown up through a great opening in the car above my head, and out on top of it. The coaches were all smashed together and dropped into the river. I was unhurt, only the shoulder of one of my crutches was jerked loose, and I replaced it before I got up.

I saw at once what had happened. The engine and tender had passed over the bridge, when one end next to the abutment sank down. The baggage car and coaches, going at the rate of thirty miles an hour, had struck the abutment with full force, and every one of the coaches had telescoped, one through or over the other. Mine was broken in two, and laid lengthwise on the baggage car, but out of the water. I walked out, dry shod, on a plank placed in position by the men on the bank, and as I reached the shore in safety I felt that the hand of a guardian angel watched over me and warded off danger, and that no matter what the duties were that I had been sent to this department to perform for my country, by the help of this same guardian angel I would succeed. Time proved that this surmise, born above that awful wreck, where a hundred and sixty fellow-passengers met death, was to be a reality.

Upon the first train out I was a passenger, and as I met General Johnston he gave me a warm clasp of the hand. As we left the dining-room that evening and entered his headquarters, he outlined my duties, and that night I left for Grenada. Here I spent but a day of two. With a flag of truce, under Colonel Foute, I went as far as the Nonconnah bridge, south of Memphis. There I left the Colonel and his flag, and purchased an old mule and a cart, hired an old negro, and carried a load of wood into Memphis and sold it. I told the old negro to take the cart and mule and continue to bring in as many loads as he could, but that he must take good care of the mule, as it was all that a band of Rebel cavalry had left me to live on.

I wore a tight-fitting wig of snow white hair; my skin was dyed daily from head to foot with a solution of weak iodide of iron, and it wrinkled up. I pretended to be an old Union refugee from Austin, Texas. I spent several days in the city, and after getting all the data I was sent to obtain, I found my negro wood pedler and mule, and together we passed out of the guard lines without molestation.

I again reported to General Johnston, and with no regard for my three still unhealed wounds and a partially paralyzed right arm, I was sent with eighteen thousand percussion musket caps and dispatches to General John C. Pemberton, who had been driven into Vicksburg by General U. S. Grant, after the battle of Champion Hill, and surrounded by over a hundred thousand Yankees. This was the most perilous undertaking that had ever been placed upon my shoulders, and especially so in my crippled condition, and I shall be very minute in my description of my journey to and from Vicksburg, as the historians have agreed that it was the most daring ever related, and fully illustrated the prowess of the Southern soldier. It is a proud legacy to leave to my children and their posterity, so I hope the reader will bear with me in the recounting and word painting of each incident as it occurred in my first trip to and from the besieged city, and not tire with my recital. To me it was a passage through the " valley of the shadow of death."

I left Jackson one bright Sunday morning as the church bells were chiming their call, summoning each and all to the house of God to join in prayer and praise to the Giver of mercies, and the God of battles. Just before leaving I gave General Johnston a pair of magnificent ivory-handled, silver-mounted pistols that I had captured in Memphis, during my recent visit, from an officer's trunk in the old Gayosa hotel. Just before I left for Dixie, as I mounted my horse, with the aid of General T. C. Mackin, of hotel fame, I received from Major Livingston Mimms, the Chief Quartermaster of the Department of Mississippi and East Louisiana, and also of Johnston's army, a *carte blanche* on the Confederate Treasurer, in these words:

" *The Confederate States Treasurer will honor any draft presented to him, signed by Lamar Fontaine.*"

This was signed by the Confederate States Treasurer and countersigned by Livingston Mimms, as Chief Quartermaster of that department of the Confederate army. I was also handed a neat sum in gold, green-backs, and Confederate money, but how much I never even took the pains to count. In this day of graft and get-rich-quick schemes, the ordinary mind does not and cannot comprehend the full significance of the trust and power conferred upon me, a poor, dis-charged private soldier. It has never had a counterpart in all the annals of ancient or modern history, and it will ever shine, like a glittering star, above the dark cesspools of infamy and corruption that make the transactions of the present day reek and ferment in rottenness around our land, in high as well as low places of power.

As I realized the immensity of the trust that this paper conveyed to me, and imposed upon my integrity, I trembled and could hardly set my steed, but there arose in my heart a something, a feeling beyond my powers to describe. I was transported to a higher, better plane than I had ever before trod, and a determination that all the gold of earth could not have purchased.

With such thoughts permeating my brain, and flashing through each fiber of my inner soul, I rode out of Jackson as the chimes of the churches swelled upon the air. I headed my steed for my father's home on Society Ridge, near the line of Madison and Hinds counties. Arriving there, I was given a warm welcome by each member of the family, and when I told, in secret, my mission to my father, his face assumed a gravity of expression I had never before seen it wear. I told him that I had but a few moments to spend with him, as I wanted to reach Big Black River as soon as possible, and cross it that night. He called the family together, and amid the assembled ones, with a fervent prayer and an earnest invocation to the Great Ruler of the Universe, he placed me in His care. While the tears were yet upon their cheeks, I shook hands and kissed each one, waved a last adieu, and, putting my horse at a canter, I rode directly across country in the direction of Cox's Ferry on Big Black River. Reaching it just as the shades of night were lending the first dusky tinge to the surroundings, I crossed over, and was soon at the hospitable home of Mr. Thomas R. Holloman, and enjoying a bountiful and delicious supper with the members of his household.

From Mr. Holloman I got a clear and distinct, word-painted topographical map of the region that lay

between me and my destination.   He had been a resi-
dent of that county for a number of years, an almost
daily traveler between his home and Vicksburg, and
was familiar with every trail or bypath that led to
and from the beleaguered city.

For hours I studied his map, until I had them all in
my brain, and could see them just as he did.   A Miss
Sue Perkins, a private tutor in his family, prepared
me some fine bandages and a nice lot of linen lint to
dress my wounds, and I got her to dip them all in
boiling tar water and dry them in an oven for me.   Mr.
Holloman promised to have me up by daylight, our
horses saddled, a lunch prepared, a bountiful haversack of provender to last me a day or two, and to
accompany me on my way toward the city as far as
safety permitted.

We could hear and feel the jar of the cannon around
Vicksburg as we conversed.   It was the last sound that
broke upon the ear at night, and the first to be heard
at dawn.

True to his promise, we were at the breakfast table
as the day broke, and as soon as we had finished we
mounted and rode off to the foot of the hills upon
which ran the Bear Creek Road into Vicksburg.

As we were about to ascend the cane-crowned hills,
there came the sound of cannon and rattle of musketry
from several miles up the road to our right, in the
direction of Mechanicsburg.   We could hear the rumble of artillery wagons and the tramp of horses just
in front of us, and I told Mr. Holloman that he had
better return at once to his home, that these troops
might scatter, and it would be best for him to be at
home to protect his little ones; to go at once and not
wait until it was too late for safety.   He took my
advice and rode swiftly back.   I put my horse in a
dense canebrake, and crawled as near the road as I
possibly could without being visible.   Flat on an old
clay root, only a few yards from the road, where I
could hear all that was passing, and get an occasional
glimpse, I lay as still as a panther ready to spring
upon its prey.

The sound of the guns and the rattle of the small arms grew louder, and soon the hum of voices and the rumble of wheels and the tramp of soldiers in retreat passed by; and then the scream of a wounded Yank in an ambulance would draw near and go by. I shifted my position, and found a place where I could not only hear but see everything passing either way. Here I spent the day. The Yankees had met the cavalry of Wirt Adams, and been defeated and driven back. I watched the retreating forces and saw many pass in the wild frenzy of a rout, and I saw the officers rallying and bringing them back to reason.

As soon as night fell, I remounted my horse and rode down the Bear Creek road, slowly and cautiously, my object being to get as close to the city as possible before I turned toward the Yazoo River, as I was satisfied that only by water would I be able in my condition, to carry my musket caps through the lines around the city.

As I was feeling my way along in the dark and unfamiliar road, there came a short, sharp cry of "Halt!" Before I could reply, or even check my horse, it was followed by a crash of musketry. I wheeled at once and darted down hill, through the cane and brush, and a shower of bullets came after me. I crossed a deep ravine and rose the opposite hill, while the bullets continued to hiss and hum around, and the spat of the musket balls, as they cut the cane and brush about me, lent wings to my horse, and he exerted himself to the utmost. As I descended the next hill, the firing ceased, and I was out of danger for the moment from those by whom I had been attacked.

The country was very hilly and broken, and the cane exceedingly thick and dense. On this account my progress was slow. My haversack and one crutch had been shot away, and the other crutch weakened by a bullet, but I was unhurt. I very much regretted the loss of my haversack of food, as there was no way to replace it, since I was now well inside the Yankee lines. With a heavy reward resting on my head for my acts in Memphis, I would have to be extra careful, and avoid both friend and foe.

Just at dawn I came to the top of a high hill that overlooked the valley of the Yazoo, and saw below almost a sea of water, as the whole valley was overflowed from the Mississippi River, all the levees having been cut by the Yankees. My point of observation was from the top of the hill, just north of the Bruce house. Mr. Bruce, being an Englishman, and an English subject, had a British flag flying from his residence. From my point of view I could see the Yankee camps to the south of me, and a mile to the north there was a large command of their cavalry. In different directions I saw scattering horsemen, and I could see them coming in my direction.

I rode straight down the hill, and followed a plantation road that led directly to the back side of the field into the overflowed district. Just before I reached the bushes and brush and tangle of the outer edge of the field, my horse staggered and fell in a soft boggy place, from which the water had recently receded. As I dismounted, and my coat uncovered the flanks of my horse, I saw a ghastly wound from which the entrails were protruding, just behind my saddle, and just under the shortest rib of my gallant horse. But a moment seemed to elapse, after my feet touched the soft muddy soil, before he was dead.

The earth was too soft and yielding for me to bear my weight on the crutch, so sinking on my knees I removed the bag of caps, unsaddled my poor steed, and lifting the caps to my back I crawled through the mud into the brush on the outside of the field, then returned and got the saddle, bridle and blanket, and hid all by covering them with brush on the dry bank of the first water that I came to. Cutting a forked stick with my saber, I went on a search for two light driftwood logs, known in the parlance of raftsmen as " Choctaw logs." Being light and full of air cells, these logs float like cork on the water. I intended to tie two together and use them as a raft to float down the river into Vicksburg with my caps.

With my halter and bridle reins in my hands, I walked along the dry bank of the back water, in the direction of the Yazoo River, searching for the logs that were suitable for my purpose. I had gone but a short distance when I came to a small, well constructed canoe, or " dugout "—a boat hollowed out of a single log—and not over ten feet long. My heart gave a leap of gladness as I saw it. In the bottom of it was an old piece of gunny sacking, and a lot of corn shucks, all as dry as could be. No paddle could I find, but I found a piece of cypress board about five feet long, and with the aid of my saber and pocket knife I soon had a fairly good one. Getting into my dugout I paddled up to where I had hid my caps. I got them on board, took my blanket and spread over them, and getting in I left the shore, made for the open water, and struck out down the stream.

I thought that I was in the Yazoo River, but soon coming into a much wider and stronger body of water, which proved to be the Yazoo, I saw that the stream I had first entered was Collins' Bayou. As I turned my boat down the Yazoo, I could hear the escaping steam from some river craft, and as I turned a bend I came in sight of a steam tugboat and seven large ironclad gunboats ascending the river in my direction, on their way to Yazoo City. I turned square across the river, and paddled with all the power I had for the opposite side. When halfway over there came from the tug a command to halt, but I paid no attention to it. Instantly there was a flash, and a shot from a small three-pound gun sung just in front and a little above me, struck the water, and went skimming along up the river. I bent to my paddle, and another shot threw the water all over me, but before the third shot was fired I was in the brush and large timber on the west side of the river. I pushed my little canoe through the vines, tangled brush, and drifting debris, and was soon in more open water. I paddled slowly along, thinking that I was safe, at least from the gunboats, but I was mistaken. They lowered a large yawl, filled it with men, and by dint of hard work forced it through the tangled vines, brush, and cane, and by using their oars as paddles, they came in pursuit of me, and the race began.   Their odds were fifteen to one, but my little dugout was made for the purpose of going through the thick brush, and in it I had the advantage. I glided through the thickets like a deer—they were the hounds and I the deer.   When the cane and brush were thick, I would gain on them, while in the openings they would gain on me.   At one point, about half a mile from where they entered the first open water, they opened fire on me, and the bullets whistled and splashed the water all around me.

For possibly a half mile or so this was kept up, I doing my best to out-run them, and they steadily getting nearer.   In the bow of their boat was a tall sailor who began shooting steadily at me.   His comrades would keep him supplied with loaded guns, so that he kept up an almost continuous fire, and he was a good shot, for several balls came so close that I could feel their wind.   They were gaining on me, and I had to act.   I placed a large tree between us, and as the bow of their boat cleared it I sent a bullet into the tall fellow that was doing the shooting, and knocked him into the water.   I paddled with all my strength, entered a thicket of cane, and lost sight of my pursuers.

I was weak from the loss of sleep and lack of food, and my wounds were painful from the fearful exertion and intense excitement of the race.   I recuperated for a while, and then moved cautiously forward through the cane, across another open space, and entered a larger and thicker canebrake.   Here I rested for several hours, and then going through it I let my dugout float with the current.   After floating for an hour or more, I entered another thicket of cane, and pushing deep into it I hid, and lying down went fast asleep.   When I awoke, the sun was not more than an hour high.   I felt much refreshed after my sleep, and got out on a large clay root of a fallen tree and stretched my cramped limbs, dressed my wounds, and made preparations for running the gauntlet of

hidden dangers that yet lay in my pathway. I felt
the loss of my haversack of provisions, with almost
the last chew of tobacco that I then owned, as well as my
pipe. But the latter loss I soon remedied from the
joint of a cane, with a stem from a smaller one. After
a good smoke and rest I sent my little canoe again on
its perilous way at a fair rate of speed. The steady
boom of the heavy siege guns around Vicksburg gave
me the direction I wished to go, and by dark I found
that I would have to turn sharply to the east, and
go back toward the Yazoo River, and enter it again,
as the water was getting too shallow for my dugout
to float, and I had to pole it along.

About eight o'clock that night I ran into the river
just above Hayne's Bluff, and as I entered the broad,
open channel I gazed upon a never to be forgotten
scene. The entire hill on the opposite side of the river
was lighted from top to bottom with colored Chinese
lanterns, and the whole was a mass of red, white and
blue lights of wonderful brilliancy. A grand ball was
in progress, and hundreds of dusky, thick-lipped,
woolly-haired damsels, with their bluecoat escorts,
were enjoying the music and promenades under the
vari-hued lights. Their coarse jests and vulgar
laughter echoed across the river to where I lay, in my
little dugout. Many couples were dancing to the
strains of the military bands, and innumerable boats
were passing from one shore to the other in front of
me, as I slowly drifted by, each loaded with a cargo
of ebon-hued men and women from the mouth of Deer
Creek, going to join in the revelry on the bluffs beyond. I laid flat in my little canoe, and let it drift
with the slow current, keeping a sharp lookout on
both sides as I drifted by.

It would be impossible to describe my feelings, or
to put my thoughts on paper with pen or pencil. I
never felt more distinctly *alone* before in all my life.
Minutes seemed hours, and my little dugout lingered
with persistence in the very channel of danger, torturing me with its lack of motion. Both banks were brilliantly lighted, and I could see the fiber of my blanket,

as I peeped through a fold of it, as I drifted on the waters of the almost tideless stream, with more than twenty thousand enemies almost in contact, or touch, of me.   Reader, can you imagine my condition, and rest a moment in my place?   With a reward of twenty thousand dollars for your body, dead or alive?   Weak, tired, and almost worn out, with three wounds torturing me with their pain and itching, it was a trial long to be remembered.   I never lost my nerve, nor abated my watchfulness, for I was determined to reach my destination, and show to those who had placed their confidence in me that I was worthy of it.   These very thoughts seemed to lend wings to my little dugout, and it began to move more like a thing of life, and moved rapidly out of the zone of danger.

As I entered between the two great search lights that lighted both sides of the river at the landing, I drew the blanket up nearer my face, and almost holding my breath, I passed by.   There were a dozen boats, yawls, skiffs, and row boats of all kinds on the river, manned by bluecoats and filled with negro women, enjoying the music and watching the dancing crowds under the colored lights along the shore.   It was a busy scene.   Ten thousand fans, waved by music-loving negroes, kept time to the tap of the drums and the cadence of the bugles.   I passed by this interesting scene, and was soon beyond the glare and in congenial shadows.   I raised to a sitting position, and sent my little canoe forward with all the force my feeble strength would allow.

Soon there loomed up in front a danger greater, if possible, than that I had just passed.   At the mouth of Chicasaw Bayou a large fleet of transports and flat boats, loaded with supplies of every kind for the army of the besieging forces of General Grant, was moored.   It seemed that a thousand flash lights were streaming across the river from each side, and the water was almost as light as the sun could have made it.   I drew the blanket up again, so as to hide my face if necessary, and as I pulled its folds over my shoulders I noticed a cane fishing rod floating alongside of my dugout. I lifted it in, and the idea of passing for a fisherman, if hailed, flashed through my brain, so I laid it full length on top of me and floated on.

Just as I entered the broad belt of light cast by the search lights, my heart rose to my mouth, for across the river was stretched a great cable, and the windlasses were at work cordelling a large flatboat from the east side of the river to the west. At times the rope would rise almost to the surface in the center of the river, as the strain became great on it, and I had to pass directly over it. I did not dare to raise my paddle or make a motion, as I was in the full glare of the headlights. Both banks were covered with spectators watching the progress of the flatboat, and of course I was in the direct line of their vision.

As I floated slowly by, passing over the cable and coming in front of the sutler's boats, crowds of negro men and women were on the front of each boat, and planks were laid from one to the other, making an almost continuous walk. Banjos and guitars were strumming, the negroes singing, and everything was in high glee. The song that seemed most popular was "The Contraband." I had never heard it before, and I caught these words as I floated by:

"Say darkies, have you seen Ole Massa,
  Wid de mustach on he face,
Go long de road very early dis morning,
  Like he goin' to leab de place?
He saw de smoke way up de ribber
  Where de Lincum gunboats lay;
He tuck he hat, an' left berry suddent—
  I spect he runned away."

This song filled the air, and echoed from shore to shore, and the chorus of:

"Massa run, Ha! Ha! De darky stay, Ho! Ho!
  It must be now, dat de Kingdom's comin'
And de year of Jubilow!"

This chorus was sung by more than a thousand voices, both black and white, in full accord. Over and over it was sung and played, until I caught the air and several verses.

With keen eyes I watched each side of the river as my little dugout would turn and drift here and there, apparently a lifeless log. Amid the din, and shouts, and songs that awakened the scenery and kept me on the alert, I drifted out into the shadows of the darkness, and another great danger was passed. But, while the music and songs were still sounding, the echoes ringing and reverberating on the air, and I was keeping a sharp lookout, I heard the puff of a boat, and suddenly the scream of a whistle just in my front. I saw the smokestacks of a stern-wheel steamboat looming up almost directly over me. I had but a moment to rise and paddle my canoe out of her path, a moment more and she would have struck and sunk me. As I darted out of her path with all the power I possessed, a voice from her upper deck hailed me:

" Where are you going there? "

I replied, " To look at my lines."

" Do you catch many fish now? "

" Yes, plenty of them,"

" Bring some up to the Hastings to me in the morning."

"All right, I'll bring you plenty of them."

Having broken the spell, I drove my little canoe with a steady hand down the river. The roar of the guns at Vicksburg was fearful, and I could see the flashes of the cannon and the light of the bursting shells, like gleams of lightning on the dome of darkness in front of me. I paddled straight ahead with a light heart, for I felt that my greatest dangers had been passed, and from the nearness of the sound of the guns at Vicksburg I felt sure that by exerting myself I could reach the city by daylight, at least.

But alas, " The best laid schemes of men and mice gang aft agley." In an hour or two I struck a broad, open expanse of water, at right angles to the course I was paddling; and down the left hand side of this I could see the flashes of the guns on the bluffs in front of Vicksburg. The course of this stream seemed to lead in a direct line to the city. I could not see across the water in front of me, and I was confident that I was in the Mississippi River. Without hesitating I drove my little dugout with increased speed directly in the direction indicated by the flashes from the guns.

Soon the gray streaks of dawn began to illumine the eastern sky, the firing grew nearer, and my river narrower. Soon I found that I was in a pocket of willows in a currentless lake. As the day broke I saw that I was not in the Mississippi but in a *cul de sac,* known by the river men as " Old River," several miles from the Mississippi and in the wrong end of it. On the bank, in front of me, a large raft of logs was grounded, the greater part in the water. It was a portion of the obstructions placed by the Confederates across the Yazoo River below Hayne's Bluff to prevent the Yankee gunboats from ascending the river above Vicksburg. It had recently been cut loose, and it had drifted down and lodged here in an unbroken mass. Much drift wood was piled around this raft and where the logs lay, part in the water and part on the land; the bank was some three or four feet high, and there was a space between the logs and the bank large enough to conceal my dugout. I took advantage of this, and pushing my canoe close under it, I was completely hidden from all outside passersby.

I had scarcely secreted myself when I heard the regular stroke of an oarsman drawing nearer and nearer, and soon I heard the bow of a boat strike the logs within a few feet of me. My little dugout was forced as far under the logs as I could possibly shove it. As I lay perfectly still there came a deafening roar of artillery, and the air was lighted with flashes of exploding shells; the fragments began to hiss and fall all around; the earth trembled at the fierce cannonading.

In about an hour I heard voices on the bank. The occupant of the boat, which had landed against the raft under which I was concealed, was a fisherman, and before the awful cannonading began I could hear the fish flutter as he would drop them from his line into the boat. His boat was not more than fifteen feet from me, and as the voices on the shore drew nearer, there was a hail from them, my fisherman answered, and then the men from the shore began to crowd onto the raft, stepping directly over my head and forcing the logs down against the top of my little dugout until I was afraid they would sink it. I concluded to try and ease it a little by pushing it out from where I had wedged it against the far end of the raft. As I raised my arms for this purpose, and glanced back the way I expected to move to see if there were any obstructions in the way, a huge, black, rusty, cottonmouth snake of the most venomous and vicious kind, gave a warning hiss, and from his open mouth sent his forked tongue almost into my upturned face. I did not make any further effort to get any nearer to him, or to change my position; I was satisfied to let well enough alone, as I was not yet sinking.

I laid very still for a while and gazed at the horrid glare of my new enemy; his eyes seemed to spread farther apart and grow to an immense size, and I felt a cold shudder pass over my whole body. I turned away from the contemplation of his snakeship, steeling my nerves to endure his presence, nor did I again glance toward him during the entire day. I have spent many long, weary days in my life, but I can truthfully say, that this one, under that raft of logs, with the Yankees and fisherman in such close proximity above me, and that venomous, hissing reptile so close to my head and face that I could almost feel his breathing, was the longest and the most dreary of all.

The night I spent at Strasburg in the Shenandoah valley, with my head pillowed upon a dead Yank, was dreary enough, but it was unaccompanied by any unseen terrors, and I was too badly hurt to have all my faculties about me. Here I suffered from the pangs of hunger; the consciousness that I was within a few feet of an overwhelming number of enemies, whose softest whispers I could hear, and should I spit, cough, sneeze, or even move, I was liable to betray myself; with a loathsome, venomous serpent within ten inches of my face, ready to plunge his fangs into my forehead or throat, and with no chance to protect myself from its attack. My thoughts came swift and fast, and in a brief space I reviewed my whole life; in fact, I lived a long lifetime in a few moments.

I watched the shadows lengthen, and listened to the conversation of the Yankees and the fisherman as well as the talk of a party of sailors from the wreck of the *Cincinnati*, a large ironclad vessel of eighteen guns, which had been sunk that morning by the fire of our batteries. The soldiers were ignorant of the movements of the land forces, and were very ragged and dirty looking; the sailors were but little better. The longest day must have an end, and as the sun began to hide behind the willows, my fisherman and the Yanks left the raft. As soon as it was quite dark I pulled my hat up on my forehead, so that if the snake was still in his position and should strike he would bury his fangs in my hat instead of in my face. Then I pushed slowly out from my hiding place, and looking cautiously around as I entered the open air and seeing all was clear, I paddled slowly along the edges of the small willows that skirted the water's edge to my left. For several hours there was but little change in the topography; it all looked alike. After a long time had elapsed and I had begun to think that I was shut up in the lake, I heard the escape of steam and the churning of the paddle wheels of a steamboat. I entered the fringe of willows and again hid. A very large ironclad gunboat and a tug passed by, ascending to my right. As soon as they had gone by, I turned into their wake, and going in the opposite direction, I began exerting myself, giving my canoe some speed. I was weak, tired and hungry, and my lower limbs felt numb and dead. I had lain so long in a cramped condition under the raft of logs that my legs were asleep, and the sides of the dugout were so narrow they compressed my body, and I was unable to turn about to relieve myself.

I paddled on and soon was in a perceptible current. The banks began to come closer together, and in about half an hour I saw the broad, open river in front of me, and as a powerful current with waves six inches or more high, lapped the sides of my dugout I knew that I was in the Mississippi, and at once made for the center of the stream, where I knew the current would be the strongest.

As I reached the center and swung around a bend, I could see the flashes of the guns and the outlines of houses, up on high hills, by the light of the bursting shells above them; the court-house steeple was often visible from the light of the explosions.   On both sides of the river were great fleets of gunboats, transports and flatboats, moored to the banks, and at regular intervals large, heavy ironclad gunboats were anchored in mid stream, with bridge headlights flashing up and down and on both sides of the stream.   I saw the danger at once, stopped paddling and let my dugout float with the current.   At one point I almost came in contact with a large flatboat with an awning over the front deck, under which was a big crowd of negro men and women.   They were shouting, dancing and eating, and a good many Yankee sailors were looking on. I could see all kinds of cakes, candies and fruits of many varieties exposed for sale.   The long rows of canned goods made my mouth water, and increased my pangs of hunger to a fearful degree.

The river was so brilliantly lighted from both sides, as I drifted along, that I could see the glitter of the brass buttons and epaulets of the officers of the gunboats as I passed them.   The Louisiana shore was covered with white tents as far as the eye could reach, and on the Mississippi side the whole shore line was a mass of all kinds of water craft.   Flatboat restaurants, sutlers' palace floating stores, and barges on whose shelves could be seen all kinds of goods for sale, were there.   I could hear the banjos, the loud laughter and coarse ribald jests of the negroes and their no less degraded white comrades, as my little craft floated along the turbid tide of the great " father of waters."

I fixed my gaze on the fireworks that enveloped the city of Vicksburg directly in my front, and with my paddle trailing and my hand in the water, I held my canoe steadily in the center of the stream and let it float. I watched the great twenty-one inch bomb shells rise with their tails of fire, stream across the heavens in parabolic curves, and rapidly descend into the city, jarring the earth with their explosions. I cannot express my feelings, nor the strange glow that swept over me as I contemplated this never-to-be-forgotten and wonderful panorama—not a make-believe act shown from a sheltered stage, surrounded by soft lights, waving fans, and fair women, but the stern ferocity of war and the living reality. It had to be seen and felt to be realized.

My viewpoint was unique in the extreme. Yes, only one, " the only one " in a hundred thousand, to see, as I saw it. Here I was alone in a tiny canoe, floating upon the broad bosom of the Mississippi River, surrounded by more than a hundred thousand men, each one of whom sought my life; with a reward of twenty thousand dollars resting upon my head, dead or alive; without a friend or comrade in the vast hosts that enveloped me; floating helpless and alone amid this weird and wonderful panorama of death. I look back through the dim glasses of the past and see more plainly as the years roll by, that I was guarded by a special angel, who led me safely to my destination. For only thus could I have escaped all the dangers that surrounded me in that lonely dugout ride down the fleet-covered waters of the Mississippi River. With her aid I defied the powers that surrounded me, and floated calmly on in my frail craft that the waves of a passing boat could have sent to the bottom of the stream, despite my every effort.

As I was contemplating and realizing the mighty events through which I was passing as a living real actor, the current was bearing me along at the rate of five miles an hour toward the Louisiana shore, and I became suddenly aware that I was very close to it, and about to be driven against it. I saw several well-manned picket boats out in the stream, crossing and recrossing it. I lowered my head, and when within six hundred feet of the shore, with my eyes fixed on the nearest boat, there came a blinding flash of light and a deafening roar that made my little canoe dance and quiver like a thing of life, and the shock almost stunned me. I was right up close to a great floating battery of twenty-one inch mortars and they had just thrown three great hissing iron globes into the heart of the city at one volley. With the blood trickling from my nose, caused by the shock, I sat up and sent my little craft out toward the center of the river with all the energy that I possessed. Had I pursued a different policy in another minute I would have drifted against this mortar raft and been a prisoner.; but I knew that they would all be watching the flight of the shells just fired, and timing the explosion of each, and would not be paying any attention to me. I kept about a quarter of a mile off the shore until I rounded the extreme northern end of the point behind which the mortar battery lay.

As I hid behind this point just opposite where the National cemetery now fronts, I ran my little dugout onto a small sand bar, and tried to get out and stretch my limbs, but I could only sit up straight; my limbs seemed to be paralyzed and from my belt down I was numb. I lay on this sand bar until I could see a faint streak of daylight breaking over the top of the hills and bluff that overlooked the river.

As soon as it was light enough to catch the dim outlines of objects near me, I pushed off and made for the Vicksburg shore, and when within a few hundred feet of it, running diagonally across, near the mouth of Glass's Bayou, a great shell exploded above me, and lighted the whole shore and river with a brilliant radiance. My eyes at the time were fixed on the point where I expected to land; this flash of the shell gave me a glimpse of the shore and I saw that it was covered with Yankees, all in a lump. I started to back out when there was a sharp hail from the shore, "Come in." Just then another and another shell lighted the heavens and I saw that the Yankees were under guard of Confederate soldiers, and I made at once for the shore and grounded my dugout at their feet. I attempted to rise, but could not, and several of the boys caught my canoe and hauled it out on shore.   They asked me where I came from, and who I was.   I told them that I was from General Johnston, and had caps and dispatches for General Pemberton.   They ordered me to get out and I tried, but could not raise above the gunwale of the dugout without aid.   Just then I was recognized by one of the boys and my name pronounced by him.   A shout went up, and when I produced my credentials no warmer welcome ever greeted a human being on this earth.   I was tenderly lifted by strong hands, a litter formed with willing arms, and with my cargo of caps, I was carried at once to the headquarters of General Pemberton.   I left my little dugout in the care of Captain Lynch, with orders to keep it ready for my use at all times.

I reached General Pemberton's headquarters just at sun-up, and was kindly greeted by the members of his staff on duty at that hour.   I was given a good breakfast and a dark room and cot, and was soon in the land of " Nod," despite the crash of the shells.

After several hours of deep sleep, I arose, and with the aid of Dr. F. F. Fauntleroy, of Hospital No. 2, I was given a warm bath and had my wounds dressed, after which I reported to General Pemberton, in person.   My dispatches, which were in cipher, had been translated, and I delivered my verbal message to him. The General expressed his appreciation of the hazardous service I had performed in my disabled condition, and the great good that I had conferred on the whole garrison. I met many friends, whom I had not seen since I left our Mississippi troops at Pensacola.   That day, as I sat on the front steps of Pemberton's headquarters, Major Fearn, of Jackson, Miss., Chief Quartermaster of Pemberton's army, rode up and hitched his fine iron roan stallion to the hitching post, and stepped inside the building.   He was hardly in, when a twenty-pound Parrott rifle shell hissed by and cut both fore legs from his horse.   As the horse fell, I arose and sent a ball into his brain, then ordered the negroes to skin and cut the animal up for beef.   It was fat and in good con-

dition and would make prime eating. I had frequently
eaten horse meat, in Buenos Ayres especially, where it
was the chief meat on the market. They dressed it
and made roast and steak of it, but though quite hungry
that night, we could not eat it, as it was rank and
musty; had it been a mare or a filly it would have been
very palatable; as it was we had to throw the meat
away.

About five o'clock that evening I rode up to Hospital
No. 2, and got a room and a good bed with Cousin
Matt Redd Fontaine and Dr. F. F. Fauntleroy, the two
surgeons who were in charge of it.

For several days I was quite feeble, and my wounds
troubled me a good deal, but under the treatment of
Cousin Matt and Dr. Fauntleroy, I was soon myself
again.

I called on General Pemberton and General Tom H.
Taylor—the latter was Post Commander of Vicksburg—
and I was given a position at a battery, consisting of
one eight-inch rifle gun and a complement of six twelve-
pound brass Napoleon guns, that stood upon the bluff,
a few hundred yards above the mouth of Glass's Bayou.
This eight-inch gun was a beautiful Whitworth rifle,
the finest that I had ever seen; it was christened " Black
Bess," and the whole upper reach of the river and city
front was within the radius of its missiles. My first
shot with it was a disappointment and I saw that it
was not loaded to its capacity. I rode back to General
Pemberton's headquarters and obtained from him a
written order to take charge of this particular gun,
and to put it to its full capacity. I then doubled the
powder charge, rechristened it " Whistling Dick," and
giving it the proper elevation, I sent a shell into the
heart of the Yankee camp some four miles away, in the
vicinity of where Grant was cutting a canal on the
Louisiana shore. I then sent a solid shot far down
the river, at a mortar schooner anchored several miles
below us. The first shot passed the schooner in a direct
line, but the second swept her decks, and scattered the
debris into the water. I then sent a shell, struck her
fair, and made a wreck of her. The rest of the fleet

dropped down the river out of range, and the Yankee camp on the Louisiana shore was moved to a place of safety.

This gun became famous during the balance of the entire siege, and was known to every soldier of both armies.   It had a mate, far down the river from us, but the mate was crippled by a shell that exploded in its mouth, compelling the shortening of the barrel.   A gun of smaller bore, a four-inch Whitworth rifle, was in position in Fort Hill, near the Sibley House, on the Jackson Road.   This gun has often been confused with the real " Whistling Dick," named and made famous by me.

I could relate many incidents and adventures that occurred during my first trip into Vicksburg, but it would take up much time and space to recount them all, and I shall confine my narrative to only a chosen few.

I slept at Hospital No. 2, which was the old Walter Brooke house, and took my meals at Mrs. Lum's on Cherry street, where the new Presbyterian church now stands.   Here with Generals Bowen and Baldwin, we were royally catered to by Mrs. Lum, and had everything that the meagre markets afforded.   General Baldwin was suffering from a severe wound, and was treated by the surgeons from Hospital No. 2.

On one occasion we were all three in the parlor, listening to the playing of Persifer F. Smith's march by Mrs. Lum, when a twenty-pound Parrott shell entered the southeast corner of the room, just over the piano, hissed through the opposite wall, and exploded on the front gallery, tearing away the post at the northwest corner, shattering the window lights and leaving Mrs. Lum, myself, and the piano covered with dust and plaster. She did not miss a note, but finished the piece, rose and got her brush and dusted the piano, and then played " Dixie."   I bowed very low to the shell, after it had passed by, and so did Bowen and Baldwin, and we congratulated Mrs. Lum on her coolness and bravery. She laughed and said, that as it did not kill her as it came through, it was no use dodging after the danger was past.

That same evening we were up on " Sky Parlor," a high peak just south of where the post office now stands, which overlooked the entire river front and the region lying west of Vicksburg, and Grant's encampment on the opposite shore of the river.   Here we had a signal station, and on this evening, under escort of General Tom H. Taylor and General Baldwin, Mrs. Lum and I were looking through the telescopes at the various vessels and encampments of the besiegers.   I noticed a Yankee leaning against a tree, on the farther side of the tongue of land that now is part of the island, which lies directly in front of the city.   There was a stack of new Enfield rifles near us, belonging to the signal station guard, and I asked General Taylor to let me try a shot with one of these guns at the Yankee leaning against the tree, nearly a mile away.   He laughed and consented. I selected a rifle from the stack and raising the sights to their full capacity, drew a bead on a bunch of misletoe in the top of the tree, in a direct line over my Yankee's head, and fired.   Every glass was directed on him, and my ball sped true to the mark, and he dropped to the earth, a dead man.   A crowd gathered around and bore him away.   A clap of thunder from a clear sky could not have produced a greater surprise, as they heard no sound of my gun and could not tell from whence the messenger of death came.

On the fourth day of June, at exactly four o'clock in the morning, a rocket from a mortar raft went soaring up into the ether vault, and when about 5,000 feet high it sent out a shower of bright stars.   Simultaneous with the explosion of this rocket, every gun around the entire city sent a shell crashing into it, every musket flashed, and a hundred thousand hissing minie balls filled the air.   The shock and roar was beyond description.   All window lights were shattered, the whole heavens were lighted with the torches of the exploding shells, and the flying fragments fell like hail on every side.

A tall, ginger-cake colored negro preacher, about sixty years old, named Jesse, as the crash came, was asleep on his blanket on the back gallery of the hospital.

Old Jesse looked out on the terrible scene and broke in a run for a large oak tree, about six feet in diameter, that had been topped, and stood within forty yards of the back door. Reaching this, he dropped upon his knees, and grasping it with both arms, at each explosion would ram his woolly head with force against it like a billy goat, and say, " Do, Lord." He was butting the tree with all his might as we reached the back door to watch the fearful display of the real fire works of war. Just as we were all out on the gallery, with a fearful shriek a large twenty-one inch shell dropped between us and the old negro, and exploded about four feet under the earth, raising a miniature earthquake. The old fellow quit butting the tree instantly, and raising his hands and eyes toward heaven, in a voice that could have been heard a thousand feet away, he prayed this earnest prayer:

"Oh, God, if you ebber gwine to help me, now de time. Oh, God, come quick; de debil gwine git me sho. Oh, God, come dine own self, don't send dy son; dis ain't no time to fool wid chilluns."

To say that we exploded would be putting it mildly. I have heard many earnest prayers in time of great danger, but I never heard one come so straight from the inmost heart before or that had so much soul pathos in it and that so fitted the occasion. Here in the calm of the present it has a ring of sacrilege about it, but in the light of that poor old negro it was a real earnest, soulful prayer. And especially when one is cognizant of the inner nature of the " old time " slave, who only wanted orders from " old master," and not from " de chilluns."

But enough of this. I met many of my friends on the lines, and on the 5th I asked General Pemberton to have his dispatches prepared and I would take them to General Johnston. At the same time I told the boys that I would take short messages to their loved ones on the outside.

I spent my last day of this, my first trip into Vicksburg, out with " Whistling Dick," getting the exact range of various points of interest around the river front, that I thought would benefit us in a night attack. The gun had a sweep of 270 degrees, and was mounted on a huge pivotal carriage with rebound spring, on a circular iron track. I practiced most of the day, trying its range at distant hidden mortar rafts and various water craft. Wherever I turned its muzzle they would disappear. I was glad to throw my shells into the mortar raft that had given me such a jar on the night in which I reached the city.

I forgot to mention one escapade that was important. One dark night the Yankees tried to pass us with a coal fleet, while I was on watch in front of our battery. I had a good glass and was looking at the upper reach of the river, when I saw an immense dark body loom up on the waters, nearly hiding the bright face of them from my view. I watched it darken the surface, and while gazing intently saw a few sparks fly upward, out of the blackness. I ordered a hot shot from our twelve pound Napoleons to be sent into a deserted cabin on the opposite side of the river, and when the cabin blazed up, lighting the river, we could see a large lot of barges, with a tug boat in their midst, slowly approaching us from above. Our small cannon began to put their shot into it, and the tug began to push her tow toward the opposite shore. This tow was protected by bales of hay, and I ordered our battery to put some hot shot into it and set it on fire, which they did in short order. Just as the tow was swung around and headed for the bank, the tug was exposed, and I sent a shell from " Whistling Dick " directly downward into her stern. The explosion was fearful, as her boiler burst and scattered fire and scalding water in every direction, and the sinking of the tug drew barge after barge down into the seething maelstrom of the dark river. There were several hundred men on this fleet, and by hard work we rescued a Capt. W. H. Ward and six men, all we could find, and brought them to our shore.

On the night of the 5th of June, 1863, I was ready to make the attempt to return to General Johnston. I gave Cousin Matt Redd Fontaine my fine new hat and took his old one. I took a long letter from Capt. James

L. Perkins to his mother, who lived at or near Madison Station in Madison County, Miss. I took this letter against orders, as he was my first cousin, and his mother my own aunt, and I knew that he would not write anything detrimental to us or the cause. Many ladies in Vicksburg cut buttons from my coat for keepsakes, and sewed others on.

I announced at evening parade to all the men in and about Vicksburg, that if they would send in their dispatches to friends on the outside I would attend to the delivery of them. I told them that they must not seal their letters and only write a line or two, thus: " Dear ——————: I am well, and so is ——————. Yours, —————— ——————.'' This, with the date, was all I was to carry out, and each dispatch was carefully scanned by a censor at headquarters. I only carried out four letters that were not thus censored.

I made my little boat ready, and at the last moment I called on General Pemberton, and received my cipher dispatch and his verbal message to General Johnston. I filled my waterproof saddle bags with the messages of the boys to their loved ones on the outside, and selecting those that lay between Vicksburg and Jackson I placed them in a beautiful oil silk tobacco pouch, given me by Miss Anna Gale, a sister-in-law of Capt. James L. Perkins. This pouch I placed in the rear pocket of my coat. When all was ready, about eleven o'clock at night, I crept down to my little dugout, pushed off into the swift waters of the Mississippi River and paddled straight for the center of the stream, where the current would be strongest. I wanted to keep on the Mississippi side until I got beyond our batteries, then I expected to be guided by circumstances as to my future course.

CHAPTER XIV

My return trip to General Johnston—Advise General Johnston of conditions at Vicksburg—Am ordered to take a rest and go to my father's home at Belvidere.

WHEN about three hundred yards from the shore, and just in front of the old Prentiss hotel, I heard a hail from our provost guard on the shore. I paid no attention to it, but laid down flat in my little canoe and let it float by. Soon a shower of rifle balls flew all around me, and several grazed the gunwales of my dugout. Three volleys were fired at me, and I heard the officer in command say, "It's nothing but a log."

I floated without giving any sign of life for several minutes, then raised up and put a greater distance between me and the shore. The firing of our pickets had put the whole Yankee fleet on the *qui vive*, as they were looking for another coal fleet to come down the river. They heard and saw the fire of our pickets, and from the lower fleet they sent out a long line of row boats, filled with men to intercept anything on the water.

As I drifted down toward them, I found that there was no way for me to avoid being seen and captured if I remained in my little craft. When they were not a great way off I eased out of my dugout into the river, keeping my face just above the water, and when I saw that they were coming directly to me, I turned my dugout over and hung with one arm over it. Just before they reached me I reached under and caught the opposite gunwale with my left arm, and when they were upon me I sank, holding to each rim of the edges, and ducked my head under it, pressing my face up against the bottom into the air space. I found that I could breathe and I lay perfectly quiet, with my legs hanging straight down, with a strong grip on each edge. I had just got my position under it when they struck several heavy blows with their oars. My canoe was very much shaken, as the blows were made in an earnest way, and the concussion was like the crack of a pistol in a closed room, and nearly deafened me. I was glad when I heard them declare that my canoe was nothing but a log. I floated under it for some five minutes longer and then cautiously drew my head from under it and looked around. I was right against the larboard side of the large ironclad gunboat *Tuscumbia* and through her open port holes I could see the men in their bunks, and the men on duty on her decks. I could have shoved a torpedo half under her and blown her into kingdom come if I had had one, and could have killed several with my pistol, as not over thirty feet separated us. The temptation was great, but I had too much at stake to try it.

I floated with my arm clinging to my canoe, without making an effort to control it, until I passed by all the boats in the fleet. I then got behind the dugout and steered it to a point on the " tow head " just above Warrenton, where I landed and righted it, wrung the water from my clothing, and got in and paddled down to Diamond Bend Landing, at the old woodyard. Here I landed as daylight broke, and as I climbed the bank, I could see a " tin clad " gunboat just across the river from me.

I fastened my little dugout securely and bade it adieu with regret, and taking my saddle bags on my shoulder and getting on my crutches, I hobbled off to the wood-yard, where I could see an old man and several negroes; the old man's son came up just as I reached the group. I asked if I could get a horse or mule to ride, and said that I was willing to pay for it in gold or greenbacks. He told me he only had a very old and poor mare, and a young three-year-old, unbroken colt, that had never been ridden or handled any. The negroes led the old mare out of a stable near by and the colt followed. I chose the colt, and after many efforts, we got a bridle and saddle on it, and with the aid of the old man, his son and two negroes, I mounted. He staggered for a while and then struck out at a pretty brisk gait across the swamp, in the direction I wished to go.   As I was about to mount I gave the old man $50 in greenbacks. My colt kept a good rate of speed down through the swamp that skirted the hills, and kept well in the swamp of the Mississippi River, but I soon found that he would not last long at the speed he was going, as he was fast giving down and beginning to reel and stagger.   I thought of dismounting and giving him a rest, but I urged him on, but he gave a short whicker, every now and then, as if in distress and calling for help.   While pushing my way through a canebrake he whickered several times, and suddenly I heard him answered by a loud, sharp neigh in front of me, and again and again it was answered.   I halted a time or two as I neared the answering neigh, and the colt seemed to grow restless the nearer I approached.   I drew my pistol, and my colt quickened its pace.

I came out of the cane, on the edge of a cypress brake, and in the edge of the cane, just in front of me, hitched with a large cable halter, was one of the finest full-blooded Arabian stallions I had ever seen in this or any other country.   I dismounted at once and transferred my saddle and bridle to my new-found treasure. This horse, I afterward learned, was imported by Judge W. L. Sharkey, direct from Arabia, a year before the war began.   When the Yankees surrounded Vicksburg it was taken down into this canebrake and hidden and cared for by a faithful old negro.

As I lengthened the colt's bridle and fitted the straps to the stallion's jaws, he would caress my hands with his nose and show signs of pleasure.   As I mounted, loosened the halter strap and set him free, I felt, as he stepped off, as if I had exchanged my dugout for a steamboat, the change was so great.   He started at once in a long swinging walk, through the cane and vines, passing by a large hamper basket of corn, some sacks and a quilt on the ground, where I suppose his keeper had his camp, but I saw no one.

He kept his course for some half hour or more through the cane, until we came to the foot of the hills; here there was a lane, leading directly up the hill, and he wanted to follow it, and I had some difficulty in forcing him to the right along the outside of the field and back into the cane. I followed along down the fence, in sight of the hills, for quite a distance, and came in sight of a Yankee camp; their tents indicated several companies. I could see the men moving about among them, and in the road in front. I got in the brush and concealed myself as much as possible, and kept a sharp lookout. I could hear shots fired occasionally in the swamps to my right, and some down in front of me nearer the foot of the hills. After reconnoitering for some time, I rode back a short distance from the hills, and then followed down the bottom, paralleling them for a mile or so. I then turned back to them and struck a lane, broad and clean, between two pieces of new ground; this lane led directly to the top of the hill, which was about three-quarters of a mile off.

I concluded that I would ride up this lane, cross the big road on its top, and take my chances on the other side, as I had to cross it anyhow. I turned and had not ridden more than a hundred or two yards, when a Yankee climbed the fence, not more than fifty yards in front of me. In one hand was a tin bucket, and swung across his shoulders were two chickens, tied together, already dressed and ready for the oven.

He sang out, " Where are you going? "

I put on a blank expression, and in north Georgia lingo, with a nasal twang, I replied, " I'se gwine to Mr. Jonson's camp, to ast him to let me go home."

" Where's your home? "

" Up in Gorgy."

" You had better go with me to my camp; I've got some nice honey here, and some good peach brandy, and we can have peach and honey and fried chickens."

" Yes, but youuns won't let weuns go when weuns git thar."

" Oh, yes, you can rest, and then go on."

" What is youuns doing now? "

" Oh, we are down here resting."

I saw from the letters in his cap that he was a member of Co. G, 25th Indiana Regiment, and he told me that they had been engaged in sapping and mining. He had no arms about him and I hated to kill him in cold blood, but I knew that if I left him he would give the alarm, and I would have a posse on my trail.   So to throw him off his guard I consented to accompany him to his camp, on the solemn promise that he would let me continue my journey as soon as we had eaten and drank.   I asked him the nearest way to his camp, and he pointed across the fields in the direction of the tents I had seen, and said it was about a mile off.   I told him that the road around the field was mighty rough, and he said he would let down the fence and we could go through the field.   I said, "All right."   He set his bucket of honey down, and took off his chickens, and as he turned his back to lower the fence I sent a ball through his brain, and rode on up the lane to the top of the hill.

As I reached the road several wagons were passing in the direction of Port Gibson, and a few straggling Yankees without arms.   I rode straight up to them, and saw that the hill was too steep for me to ascend on the opposite side, so I turned in the direction of Port Gibson and rode along side by side with them, for possibly half a mile, paying no attention to anyone, but keeping a sharp eye on my surroundings.   I thought that the boldest would be the safest course under the circumstances, and my theory was correct.

I soon came to a road that turned off to the left. This I took and rode slowly and carelessly along, until a bend hid me from sight.   I then put my horse at a gallop and he moved like the wind.   I let him go at this speed for some time before I checked him, as the road wound around on the top of the ridge for several miles.

At last it began to descend the ridge, and far down, in a valley below me, I could see a large house surrounded by a grove of china and locust trees and a fine orchard.   I took a careful survey of the country beyond as far as my eyes could reach.

As I descended the hill overlooking the house I saw six horses hitched in the shade of the trees.   I scanned them very closely as I approached, and found that they all had side saddles. I rode cautiously up near the end of the front gallery, where I had a commanding position, and sheltering myself behind a large china tree, I sent out a hail. I was answered by a boy, about fifteen or sixteen years old, and I asked him if he could pilot me to a place where I could cross Big Black river, and that if he would I would give him fifty dollars in Confederate money. He said that he would ask his ma.

He was gone quite a while in the house, and I saw and heard no one the whole time he was out of sight. I had an uncanny, restless feeling while waiting his return, and I kept my pistol in my hand at a ready, and my eyes scanning every part of the premises, especially the windows of the house. I am satisfied that if a curtain or window had been raised in sight of me, I would have sent a bullet crashing into it. The young man came at last, and taking the side saddle off one of the horses he replaced it with his own, and mounting, led the way. As we passed the house I rode directly behind him, and kept my head turned so as to cover it. I thought it very strange that with all these side saddles visible, not a woman came in sight.

As soon as we were out of sight of the house I rode alongside of my guide and asked him where he thought that I could cross Big Black. He said that he would try Dr. Nailor's first, and if we could not cross it there, that we would try Hankinson's Ferry. Our road led directly to the Nailor place, and when we rode up to the quarters and inquired for a boat, we were informed that the Yankees had taken every one they had. I examined the banks and found that they were too steep for me to descend, and the opposite bank too muddy and boggy for my horse to get out of the water. The negroes all looked mean and sullen when I would ask them a question, but with one consent they agreed that the only place I could cross the river was at Hankinson's Ferry, several miles up the river. I asked the boy if he knew the route; he answered that he did, and I told him to take me there.

We left the Nailor place and rode up the river bank

for quite a distance, and I tried several times to find a suitable place to swim the river, but on account of recent freshets I could not find any.

When we were within about half a mile of the ferry, my guide wanted to leave and return home, as it was growing late, but I demurred and told him to ride up to the ferry and see if there were any soldiers there, and if there were, and they asked him any questions about his being there, to tell them he was hunting some of his cattle, and then they would not bother him.   I told him to return as quick as he could, and to let me know if I could cross.

After he left I slowly followed in his trail until I came to a thicket of cane, in which I could hide, and see and not be seen.   I waited long enough for the young man to have ridden several miles, and my patience was nearly exhausted, when I saw him coming at a fast trot.   I hailed him, and I saw that he had a scared face, and did not seem to be in the same frame of mind as when I last looked at him.   I asked him if he saw any soldiers at the ferry, and he said he had not, but that there had been some there the Saturday before, but none since.   He said the old ferryman told him this.   I asked if there was a boat that I could cross in, and he said there was—a good new one at that.   I asked how far it was to the ferry, and he replied that it was not a great way; that when I struck the road, I turned to the right and would soon be at the ferry.   I paid him the fifty dollars promised, and he rode off in a gallop.

The sun was just below the tree tops as I got back into my saddle and rode slowly and cautiously toward where my guide said I would strike the road.   As it grew dusk, I entered the road, and could see that it had been well trodden, all tracks going toward Vicksburg, and I, fool-like, never once thought that these were the tracks of the soldiers who had just been relieved from guard duty.   At once I turned down the road and followed it for a few yards, when my horse pricked up his ears and looked steadily ahead.   I halted and turned out of the road and struck out into the swamp on the opposite side, and then toward the river.   As I approached the river, the ground became very boggy, and I was forced to keep on the ridge. Here the river makes a large bend in the shape of an " S," and I followed as close as I could to the brink, looking for a place to swim it. I again struck the road, and turned toward the ferry; my horse again became uneasy, and I kept my pistol in my hand, and my eyes in all directions. As I rode into a patch of cane, on my right, I saw that the bank of the river had caved and cut the road nearly in two. By this time it was growing dark, and as I reached the cave in the road, up sprang a Yankee soldier from the bank under me, and, with his gun almost touching me, yelled out:

" Surrender, you Rebel s——— of———."

I cut his sentence short with a bullet where the ribs part. My horse wheeled at the crack of my pistol, and as he did so, I was enveloped in a sheet of flame, in a half circle from river bank below to river bank above, and the ball and buckshot from a hundred and fifty muskets flashed, hissed, stung, and sung around me. My hat brim dropped across my eyes, both arms, legs, breast, head and body tingled, my right arm hung limp and my left heel pained me fearfully. My horse sprang forward with a fearful snort and two Yankees grabbed his bridle. But with my left hand I sent a bullet into each, and cut down a third one who put himself in my track. My horse broke through the cane like a deer, and for a half mile or so, such speed I never saw excelled, and then without warning he sprang high in the air, and fell with a crash, and rolled over, pinning me under him.

My horse had fallen on his right side and my right leg was fast under him. The ground was soft and yielding. I drew my extra pistol and laid it by my side, took my dispatch, which was in a small glass vial, and sank it below the surface of the earth, and then with considerable trouble reloaded the pistol from which I had fired at the four different Yanks in the melee. Then I calmly awaited my fate. My horse lay between me and the Yankees; I saw that he would make a good breastwork, and here I made up my mind to die.

After waiting for some time and hearing no attempt

to follow me, I began to look about for some way to escape. I made many efforts to pull my limb from under my horse, but all my efforts seemed futile, but, by herculean efforts, I at last succeeded. As I rolled free I found that both crutches had been shot away, and that my saber scabbard was cut nearly in two; the hook that held it up was missing and my left boot heel was gone; my breast and left hand were bleeding, my head ached, my right arm was quite numb, and my body burned and tingled. I drew my saber and cut a small forked bush and trimmed it for a crutch; taking off my saddle bags, I loosened the saddle, removed my blanket and bridle, and laying them across my shoulders I bade my gallant steed, from whose side I could see the entrails protruding in seven places, a sad farewell.

I hobbled down to the river bank, gathered some dry brush and small logs, covered them with my blanket, and bound them together with my bridle reins. Placing my coat and saddle bags on my improvised raft, I shoved it off and swam the river, landing not more than two hundred yards above where I had been ambushed. Putting on my coat, and taking my saddle bags, I began a slow and painful journey toward the southeast.

I forgot to mention that after I got out from under my horse, I had a long hunt for my dispatch before I found it, and it must have been eleven o'clock before I got to the river. I suppose that the Yankees thought, from the speed my horse made when he dashed away, that it was useless for them to try and overtake me on foot.

My path and course led me across a wide, open old field with serrated hills and deep gullies. As soon as it was daylight, I could see a large white house on a hill, and a deep gully led up to the rear of it near the smoke house. I stopped and took an inventory of myself, as the sun was now well up and I within half a mile of succor I hoped. I hid by a water hole in a gully; took off one of my shirts, made some bandages of it, and proceeded to make myself presentable.

I was wounded in the right leg, my right arm was partially paralyzed and of but little use; my left hand badly torn with a ragged hole through it, and the end of my little finger cut off and hanging by a thread. A ball came out of my breast with the clothing, as I removed my shirts; my forehead, neck and jaw were bleeding slightly, and I could feel a great welt across my forehead; my left boot heel was shot away, and my heel considerably swollen and painful; my sword belt and the sword scabbard were cut nearly in two, while the blade was slightly bent; my clothing was cut up with many bullets, and looked more fit for the rag bag than to be worn, especially as they were very muddy as well as bloody.

After making myself as decent as the circumstances permitted, I cut a cane from a small clump on the side of a ditch; splitting open a joint, I laid my finger in it and pressing the ends together, I bound it securely in the hollow joint so it could not slip. Having completed my toilet, I began a slow and painful ascent of the gully that led up to the back of the residence that I saw on the top of the hill in front of me.

In about an hour after my wounds had been dressed, I climbed the gully bank just in the rear of the smoke-house, and reached a plank fence covered with vines, on the edge of a plum thicket, and here I laid in wait, listening and watching. I had been on watch but a few moments, when a little negro, about ten years old, came within a few feet of me. I drew my pistol and pointed it directly at her and asked if there were any Yankee soldiers about. Scared almost to death, and with eyes bulging out, she answered in a stammering voice that I knew was the truth on the spur of the moment.

"No, sir! hain't been none here since lass Sunday."

I did not hesitate another moment, but climbed the fence and walked out past the smoke-house into the back yard, between the house and the kitchen. A yellow negro man, with an apron on, was just coming down the steps out of the kitchen, and a tall, fine looking lady, dressed in deep black, was on the back gallery.

I addressed her with, "Good morning, ma'am! Can I get a horse or a mule from you? I am badly wounded, and must go on."

She replied, " No, you Yankees have not left me a four-footed animal on the place."

" Can I get something to eat?   I am very hungry."

" Yes, but you don't deserve it at my hands."

" Can you let me have some lint and a few bandages? "

" Yes."

" Would you let that boy get me a tub of hot water, and aid me in dressing my wounds? "

" Yes, get him the water, and take him in the office, then come in the house and get the lint and bandages, and help him dress his wounds."

I hobbled into the office, and the negro brought a tub of hot water, and I made him bring a small bucket of pine tar and dissolve it in the water and add a little turpentine.   And after a good bath in this, with his aid, I laid on the lint and bandaged all my wounds well, and taking the best looking shirt I had, put it on top, and soon I felt like a new man.

The darky carried me around to the front on a pair of very good straight stick crutches with red cushioned tops, and from there into the dining room.   Here I saw seven ladies.   The tall lady whom I met on the back gallery and who gave the boy his orders, was seated at the head of the table, and at the foot was a small, pale, delicate lady, about thirty years old, who seemed to be very sad and suffering greatly.   Just opposite me sat a beautiful dark-eyed, curly-haired girl, a perfect Hebe, not more than seventeen or eighteen years of age.   She seemed to have been chosen as the spokesman of the party.   I bowed as gracefully as my condition would permit, and said:

" Good-morning, ladies. We have promise of a beautiful, bright, warm day."

They all bowed very stiffly in return, but uttered not a word in reply.

As I took my seat, Hebe asked, " Where are you from? "

I replied, " I am just out of Vicksburg."

" Oh, you are a Yankee then? "

" No, I am not."

" How did you get out? "

"Only my God and General Johnston will know that for some time to come."

"Is that so? Well, sir, do you know many people in Vicksburg?"

"I know a great many soldiers, and some of the citizens."

While this conversation was going on I was doing my best to get the little tobacco bag, in which I had placed the dispatches from the parties living between Vicksburg and Jackson, that the boys had given me. And after getting it out, I had some difficulty in opening it. I finally succeeded, and the thought struck me that these intensely Southern ladies would be the very ones to intrust with the delivery of these dispatches. I pulled one-half out, and left it loose. The little dark-eyed Hebe plied her questions, and as luck would have it, as she named her friends, I knew the most of them and I saw the ice in their manners was slowly melting; all were growing more pleasant toward me. The pale, delicate lady at the foot of the table cut up my food, and the negro boy poured a thick glass of cream and placed it before me, and was extra polite and attentive at a signal from his mistress.

In a short lull from the fire of Hebe's questions, the pale lady asked: "Do you know Major McCabe of the 33rd Mississippi Regiment?"

"Yes, ma'am," I replied. "He has been quite ill for some time with typhoid fever, but before I left he was able to return to duty with his regiment, and I had the pleasure of telling him good-bye just before I left Vicksburg."

As I finished speaking, I glanced at the dispatch that I had partly drawn out of the tobacco pouch, and saw it was his note to his wife, informing her of his recovery and return to duty. I drew it out and said, "I have a note from him to his wife, and possibly you may know his handwriting?"

With this I handed the note to her. She gave one glad shriek, kissed it and nearly fainted. All the ladies rushed to her at once and read the message. She recovered, and throwing her arms around me gave me a loving kiss. Every eye was wet with tears of joy, and such a greeting as was awarded me by these ladies can never be forgotten while life lingers.

But I can assure you my wounds felt the pressure of each tender, warm-hearted hug, as they attempted to make up for the cold and callous reception given me while I was supposed to be a Yankee escaping from the beleaguered city, and bent on plunder and possible murder. The revulsion of their feelings was beyond control and I appreciated and understood them. I felt that I was a Southern soldier, and all that that meant.

They all introduced themselves, but I only remember Mrs. Lum, the owner of the plantation, and Mrs. McCabe. Mrs. Lum said she had an old mule on the place that was twenty-one years old, and that I could have her. After breakfast an old gray mule was brought up from some hidden recess or hollow among the hills, and a lot of old quilts, and a sheep skin was rigged up into a saddle, with rope stirrups. I gave them all the dispatches that they could send to the families of the boys in the neighborhood, and bidding all farewell, mounted my old mule and rode away. She traveled at a very slow and dignified gait,—a gait all her own,—and after worrying myself and nearly breaking my crutches over her head trying to increase her speed, I gave up in disgust and concluded to let her have her way. She carried her head crooked a little to one side, and had a very knowing look in her eyes, and I christened her the " Widow Bedott," and let her jog along on her own account.

I did not follow any beaten trail or road, but cut across the country so as to avoid all thoroughfares. While pursuing the course I had marked out, I came directly into a road that led due south to Rocky Springs. From my point of view I could see down this road for about a mile, and about a half a mile off I could see a man approaching riding a fine horse. He was dressed in fine, dark clothes and looked like a Yankee. I dismounted from the Widow Bedott, and fastened her to a sassafras bush near a clump of blackberry bushes, and hid myself in a slight depression on the left of the road.

On the opposite side was an open field with a high rail fence.

From my position I had a good view of the road both ways and I waited patiently for my victim. He soon came in sight. I saw he was a doctor, and I waited until he was opposite me, and had no chance to escape. I brought my pistol to bear on him, ordered him to halt and dismount. I never saw an order more quickly obeyed in my life. I commanded him to hitch his horse to the fence and move off. He obeyed at once. I then rose from my position and mounted the mare, and laid his saddlle bags on the fence. I then told him that I was ready to parley with him, and would pay him any reasonable price for the mare, in gold, greenbacks or Confederate money. He found his tongue for the first time and told me that the mare was not his, but one he had borrowed from a Mrs. Payne. I told him that made no difference to me, that I was going to take her anyhow. He would not accept any kind of money, and insisted that he could not dispose of her, as she did not belong to him, but to a widow. I finally gave him an order to take her, wherever found, and told him that I would leave her at some point on the road to Jackson, and I gave him the order. I then pointed to the Widow Bedott and made him a present of my late steed.

I rode off at a brisk pace, still avoiding all roads as much as possible. As night fell, I concluded to leave the woods and take to the main traveled road. I came to a place where there had been a camp of soldiers; a few fires were smouldering, and as I rode into it a gruesome sight broke upon me. My horse shied to one side, and I saw hanging to a tree, swinging to and fro, two men, one a negro and the other a white man. Their eyes and tongues peeped out and thousands of flies swarmed over them. They looked as if they had been hanging several days, and I felt a cold shiver run through my veins as I almost came in contact with them.

About fifty yards from this spot, I came into the road leading from Rocky Springs in the direction of Raymond, and I rode rapidly down it. At about one o'clock at night I was in sight of Raymond, and as I entered the suburbs of that place I saw two Yankee officers just about to enter a yard. I drew my pistol and was in a few feet of them when I ordered them to halt and surrender. They informed me that they were prisoners, both wounded and on parole, and that there were a good many more in Raymond at the hospital in the courthouse, in charge of Dr. Rice of Vicksburg, and that they had been there ever since the battle of Raymond.

I let them pass and rode on to the court-house, and found a sergeant and several men on guard. I dismounted and showed my orders to the sergeant, and told him to get me the best horse in the place, no matter to whom it belonged. He said the doctor had the best. I told him to have the horse at the door as soon as possible. I then went up the stairs and had my wounds redressed and bandaged, left a large number of dispatches to be delivered around Clinton and Raymond, and then gave orders to let the doctor (from whom I had taken Mrs. Payne's mare) have her upon presentation of my order for her.

I mounted my new horse, and set off at a brisk gait for the city of Jackson, just eighteen miles away, which place I rode into hungry, tired, and very sore. I went at once to headquarters and delivered my dispatches and receipts to Col. Benjamin Ewell, General Johnston's chief of staff. I then went at once to the telegraph office, and turned over all the dispatches from the soldiers in Vicksburg, to be sent to their loved ones in the different States. I spent several hours, in writing and mailing others, telling their families why their messages were so short. I then walked all over Jackson and delivered in person all that had been intrusted to me.

I tried at many places to get lodgings, but did not succeed; I could not even get a drink of water, nor could I get a mouthful to eat. I returned his saddlebags to General McMackin, and to Major Livingston Mimms, the gold, greenbacks, and Confederate money, less the $50.00 in greenbacks that I paid the old man at the woodyard at Diamond Bend for my young colt, and the $50.00, in Confederate money, I paid the youth who piloted me into the hands of the Yankees, at Hank-

inson's Ferry.   After my settlement I had but $2.00, in
Confederate money, left.

I walked up to the Bowman House and asked if they
would give me a room and board until I could hear from
home, and get some funds, but the proprietors refused.
I bought two small round black ginger cakes, from a
little negro, who was peddling them on the street, and
paid her a dollar a piece for them.   I got a drink of
water out of Pearl River as I ate them.   As a last resort,
I made application to the hospital for a cot, and that
too was refused on the ground that they were full.

General Johnston did not come down to Jackson from
Canton, that day, and I could not leave until I had com-
municated with him.   The day was a very tiresome one
to me, and late in the evening I again went to the hospital and had my wounds dressed, and as the night wore
on, I laid down on the stone steps of the capitol building and slept as sound as a babe until daylight, and
woke considerably refreshed, as it was the first sleep I
had had since leaving the city of Vicksburg, the night
of the fifth of June, and this was now the morning of
the ninth of June, and only about six hours of sleep to
my credit.

At ten o'clock General Johnston came down from
Canton, and I repaired to his headquarters, gave him
Pemberton's verbal message and told him the exact conditions prevailing in and around Vicksburg as I saw
them.   He gave me a cot at headquarters, and I slept
until about 2 p. m., when I was roused up and ate my
first meal since my breakfast with the ladies at Mrs.
Lum's.   I had turned Dr. Rice's horse over to the Quartermaster, and General Johnston had given me another,
telling me to ride out somewhere in the country, where
I could get a place to stay, to have my wounds dressed
regularly, and to take a good rest until I heard from
him.   I then decided that I would go out to Belvidere
and spend my rest at my father's, who was at the time
Chief of Ordnance of the Department of Mississippi,
and at home on furlough.   General Johnston furnished
me with all the money I might need.

CHAPTER XV

Am ordered again to Vicksburg—At Yazoo City—Return
to Jackson—Am wounded and sent to hospital at
Selma, Ala.—Report to General Bragg and join General Longstreet—Receive major's commission.

I LAID in a good supply of underclothing, several
negligee shirts, and a pair of new crutches, and hanging
these upon my arm I mounted my horse and rode off to
Belvidere. For a week I enjoyed myself and got all the
real rest I needed. At the end of a week I got a message
from General Johnston to report at once, and I answered it in person. My orders were to go again to
Vicksburg, and this time to establish, if possible, a
route for a line of couriers, to and from Vicksburg,
either up and down the Yazoo River by the first line I
took, or by the Mississippi River, from a point above
and outside of the line of the land forces.

I went by way of Cox's Ferry again. I met General
Cosby near Mechanicsburg, and taking Captain Saunders with six men, I crossed little Sunflower, and keeping
in the swamps and thickets we crossed Deer Creek, and
got to Old River. Here we made a depot in the brush,
and had our dugouts nearby. As the caps were brought
on horseback, we would load our dugouts and paddle
down the river into the city before daylight. I only
made one trip with Captain Saunders, and we carried in
200,000 caps with us, reaching the city without any
serious trouble.

I was quite weak, and remained in Vicksburg, as I was
not strong enough to paddle my boat up stream against
the current of the Mississippi, with only one sound arm.
I took my place with "Whistling Dick," and let the
Yanks hear from me as the opportunity offered. I
visited many of the boys at night, and chatted with them
of home and the loved ones there, and helped to make the
horrors of the siege as light as possible.

The night of the third of July, after the white flag of surrender had been hoisted and the guns had ceased their thunder, I got about four hundred men together, and lowered old " Whistling Dick " into the bottom of the Mississippi River, and she sleeps there now under two hundred feet of mud.   Then I got in my little dug-out, and tying my crutches into a cross I fastened my coat and a shirt to them, hoisted and lashed them to my dugout seat, and taking my paddle for a rudder, with a strong wind in my favor, I floated out on the river. Daylight overtook me just opposite Millican's Bend; here I landed, and on my crutches walked up to the Duval place.   There I got an old " box-ankled " mule into a stall, and after a little coaxing, I got a rope halter around her neck; I then got some bagging and hemp rope, and rigged a saddle and halter bridle, and by tying loops in the rope girth I had very comfortable rests or stirrups for my feet.   My saddle was soft and pleasant, and, after a short trial, everything was adjusted very comfortably.

I rode across the swamp in the direction of Yazoo City.   I came to a large pile of cotton, possibly a thousand bales, hidden on the back side of a plantation; this I immediately set on fire, as I knew the Yankees would soon take charge of it, as they would cover the whole country.   The cartel for the surrender had been signed on the third of July, and to-day, the fourth, they were marching into the city.   With these thoughts in my mind I had no hesitancy in applying the torch to this huge pile of cotton, then worth about one dollar a pound in the marts of the North.

After firing the cotton, I rode away from the smoke of it as swiftly as my old gray mule would permit, following an old blind road, seemingly that had not been traveled for years, as it was grown up in places with vines and small bushes.   I came to a lake, that seemed to have once had a bridge or ferry across it, and on the opposite side I could see the road leading away from it. I urged my old mule to enter the water, but she would back her ears and plant her feet and positively refuse to budge in the direction of the water.   At last, weary and mad, I drew my pistol and was about to send a bullet into her brain, when I thought of an expedient I had once read of, used by a Mexican on the Rio Grande River years before, to compel his pony to take to the water when he had stubbornly refused, as my old mule was now doing. In imitation of the Mexican, I pointed her head straight at the water, laid my pistol barrel parallel with and flat upon the top of her tail bone, and gripping a firm hold with my feet and hand, I pulled the trigger. She gave a mighty leap and landed far out in the lake, and I went down to my ears. She rose in a second, as her feet touched the bottom, and made fast time for the opposite shore. My bullet did not touch her, but the flash took some of the hair off and scorched her hide and tail, and raised a small blister.

I crossed several streams after this, notably the Big Sunflower River, before I reached the eastern edge of the swamp, but at none of them did I have any great trouble, for upon reaching the water's edge, I would simply point her head straight at the spot I wanted her to enter it, and when all was ready I would touch her, and she went in like a flash, reminding one of a boy touching off his toy cannon to celebrate some holiday. As I would place my hand behind the saddle, and cluck, she never hesitated; in fact her movements were so quick, I had all I could do to stay on my pile of bagging.

On Deer Creek I rode up to a house and asked if I could get something to eat, and also asked for an old saddle, if one could be spared. I was told to get down and come in. I did so.

As I entered the door a man met me and said, "You are my prisoner."

"I reckon not," I replied.

He sprang for a double-barreled gun near him in the hall. I drew my pistol and ordered him to halt, told him not to touch the gun, if he did I would kill him. I then commanded him to surrender. He refused and reached for his gun, and I sent a bullet into his brain, and he dropped dead upon the floor. I picked up his gun, retreated down the steps and remounted my mule. I have thought since that from the way he acted he was under the influence of whiskey, and somewhat intoxicated, but under the circumstances I was forced to do what I did. I saw several negroes at a distance, but they did not attempt to molest me. I think that he was the overseer on the place, not the owner, and if I had not killed him he would have given me much trouble and annoyance. I was anxious to get out and report to General Johnston and wanted no unnecessary delays.

I rode on across the valley, and before dark I crossed the Sunflower River, and at daylight came to a large plantation on Silver Creek, belonging to a Mrs. Denman. I rode up to the front gate and hailed. A negro woman came to the front, and I asked if I could get a saddle and something to eat. She retreated into the house and after a while a negro boy came round with an old English saddle tree, without stirrups, and said it was all the man's saddle " Mistes " had. I put it on the old mule and it rested me very much.

I followed up the creek for several miles, and came to a road leading directly across the swamp to Yazoo City. Here I stopped in front of another dwelling house and asked for something to eat. An elderly lady of the true type of Southern womanhood, a Miss Mag Bennett, came to the gate and gave me two hoe cakes of corn bread, with honey and butter spread between their covers. She said that breakfast had long been over, and that this was all she had in the house. I thanked her, and asked how far it was to Yazoo City, and if I would have any trouble in finding my way across. She answered that the road was clear, and no Yankee soldiers were in the way. I thanked her for her kindness and rode off, pinching small chunks from my corn pones and chewing and swallowing the fragments very slowly, realizing fully how hungry I was, as I had not had a mouthful to eat for four days. As I finished the last morsel I felt rested, but still very hungry.

The region I was crossing is very low and uninhabited, and subject to deep annual inundations from the Mississippi River, and is drained by Panther Creek. About twelve o'clock M., I came to a large two-story residence, that was set back some distance from the road. It had a large lawn in front, and I could see a number of horses hitched about in various parts of this lawn, and some twenty or thirty Confederate soldiers lolling around. I rode up to the gallery and asked if I could get dinner. I was answered in the affirmative, and one of the soldiers aided me in dismounting and fastened my old mule.

As I took my seat on the gallery, I asked if they had any news from Vicksburg; and they answered that they had none. I told them that it had surrendered on the third of July, and that the Yankees had marched in and taken possession on the fourth. They would not believe it. I told them that I had just made my escape from there, and they merely laughed at me. I said no more on the subject, but merely asked if they had heard any heavy firing from that direction lately.

A few moments afterward I was invited in to dinner, and took my seat at the table. Several ladies were present, and one was particularly kind to me. Seeing my crippled condition, she aided in cutting up my food. As my crutches were leaning against the wall, a little negro girl brushed against and knocked them down; this lady picked them up and apologized for the servant's carelessness.

At that time I was too much engrossed with the business before me to pay much attention to anything else. I was somewhat riled because they did not believe that I told the truth about the surrender of Vicksburg. I did not know then, nor did I have the faintest idea, that the young lady who cut up my food and picked up my crutches was to be my companion and loving helpmate and guide through more than forty years of life, after peace had spread her snowy wings over the whole land. I was certainly a forlorn looking being at that time; worn out, wounded, and half starved.

As soon as I finished eating, I mounted my old mule and rode into Yazoo City. Here I telegraphed General Johnston the news, and the conditions of the surrender of Vicksburg, and my safe arrival in Yazoo City. I received a telegraphic order from him to take charge of all the straggling forces, and all the public property of the Confederate States, in and around this vicinity, and bring all to Canton. I got a good large sorrel mule from Judge C. L. DuBuisson, and got all the government property out of the city and well on the road to Canton, with a guard of something over three hundred men belonging to various commands. Our camp was out at the Know Nothing Spring, on the plank road toward Benton, and about six miles east of Yazoo City. In this camp I organized a battalion, and placed a guard in Yazoo City; and none too soon, for the gunboats and the Yanks were almost in sight, and came swarming up the river to Yazoo City by thousands. They landed troops of negro cavalry and proceeded to raid the country. I laid my plans accordingly, and sent my wagon trains under escort to Canton, built a pontoon bridge of fence rails across Big Black, at Moore's Ferry, and got everything ready for a retreat. After everything was propitious, I had a running fight with them on the plank road between Yazoo City and the Know Nothing Springs, led them into ambush and let very few of the negroes escape. Just east of " The Ponds " on the north side of the road, we buried thirty-two of them, and from about three miles this side of Yazoo City, to the " Ponds," they left most of their number.

After this skirmish, we retreated to Canton. Beyond Canton, across Bear Creek, I again had a skirmish with the Yankee cavalry and drove them back. I did not not do much rifle or pistol work in either of these engagements, as I was in command and had to take care of everything. I crossed my wagon trains over Pearl River, at Ratcliff's Ferry, and got them beyond Jackson, in the direction of Enterprise, and then reported to General Johnston in person.

I spent several days in Jackson, and received a severe wound through my left lung on the 16th of July, and was sent to the hospital at Selma, Ala. I was delirious when I reached there, and in a very feeble condition, and have no remembrance of my journey or arrival at that point. A high fever set in from my exhausted condition, and very little care was given me, until nature began to assert her powers and I rallied and demanded more and better treatment.   Neither the hospital attendants nor the surgeons knew my name.   I was only a sick and wounded soldier.   When Drs. Tuttle, Mellon and Cabell found out who I was, no man on this earth ever received better or closer attention that I did.

About the last of August, or the first days of September, 1863, I was carried to the hospitable home of Judge DuBose, not far from Faunsdale station, between Selma and Demopolis, and here, under the gentle ministrations and kind nursing of Mrs. DuBose and Misses Gussie and Rose, I was soon myself again.

From the home of Judge DuBose, I was ordered to report to General Bragg at Chickamauga, and to join General Longstreet, who was then on his way to reinforce General Bragg at Chickamauga.   I reached that point on the 16th of September, with a full major's commission.

CHAPTER XVI

Battle of Chickamauga—I make frequent raids—My first spree—Battle of Missionary Ridge.

I was now again a Confederate soldier, and a commissioned field officer in the regular army of the Confederate States, for life and not for the war alone.

On the 18th of September I went into the battle of Chickamauga a staff officer, without my rifle, and I felt like a fish out of water. I was sent out to the extreme left wing of our army in that great battle, and led a small squad of cavalry in the rear of the Yanks, dismounted, and opened fire into their ranks, and doubled them back on their main line toward their center. I tried to practice Jackson's tactics, as he did at Chancellorsville, to the best of my ability, without orders, as I had none. Our little squad did some heavy flanking and fighting, for two days, which our Yankee friends will long remember. I was disabled by a shot, near the close of the second day's fight, and sent to the hospital at Atlanta.

On the 10th of October I again reported for duty, and was sent by General Bragg to Gen. P. D. Roddey, at Tuscumbia, Ala. Upon my arrival, I was put in command of the post at that place. Here I remained until we were ordered to Missionary Ridge, just before the battle of that name.

While at Tuscumbia I made frequent raids in the direction of Iuka, Miss., as far north as Columbia, Tenn., and in around Pulaski, Tenn., and other points, capturing many prisoners and destroying Yankee supplies.

On one occasion I was ordered to make a raid in the direction of Iuka, to see what the Yanks were doing. It was a cold, bleak, drizzly day, and as I approached the road leading from Iuka to Eastport, my scouts reported a heavy body of Yankee troops moving in the direction of Eastport. I got within half a mile of the road, and dismounting half of my men, I left the others with the horses, and taking one hundred and fifty dismounted men I marched them up to within three hundred yards of the road, and placed them in a clump of pine and small black-jack bushes, facing the Bear Creek road, with their right flank at right angles to the Iuka and Eastport road. Here I left them in command of the senior captain with orders to remain in concealment until my return. I then buttoned my own coat, which was a Yankee one dyed a dark hue, and having on a Yankee cavalryman's hat, spurs, bridle and saddle and a horse branded U. S. A., I made a very fair Yankee. Taking a large wagon whip, I rode down to the Yankee lines.

As I struck the Eastport road, the whole column was halted, as some of the artillery was stalled or mired in the mud in front. Just at the point, ready to turn out into the Bear Creek road, stood a large surgeons' wagon, filled with all the necessary instruments and drugs, and drawn by four tremendous Norman horses. I spoke sharply to the driver and told him the doctor wanted that wagon at the front at once and to follow me, as the artillery was stalled in front and if he waited he would not reach Eastport before midnight. He obeyed at once, and all the wagons, sutler's stores and many straggling Yankees followed. I rode at their head until I passed my dismounted men, then I changed sides and slowly dropped back until I came in sight of the mounted men and loose horses. I found them in line of battle. I was just opposite one of the sutler's wagons, when I saw my dismounted men close in behind. At the same time a little clerk in the wagon caught a glimpse of the starry cross banner glittering in the ranks of my mounted men.

He leaned out of the wagon, and looked at me and exclaimed: " We are off to the Confederacy, by God, sir ! "

" You are mighty right, young man," I answered.

I hurried the wagons up, and told the stragglers to

climb in and not try to get away; if they did not obey I'd kill them all. I never saw men more obedient. My men were soon mounted and we put everything in a trot and drove with all speed back to Tuscumbia and never fired a gun. I had twenty-nine wagons, a doctor's complete outfit, seven large sutler's shop wagons and fifty-one prisoners. The wagons contained quartermaster and commissary stores that we were badly in need of.

The sutler's stores were a real godsend, as there were quantities of calicoes, domestics, pins, needles, hairpins, ladies' hose, shoes, boots, etc. And in the stores I found seven baskets of champagne, a great deal of quinine and other much needed medicines. Among the quartermaster's stores was a large supply of cavalry boots, shoes and men's wear. I kept a fine pair of boots and took several bolts of calico, domestics, hose, gloves, pins, needles, thread, hairpins and so on, for distribution among my lady friends, and took charge of three baskets of champagne and a pair of gold spurs presented by the ladies of New York to Gen. Morgan L. Smith.

The little sutler's clerk who had waved his hat and exclaimed, "Off for the Confederacy," I paroled, and sent an escort with him into his own lines and told him to go back home to his mother, and to stay there, and not come South again until after the war was over. I gave him a note to hand to General Dodge, commander of the left wing of the 16th Army Corps, thanking him for the liberal donation of so many wagon loads of army supplies, stores, and medicines for our needy hospitals, that he had delivered into my hands so generously, without my having to lose a man, fire a gun, or pay a cent. I sent one basket of the champagne to Miss Ella Winston, and one to Miss Kate Armistead, both cousins of mine, living near Tuscumbia. I kept one basket at my headquarters, and sent the rest to the hospital. I also sent cousins Ella and Kate a donation of ladies' shoes, gloves, domestics, calicoes, thread, pins, needles, and other etceteras for themselves and the other lady members of their families.

The next day, I received a card of thanks from each, and two negroes brought a great tray loaded with the

choicest viands—a roast turkey, baked and fried
chickens, butter, bread, jellies, celery, cakes, and other
good things. I received their donations with thanks. I
sent my servant to Dr. Abernathy's and borrowed from
Mrs. Abernathy chairs, napkins, goblets and a table
cloth, and also some knives, forks, and spoons.   I sent
invitations to Dr. Dan German, and four of the officers
who were with me in the expedition, to come at three
o'clock that evening and dine with me at headquarters.
I had the table elaborately decorated, and waited for my
guests.   Only one came, and that was Dr. German. The
others all being " on duty," could not attend.

We sat long at the table and enjoyed the rich feast,
sent by our fair friends, and when we were fully satisfied, at Dr. German's request, my servant opened a bottle
of champagne.   I had never in my life tasted any kind
of intoxicating liquors; no kind had ever passed my lips.
Our glasses were filled, and the doctor drank his with the
true enjoyment of a *bon vivant;* I tasted mine, and although it had a sweet, fiery, pungent flavor, it was not
bad to the taste.   Again and again I filled my goblet,
and kept up with the doctor, until two whole bottles had
been emptied by me, and two by the doctor.   Then the
chairs, table and the walls and ceiling of the room began
to spin around, and my glass would not set upright on
the table but insisted on turning over; I drove it, with
considerable force, down upon the table to make it stick
and it suddenly disappeared, as if by magic, or the ghost
of a dream.   I, myself, seemed also to disappear and
the doctor, too, went into the land of invisibility in a
whirling, shadowy form.   Everything grew dark, but
the gyrations and twisting motions kept going unceas-
ingly, until I was spun out into a seemingly fine thread
of gossamer and lost in infinity—floated away on the
subtle fumes of the treacherous sparkling wine.

The sunlight was streaming in from the wrong side
of the room when I came to.   Chairs, table, ceiling,
and all things visible were still in a whirl, and a
pain was throbbing and scooting through my brain as
if my old head had been pounded with a sledge hammer,
or pierced with a Yankee bullet.   My leg was fast above

my head, my spur driven through the bottom of a chair, and it was as immovable as a ton of lead.   On the opposite side of the table, still whirling round, though pale, stark and stiff as an iron poker, lay the doctor.   I could hear the rattle of dishes and the stir of my servants in the kitchen.   I tried to speak, but my tongue was way down in my throat, and was glued to it.   I tried to shift my position and turn over, but I was numb and seemingly dead.

I concluded that there had been a sudden raid into the town by the Yankees, and that the doctor had been killed and I shot through the head and paralyzed.   I tried to move my leg, and lift it out of the chair, but I was absolutely unable to control a single muscle of it.   I could hear my negro grinding the coffee, smell the meat frying and hear it sizzling in the frying-pan.   I made effort after effort to speak, but only a gurgling sound could I produce.   At last, as I became more sane I got my voice, and as I called my negro, my voice seemed to come from a great distance and had a deep, sepulchral cadence and was very indistinct.   When he came in sight he, too, was spinning round and going through various gyratory motions that were very annoying to me.   I ordered him to stop, and stand still so I could look at him.   I asked him how many had been killed in the fight when we were surprised by the Yankees.   He said that there had been no fight, and no one killed.   I knew he was telling me a lie, for I could see with my own eyes that the doctor was dead, and I knew that I had been shot through the head, and couldn't move hand or foot.

My negro went back to his cooking, and soon I could hear him singing, " We'll anchor by and by," and it made me feel that I was anchored, without waiting for the " by and by."   I called him again and asked how many were killed.   He came, and in very positive tones he said: " No, Massa, 'taint been no fight; 'tain't no one kilt; Dr. German ain't dead, and you ain't hurt; it's jist dat air shampain what you and he dun drinked."

I lay still, for I had to, and tried to gather my still whirling thoughts together, and the more I tried to think the less progress I made.   Finally I had a rift of reason, and it came like a flash. I was *drunk,* champagne drunk at that. I was lifted to my cot and for a whole week I laid, as it were, in a drunken stupor, and when I tried to raise my head in bed, I would get still drunker. And now, looking back over a lapse of forty odd years, I can truthfully say that that drunken spree has been enough experience in that line to last me through life. Nor can I to this distant day conceive how anyone, after passing through the pangs of a champagne drunk, could ever wish, voluntarily, to indulge in another.

As soon as I got over my spree I was ordered to report to General Bragg, at Missionary Ridge, near Chattanooga, Tenn. I found our army in position on the ridge, with our lines extending to and including Lookout Mountain. On the latter we had a signal station. I rode up on this mountain, and had a magnificent view of the whole surrounding country.

Chattanooga and the entire Yankee army lay at my feet. Grant and his lieutenants had thoroughly recuperated it, since Bragg's inertness had permitted them to do, after their defeat at Chickamauga. Why Bragg let them lie unmolested in Chattanooga so long after Chickamauga, I have never been able to comprehend. I have always thought that we should have driven them out of Tennessee without halting, while the veterans of Longstreet were with him. We could have cut off and destroyed his long, thin line of communication and captured his legions in detail. If only Stonewall Jackson had been in his place, a different tale would have been told to the coming generations. Grant had no real safe base of supplies, and what he did have would have been in Jackson's hands and destroyed, and Grant's army would have been a thing of the past in less than a week.

At the battle of Missionary Ridge, I was near Bragg's headquarters, to the right of our center, about a hundred and fifty yards, as we faced Chattanooga, and could see the city and the river. On the morning of the battle a heavy mist obscured the mountains and valleys; Lookout was entirely hidden. I could hear the distant rattle of musketry skirmishing, far away in the direction of the mist-shrouded crest of Lookout Mountain, but everything was hidden from my vision. As the fog lifted from the fields in front, I could see long lines of skirmishers leaving their rifle pits, that extended from Missionary Ridge to Lookout Mountain, and coming toward us. While watching them, a fierce firing began on our right, and I saw long dense lines of bluecoats, extending from the river on our right wing to as far as my eye could reach on our left.

I was sent to General Hardee by Bragg, and as I rode up and reported for duty, Sherman's whole corps made a charge on our skirmish line and drove out the skirmishers by overwhelming numbers alone. Then they made a charge and attempted to reach our breastworks. The fighting here was desperate in the extreme. We met them with a perfect storm of grape and canister, and a deadly rifle fire; time after time they rallied and came again, until the whole mountain side was blue with their dead bodies, and the gullies ran streams of blood.

Later in the day after carrying several dispatches to and from Generals Bragg and Hardee, while resting behind a breastwork near some tall poplar trees, I asked permission to use my rifle. It being granted, I brought it into play and did some good execution among the mounted Yankee officers.

Our part of the line was victorious, and we drove Sherman from off the field and back to the Tennessee River, and we occupied the battle ground. Our lines rested and cooked their suppers, and I, with many of the men, was fast asleep, when we were aroused and told to fall in, as our army had been defeated, and the greater part of Breckinridge's corps destroyed. Many would not believe the rumor, and much confusion ensued as we were hurried through the darkness in the direction of Chickamauga. We marched the whole night, we knew not where, not seeing or hearing an enemy on either hand. Daylight found us still retreating, and everyone very much exhausted and worn out.

We halted at last, and kindled fires, and prepared coffee. I rode among the men as they were resting, and I never before saw as disheveled, disordered, and disheartened a set of men in my life.   I was perfectly disgusted.

The next morning I met General Bragg, and asked if I could return to Tuscumbia. He assented and gave the necessary orders. With my servant, George, I at once set out on my return by way of Rome, Ga., and Gadsden, Ala., and reached my old headquarters at Tuscumbia, Ala., without any delays.

A few days after I was ordered by Gen. N. B. Forrest on a scout with twenty-one men, toward Murfreesboro, with orders to tap the railroad at some point, and blow up a down train loaded with supplies. The journey was a long and dangerous one, through a country filled with renegades and cut-throats. I selected my men principally from the Fourth Alabama, and only took young unmarried men, who volunteered willingly, and unhesitatingly. I carried on mules nine large cap-torpedoes to place under the rails, to be exploded by pressure or from a small electric battery, which I had given a thorough test before I started by firing several blank cartridges, at the distance of half a mile from the battery. I had a good telegraph operator with me, and I put him in charge of electric appliances.

We arrived at our destination, in Rutherford County, on the railroad from Nashville to Chattanooga, just at daylight one morning, without having any serious delays or having to make any great detours from the original line mapped out for our journey. We captured the guard in the tunnel, without firing a gun, as they were so far in the enemy's lines, and surrounded by a friendly community, that they were careless and off guard. I compelled the operator at the tunnel, by threats of death, to give my operator his code and signals. I placed my torpedoes where they could do the most damage to the tunnel, and then dressing my men in the uniforms of the Yankee guards, I put the battery in position, and awaited the train's arrival.

The telegrapher gave warning of the approach of an " up " train, loaded with Missouri Yankee troops, going home on furlough, and to tell of their victory at Missionary Ridge. My orders were to destroy a *down* and not an *up* train, but I did not hesitate to disobey this order, as I thought a train load of live Yankees, put out of business forever, would do the Confederacy more good than a train load of army rations. So when the entire train was well in the tunnel I sent the fatal spark on its mission, and buried the whole under a crushing mass of clay and stone. I waited until the last fumes of steam and powder smoke escaped from the awful wreck, and then with my nine prisoners I began my retreat.

CHAPTER XVII

Receive orders from General Forrest—Am captured by
Col. C. W. Gaines—The Dutch jailer—Offered freedom
—Am forwarded to Louisville—My escape—Am ordered
to report to General Stuart in Virginia—My journey to
Virginia.

WE had to make some long and hard rides to escape
the numerous bodies of cavalry that were soon following
in our tracks, as we were in a regular hotbed of Union
renegades, and every man's hand was against us. My
Yankee captives were mounted on the mules that had
borne the torpedoes, and they were not anxious to keep
up with us, but rather retarded our progress. I held
onto them until I crossed the Tennessee line, not far
below Pulaski, and here one dark night, in a dense strip
of woodland, I halted and built a fire, as it was intensely
cold, and paroled every man, and gave him a mule to
ride. Each gave his word of honor that he would not
tell which way we had gone.

I left them at the camp-fire about midnight, and about
daylight on the morning of the 14th of December we
were on Hurricane Creek. As we halted, we sent a
picket out behind us, and were just preparing to get a
cup of coffee and broil some bacon, when our pickets
fired their guns and were in our midst with a regiment
of Illinois cavalry at their heels. I ordered the men to
escape into the fallen timber and scatter and cross the
river wherever they could. We met the Yanks with a
feeble fire, and I was shot through the thigh and received a serious wound in the knee of the right leg. I
and four of my men were captured by Col. G. W. Gaines,
of the 9th Illinois Cavalry. My men were all scattered
in the fallen timber, and save the four who were with me,
all escaped.

My wounds knocked me senseless and my knee was
very painful. When I came to my horse had been killed
and I had been a prisoner some moments before I was

aware of it.   I was carried at once to Pulaski, escorted by a Captain Pickett of the 9th Illinois Cavalry.   At Pulaski I was turned over to the provost guard and escorted to Columbia, Tennessee. Here I was confined in the inner cell of the jail; and here, sore, weak, tired and wounded, I lay all night on the stone floor, very cold and without a blanket even.   There were several inches of snow on the outside.

The next morning I was taken out into the hall of the building and carefully searched by a large, red-faced jailer, named Truitt.   He was a big, rough, fat, cruel-looking specimen of humanity, and just fitted my idea of what a Yankee prison-keeper should be.   Soon after he had finished his search, a tall, red-headed Dutch captain, with bleared eyes, came in, and held a consultation with my jailer.   My Dutch captain was as beastly a specimen as I had ever looked at.   He wanted to know if I had been searched; and Truitt told him I had been.

Upon my left-hand fourth finger I wore my mother's wedding ring, placed there by her own sainted fingers only a few hours before her death, with a request that I give it to the companion I should choose to be my help-mate through life.   In my undershirt, just under the left arm pit, in a specially constructed pocket, I always wore a small miniature of my mother, in a round gutta percha case, about as large as a dollar; I had had it made long years before and it and her ring were my *talismans*, and I held them as very sacred treasures.   This Dutchman saw the ring and ordered me to pull it off and give it to him.   I refuséd and he caught my hand. I bent my finger but he was too strong for me and tore it off.   In the struggle he felt the gutta percha locket, and thought it was a watch.   He ordered me to pull it out.   I again refused, and he drew his knife and was about to cut a hole through my clothing and take it by force when I told him I would get it out.   I steadied myself on my crutch, and taking the picture out, I dropped it on the stone floor, and ground it under my heel, saying as I did so, " No damned Yankee looks at that."   He stepped back, drew a small Smith & Wesson pistol, and fired a shot that entered my left side, glanced a rib, and passed out, making a small flesh wound.   I told him he was a damned coward, and that some day I would yet meet him and have a settlement, even if it was in another world.   Truitt and the guard interposed and I was carried out and put on the train for Nashville.

Before going on with this trip, I will remark that in October, 1866, I had the exquisite pleasure of meeting this Dutch captain in a canebrake on Steel's Bayou, between Deer Creek and the Mississippi River, in Issaquena County, Miss.   I asked him for my ring and he told me that he gave it to a " woman of the town," in Detroit, Mich., and did not know what she had done with it, as he had never heard from her since.   I left his bones to bleach, unburied, in that same canebrake.

As I was removed from the prison to the cars to Nashville, every fiber of my frame was smarting with indignation ; a demon of revenge possessed my soul and I was almost a maniac.   I was carried at once to the penitentiary and placed in cell No. 3.   Here I laid for several days in a kind of torpor.   I tore up one of my shirts, made bandages of it and dressed my wounds as best I could.   My food was pea soup, pickled fat pork, and a coarse, sour kind of bread, and miserable tasting water.   A large wooden vessel was used as a sink.

My cell was about four feet wide, and about eight feet long.   I could sit on my iron cot with only its coarse gray blanket, and rest my feet against the opposite wall, as I often did.   A guard paced his beat constantly in front of my door ; I could hear his steady tramp and soon became accustomed to it.   The stench from my wooden sink was almost unbearable, and each day as I endured it I became more and more filled with venom and hatred.   The act of my Dutch captain at Columbia had maddened me, and I was more like a beast than a man.   Each day I nursed my wrath and it intensified.   I blamed myself for not trying to crush his skull with my crutch at the moment he did me such an injury.

One day, while these thoughts were seething through

my brain, the door of my cell was thrown open and an old, gentlemanly looking man, wearing a tall silk hat and a high standing collar, accompanied by General Dodge and several other officers, presented themselves at my door; but as it swung open the awful stench drove them back, as my sink had not been emptied since my arrival. In a few moments two soldiers entered and carried it out, then returned and sprinkled chloride of lime all over the cell floor and closed the door. The fumes of the lime almost suffocated me. I laid back on my cot, and I know that if my words and thoughts had had the power to do so the whole Yankee nation would have been assigned to the bottomless pit.

In about an hour the old man returned; the door was left open and the officers stood on the outside, but he entered. He spoke in a mild and kindly tone, and said:

"Good morning, my young friend. I have come to offer you your freedom; yes, to give it to you."

I arose and thanked him, and said that I was very glad, as this was a horrible place in which to keep a human being.

He took off his hat, drew some papers from it and in rather pompous tone said, "Our great and glorious President, in the goodness of his heart, has seen fit to issue an amnesty to all repentant rebels. Now all you have to do is to sign these documents before me, and we will send you north of the Ohio River and take good care of you until the end of this cruel war."

As his meaning dawned upon me while he was repeating this formula, I never was angrier in my life.

I asked, "Is that the oath of allegiance to the Yankee government you want me to take?"

"Yes," he replied.

As mad as a hornet, I said, "Well, sir, when I die, I want my winding sheet made out of Yankee scalps and I want the fun of killing them myself."

I drew myself back and gathered up my crutches, and as I did so the old man jumped back and out of the door, as if I had struck at him. My cell door was slammed to and I heard the officers on the outside

laugh heartily. I laid back on my cot madder than
ever at this new insult offered me by the old man, whom
I learned was a Judge Campbell. I felt exhausted and
every muscle in my body ached. I studied how I could
escape this life, and how I could best avenge myself.

As I thus lay, my cell was again opened and a polite
sergeant said General Dodge wanted to see me. I
arose and followed him. We got into an ambulance
and drove to the capitol. Here I received a good bath,
shave, hair cut, and shampoo. My wounds were dressed,
clean underclothes and a citizen's suit with the exception of a coat furnished me, and I was driven in a hack
up to General Dodge's headquarters. Here I was introduced to General Dodge and a number of officers,
and we had a splendid dinner. I was asked a good
many questions, but I was on my guard in a moment,
and soon they all saw that I was too sharp to be caught
in any trap set for me, so after a while they desisted.
After a good cigar, which I really enjoyed, General
Dodge gave me a letter addressed to "The Commandant of U. S. Military Prisons," and also one addressed
to the chief surgeon in charge of the Broadway prison
hospital, Louisville, Ky. He told me that I would be
forwarded to Louisville that night, but that I could
stay at his headquarters, on parole, until time to take
the train, which I did. He handed me several late
papers, and I took a seat in a large arm rocking chair,
with a soft cushioned seat, and in a few minutes I was
sound asleep. A Captain Pratt, a Kentuckian by birth,
roused me from my slumbers, and went with me to the
train, and saw me aboard and in charge of the guard.

We reached Louisville about daylight, and I was
placed in the Broadway prison hospital, under charge
of a Dr. Dalrymple, who told me his residence was 202
Hudson street, New York. He was a great big, fat,
jolly, kindhearted man, with a touch as gentle and
soft as that of a woman. He was soon interested in
my wounds, and dressed them with his own hands. He
informed me that General Dodge was an intimate friend
of his and that he would take good care of me, and
see that I had the best of treatment while in his hands.

I was given a nice room, all to myself, and I was well cared for in reality. Many Southern as well as Yankee women called on me, and one evening my kinswoman, Mrs. Z. P. Zanone, accompanied by Miss Annie Fontaine and others, whose names I cannot recall, came to see me. They brought me some nice cigars, canned strawberries, pineapples, lemon sherbet, cakes, and other delicacies, and I ate as long as I could swallow.

That night I was taken with cholera morbus and terrible cramps, and about two o'clock in the morning I put on my citizen's overcoat and went out to the large main prison sink. There was a separate hospital sink, and one common one, divided by a wall of plank, for the Federal and Confederate general prisoners; and it was to this general sink that I made my way. It was about thirty feet long, and had a flattened pole to stand upon; it was some ten or fifteen feet deep, and half filled all the time with quicklime, copperas and other disinfectants. I stopped at the end, and while on the pole, grasping the corner post and in terrible agony, the main prison sergeant, another great brute of a Dutchman, entered at a small side gate from the street. Leaving it partly open, he came in a rush to my corner position. As he saw me bending over he raised his foot and kicked at me, just grazing my chin and nearly sending me into the pit below. I arose at once; all pain was gone in an instant. I stepped aside, boiling with anger, and he took my place. I fastened up my clothing, and as he bent his head forward, I drew back my crutch, spear fashion, and sent the iron heel straight at his neck, striking him just under the chin with all the force I could exert. He fell backwards, head foremost, into the pit of quicklime, and sank like a rock. I bent over to give him a finishing blow, but only the bottoms of his boots ever came to the surface; I gave them an extra tap, and sent them back out of sight.

The snow was about six inches deep and a cold north wind blowing. I went out at the gate the Yankee had left open, and walked straight down toward the river. I struck a road or pike running parallel with it, and down this I turned.   I followed it for about ten miles, walking very rapidly to keep from freezing.   I met several market wagons, but merely bowed to the occupants and walked on.   About eight o'clock I came to a small thicket of bushes; this I entered and left my gray uniform coat, and only retained my light citizen's overcoat, given me by General Dodge.   Being now in full citizen's dress, I felt much safer in meeting people, as I was on my crutches, and did not attract much attention.   About a mile from where I hid my coat I came in sight of an old-fashioned Southern homestead, with negro quarters and outhouses.   As I neared it I saw a young boy come out of the gate, put his foot up on the horse block and adjust his skates. I walked up and said, " Your folks are good Union people, aren't they, son? "

He looked up quickly.   " No," he said, " my mamma is a good reb, but my papa don't say much."

I opened the gate and walked into the yard, straight up to the front of the house, and up the steps onto the porch.   I saw through the side lights a negro woman go out through the back door.   I only saw her back as she passed out and shut the door.   I walked right into the hall without knocking, and as I entered I met an elegant lady—tall, dignified and graceful.

She looked me over, and said, " Why did you not knock, sir, before entering my door? "

I answered, " I did not wish to attract the attention of the servant who was just passing out the back door, as I am an escaped Confederate soldier, and came here for help to get back to Dixie."

She gave me a sharp look, as if to pierce the inmost fiber of my soul.   " And what made you think that I would aid a reb to escape, sir? "

" I gathered as much from a short conversation with your little son, whom I met a few moments ago at your front gate."

" Come this way, sir; walls have ears."

We ascended a stairway into an attic, and here she told me to stay and keep quiet.   Not long after I heard her coming back, and with her was a young lady about sixteen years old; they brought me an elegant breakfast, and she told me her husband was away from home, but would return some time that evening. I told her that I had escaped from the Louisville prison hospital on Broadway, and if caught I would be shot or hung; that I must get away as soon as possible.

Soon after the noon hour, I heard her again ascending the stairway, and with her came her daughter. They brought me an elegant lunch and I enjoyed it. They spent but a few minutes with me in conversation after I had my meal, for fear that their absence would attract the attention of the servants down stairs.

Some time after dark I heard heavy steps ascending the stairway, and an elderly gentleman entered and shook hands with me. He remarked that his wife had informed him that I was an escaped prisoner from the Broadway prison in Louisville. I told him that I was. And then I gave him an exact account of my escape and the death of the Yankee Dutch sergeant. I wanted him to see clearly the danger that I was in, as I believed him to be a true Southern man, and would do all in his power to aid me in escaping, especially when the peril I was in was so great. He asked what I would need. I told him a good horse, a few dollars, and a pistol. Then he gave me a splendid new Colt's 45-calibre pistol, about fifty dollars, and told me that a good horse was hitched at the front gate at my disposal; that I could mount at any time that suited my pleasure. He told me the route that I had better take to avoid the Yankee camps, and a minute description of the country. I arose at once, and said that I thought the sooner I started the better.

We descended, and as we were passing through the hall his wife came out of her room and placed a large, heavy chinchilla overcoat on my shoulders, and told me that it would keep me as warm as a blanket. I thanked her, and she aided me in putting it on. I then bade them good-bye and passed out of the gate. I told them my name just as the door was closing behind me, and asked for a pencil and paper and wrote it down and said that if it was ever in my power I would aid them, or any of their family. Long years had elapsed when their son, Dr. W. A. Alsop, became my family physician in the Yazoo Valley, at Shaw, in Bolivar County, Miss.

The air was bitter cold, and as I mounted my horse he was shivering. I took the first pike or road leading southward and away from the river. I rode steadily all night, and as day began to dawn I went into a dense wooded place between two hills, and rode a mile or so away from the pike. Here I spent the day. As soon as it was night I turned into the first barn near the pike, and seeing a negro, I asked where I could get some corn and oats for my horse, and how far it was to where a traveler could stay all night. He let me have corn and oats for my horse and told me that down the pike about a mile I could get lodging and something to eat.

As soon as my horse had finished his meal I mounted and rode steadily until daylight. I would examine the sign posts along the road and could tell pretty well where I was, and the direction I wished to go.

My daily and nightly program was about the same for two weeks, and I only had to use my pistol four times to avoid capture. I exchanged horses twice on the road, but never with the owner's consent, relying solely on my judgment and knowledge. I fared very well, generally through the aid of negroes, and often from the kindness of Southern ladies. The ladies would fill my haversack bountifully and give me all the information they possessed regarding the positions occupied by the Yanks in my line of travel. Thus I was enabled to avoid many dangers, and to know to whom to apply for aid.

At the beginning of the third week of my journey, I rode into our picket lines near Decatur, Alabama, and met several of the 53rd Alabama Cavalry. I reported my arrival by telegraph, and was ordered to report for duty to General J. E. B. Stuart, in Virginia.

My liberty was of but short duration. I was riding with a small escort about fifteen miles north of Florence, Alabama, when we were ambushed and fired into by a band of renegade Tennesseeans. I was knocked from my horse and wounded in the thigh and knee, and two of my men were killed and several others wounded. I never even got a glimpse of the villains. I was carried to Dr. Mitchell's in Florence, and for two weeks I was carefully nursed by the doctor and his family. Why the renegades did not take me prisoner or kill me I have never been able to learn.

As soon as I was able to travel I started on my journey to Virginia, and after a three days' journey from the doctor's I rode right into a whole regiment of Yankees. My horse was shot and killed and I was again captured. This time I was not halted at any prison until I reached McLean's Barracks, in Cincinnati, Ohio. From there I was sent to Johnson's Island prison, near Sandusky City on Lake Erie. Here I only remained twenty-four hours. I was forwarded back to Columbus, Ohio, and sent out to Camp Chase, about four miles in the country, from the city. Here I met many of my old comrades in arms, and there were daily accessions to our ranks.

All branches of the service were here represented, cavalry, infantry and artillery, as well as the navy of the C. S. A. Many citizens were prisoners here, and not even women were spared.

I set to work at once to plan a way of escape. I laid out an elaborate tunnel from the inside of our room, and we dug it; but the prison had detectives in our midst, who passed as Confederate soldiers, and they betrayed us, and only three out of the eighteen engaged in the work escaped. Our rations were horrible: pea soup water, pickled salt pork, which was very thick and fat, and a sour, coarse, prison bread.

While I was there I got a written permit from Sancho, the prison provost, countersigned by Colonel Moody, the post commander, to make and use a *bow* and *arrow* with which to shoot *rats*. After I made my bow and arrow, our *mess* had plenty of fresh meat, and occasionally we would make a sale of our surplus rats to some other mess not so fortunate as we. My way of hunting was to buy a soup bone of fresh beef, that had been used by the sutler or some other outside party; take this bone and place it in the snow just outside of our door, and leave a small crack so that I could peep through and watch a rat as he came to take a nibble; and while he was gnawing it I would send an arrow through him and draw him inside, and one of the boys would take charge, and skin and clean and prepare him for our camp kettle. We would buy rice, pepper and salt, from the sutler, and cook it and our rats together, making an elegant rat and rice *pillau*. It was a very palatable dish, and I can assure you that we all enjoyed it, as the rat closely resembles the squirrel, and any old hunter will tell you that the sweetest meat known to the hunter is a nice, young, tender squirrel, either broiled or barbecued.

While in Camp Chase, our mess edited a weekly newspaper, called " *The Rebel Sixty-Four Pounder, or Camp Chase Vindicator.*" It was all written in small columns on four pages of large foolscap paper; eight columns in all. Each copy was beautifully illustrated by our special artist. One column was devoted to poetry and one to " grapevine" telegrams from Dixie. Everything was original, and we had no " exchanges." Colonel W. S. Hawkins, of Tennessee, and myself kept up the " poet's column." Captain Moody, of Port Gibson, Miss., a brother of the prison commandant, and Captain Thomas F. Perkins, Major G. Hamp Smith and someone else whose name I have forgotten had charge of the " locals." Our editorial corps consisted of about a dozen as bright minds as you could find in any community. Every number we issued, after being read by our prison comrades, was sold at twenty-five cents a copy on the outside to " souvenir hunters," and the Yankee guards became regular subscribers. It was a money-making business with them, as they received a fancy price for them from visitors.

We had a fine band, which played on prison-made instruments, and we had variety shows and vaudeville acting quite often, which did much to relieve the tedium of the long, weary days and nights, when the north winds howled, and we shivered in our cold, open, windswept shanties.

One day, while passing the open doorway that separated barracks No. 2 from barracks No. 3, I saw a young lady in the opposite prison, and Sancho, the provost, was with me. I asked if I might speak to her, and he told the guard to let me talk to her at the window for five or ten minutes. I stepped up and asked if I might have a few moments' conversation with her. She stopped and looked up at the guard, and he said, "Talk to him if you want to. I won't hinder you for a while."

As she came to the window I stretched my hand through, shook hands with her and introduced myself.

She merely bowed and said, "What do you want with me? I don't know you."

"What have they put you in here for?"

"Is it any of your business what I am in here for?"

"No, ma'am; I only had curiosity to know why so young and beautiful a lady should be made the inmate of a Yankee prison pen." ·

"Well, sir, if you are so anxious to know, tell me what are you in here for?"

"I am in here for killing Yankees."

"Well," she said, "I'm in here for telegraphing to hell to see if there was room there for any more of them, and they caught me before I got my answer."

I turned away and said nothing more, as I had quite enough. I asked Sancho if he could tell me the charges against her, and he said that they had found her with the end of a telegraph wire, that she had cut and stuck in the ground, and that it was an actual fact that she made the same remark to the officer who captured her, somewhere in West Virginia.

In March, 1864, a trainload of us were put in box cars and sent to Fort Delaware. The snow was very deep and the cars very cold, and especially did we suffer when they slowly ascended the winding track that led up to Altoona, and again at a place called Lancaster. At this latter point an amusing thing occurred. We had a captain of a Tennessee regiment—Webster, I think his name was—but we called him "Jack of Clubs." He was, a singular looking man, with very long, tawny beard and hair to match, that stood, each by itself. His arms were very long and reached almost to his knees; his forehead projected and seemed to hang out over his face, which was rugged and seamed; his nose turned up like a pug-nosed bulldog, and you could look right into his nostrils; his under jaw was fully half an inch longer than the upper, and his teeth were always visible. He had a fierce gray blue eye that looked straight into yours, but on the whole with a genial, kindly expression that won your heart. He was a genial, kind-hearted, good fellow, and as brave as a lion. You could meet no kindlier comrade, despite his peculiar makeup, in any clime.

He sat beside me as our train rolled into the station at Lancaster, Pa. An immense crowd had gathered, cold as it was, to catch a glimpse of the rebel prisoners as the train stopped. I had cut nearly through the white pine walls of the box car in which I sat a hole big enough for me to escape through, if an opportunity presented itself, but had not removed the severed boards.

The sun was shining brightly, and the landscape was glittering in its mantle of snow, and the platform of the depot was densely packed with women and children sightseers, with a fair sprinkling of men.

My peep-hole was just ready to be shoved out; I gave it a push, the boards fell, and I stuck my head in the hole and looked out. I was within two feet of a boy about fifteen or sixteen years old, and he turned to his mother and said, "Mamma, what do the rebs look like?"

She replied, "Hush, my son, they look just like our men, only they have on gray uniforms, instead of blue."

This did not satisfy him, and he continued to peep, and ask the same questions over and over. "Jack of Clubs" pushed me to one side, and just as the boy was stooping low and trying to see the whole inside of the box car, he rammed his head almost against the boy's face, and shaking his bushy long hair and beard at him he gave vent to a loud, hoarse lion growl that shook the car. The boy gave a tremendous spring backwards, striking his mother fair in the breast and felling her like an ox. He went through the crowd like a catapult's missile. Such a stampede as took place from that platform when Jack's growl and wonderful head sent the youth flying through the multitude, was never before witnessed, and I would give a good deal to know to-day what that boy thought a reb looked like, as Old Jack's head and growl broke upon his vision and hearing.

Quite an hour elapsed before the excitement subsided, as it was reported that the rebs had made a break for liberty and many had escaped. Even the guards could not tell what had happened. We were at last mustered, the roll of prisoners called and all accounted for. The guards were very much frightened, as they were not soldiers, and had never heard the hiss of a bullet on the field of death. The excitement died down after the roll call and our train moved out.

We passed through a wild, hilly region, with deep cuts, and the snow in many places was piled deep, almost touching the sides of the car. Soon after passing a small station called " Bird in Hand," I was looking out of my hole, and in a dense wooded cut, where the snow was deep on each side, I sprang head foremost into a snow bank and was buried out of sight. I waited until the rumble of the train had died away before I made a move. When all was quiet I crawled out and climbed the hill on the south side of the track and took a survey of the country as far as I was able. There was only one farm house in sight from my point of view.

I had about twenty-five dollars in greenbacks left from a purse given me by a young lady, as I sat in the train at Cincinnati after leaving McLean's Barracks for Camp Chase. I started at once for the farm house, as the sun was just about setting and it was bitter cold. As I came to an elevation overlooking the farm house and not more than two hundred yards from it I saw a bluecoated soldier, apparently the owner of the farm, come out to the barn, open the door and lead two fine Norman horses out, and water them from a long-handled wooden pump. He led them back and brought out a beautiful little red roan mare; she was a perfect picture of an ideal horse and I made up my mind at once that I would ride her to Dixie.

I saw my soldier-farmer close the barn door and take something from the outside wall near the door, place it like a key in a lock, turn it and again replace it in position, and return to his house.

I got out of sight behind the hill in the woods and stamped and worked my arms and hands to keep up circulation and warmth. As soon as it was dark I crept as near the barn as possible and waited until the lights were extinguished in the house and all sounds died out. I then approached the door of the barn and found it fast. I remembered seeing the farmer hang something on the wall near the door, and found a bent wire hanging there. Taking it, I found a small hole in the door and inserting the wire I turned it down, and it caught against a knob inside, and by exerting a little force a bar moved, and the door opened. I went in and felt the various horses and found my little mare. After some time I found a saddle, bridle and blanket, and putting these on the mare I led her out, carefully fastened the door and hung the wire key back in its place. I mounted and rode across the country in a southerly direction. There are many low stone fences in this region, but as the snow was deep and hard frozen and piled against them, I had no difficulty in getting over. I had to make a gap in but one, and that was the one around the barn where I got my little mare.

The night I got my horse it was very dark, which was in my favor. After crossing several fields I came into a good macadam pike, which led in the direction I wanted to go, and I followed it until about midnight, when I came to a broad, shallow river, which was frozen over. I got down and led my horse across. I felt the ice sway under our weight, but we crossed without accident.

I continued my course beyond the river until day began to dawn, and seeing a dense timber nearby I turned into it and rode some distance into the thickest part. Here I dismounted and hid my horse, then walked some distance, until I could see out across the country

in the direction I was going to travel the next night.   I
could see, not far from the edge of the woods, a stack
of hay and a field of corn in the shock.   This field was
in a small bottom near the woods, and no house nor
any human being was visible.   I walked out to a corn
shock and gathered an armful of corn, took it to my
horse, fed her and then returned and got another.   I
ate an ear or two myself, and then taking the blankets
from under the saddle I sought a warm, sunny spot on
the south side of a large log, sheltered from the north
wind, laid down and was soon fast asleep.   I slept like a
log, and late in the afternoon I awoke, fed my horse,
and as night fell and darkness again covered the land,
I rode back into the pike and continued my journey.

I pursued these tactics for several days and nights,
never venturing to approach a house to ask a question
except once.   As I was passing an isolated region my
way led just under a window that jutted over the road,
and I paused at the sound of voices and listened.   I
found from their conversation that they were Quakers
and deplored the war and hoped the South would win.
I stopped and bought part of a cooked ham and some
homemade bread and sausages, well boiled, from them.
I inquired the way to Poolesville, Maryland, and found
I was not more than two days' ride from the Potomac
river.   My only regret was that I had no arms, only
a small, broken-bladed pocket knife.

When nearing Poolesville, about ten o'clock one night,
I could see lights in a house in front of me, and as I
approached I could hear the sounds of a piano and the
swell of voices singing some familiar air.   I rode up
slowly, and found four horses, with officers' trappings,
and each saddle had a pair of Colt's pistols on the front,
with ammunition in the cartridge boxes.   I secured all
these, turned the horses loose and let them go; and I
got a splendid pair of fine blankets, which were a great
comfort in the chilly wind.

Just before daylight I reached the Potomac, which
was not frozen.   I forded it and crossed to the Virginia
shore, just as day was breaking.   Many familiar landscapes greeted me as the daylight appeared, and I

again went into hiding until dark. I gave Leesburg a
wide berth and rode steadily at night by many a well
remembered path along the foot hills of the Blue Ridge
Mountains, until I crossed the Rappahannock River.

Many nights I could see the camp-fires of the
Yankees, far to my left, and I did not encounter any
of our pickets until I was across the Rappahannock. I
was escorted down to Mine Run by a squad of my old
command, under Corporal Moon.

CHAPTER XVIII

Arrival at General Stuart's headquarters—Battle of the
Wilderness—"Jackson's Ghost"—Death of General
Stuart—At Spottyslvania Court House—Captured and
sent to Fort Delaware.

As soon as I reached General Stuart's headquarters
I reported to him and apologized for my delay in not
reporting sooner. I fell into my old scouting habits,
and on familiar grounds I was soon myself again, and
with my rifle I made it *warm* for Grant's pickets on
the Rappahannock and other points.

The Yanks were on the move as soon as the sun began
to warm the earth, in the latter part of April, and as
the first days of May peeped into the calendar real
hostilities began. Sharp fighting occurred at Mine
Run, and General Lee, with his keen rapier, began to
fence against the overwhelming sledgehammer blows of
Grant. Again, on the old field of Chancellorsville, in
the Wilderness, Grant had a grand army three times
the numerical strength of Lee's; yes, one of the largest
and best equipped armies ever marshaled on any battle
field in America. Against it was opposed the ragged
veterans of Southland, half-clothed and half-fed; but
the *morale* and stamina of that ragged band were worth
many a division of the hirelings and negroes of the
mighty hosts that confronted Lee.

On the sixth day of May the battle along the old
plank road raged all day, and we fell back from off the
field some half-mile. We captured an old gray mule,
and had her on our extreme left wing, on the picket
line. She was extremely restless and made constant
endeavors to break away from the boys and get back
into the Yankee lines. We had to tie her in the center
with two ropes between two trees to keep her from
tangling and hurting herself.

After dark I rode to the extreme end of our lines,
on the old plank road, and dismounted, leaving my sword,

spurs and everything that would rattle or make a noise with the pickets.   I then visited the vidette and learned from him that the Yankees were not more than a hundred or so yards from us, right in our front.   I crawled along the berm of the plank road, through a small covering of pine sprouts, to the edge of a culvert bridge that had been destroyed, and on the opposite side, not over seventy or eighty feet away, was their squad of videttes.

I laid still and listened to their conversation.   I found at once that they were all negroes.   They were telling what they were going to do to " de rebs " the next day.

I listened breathlessly for a while, until one negro broke into the conversation with, " I spec it war about here whar dat old he reb, Stonewall Jackson, wur kilt."

" Say, Sam, whut wud you do if he's ghost wus to cumb here now? "

" Oh, hush, nigger, dey hain't no ghostses."

" Yes, dey is, 'ca'se I'se seed um."

And an argument began about ghosts, which I knew would shut off anything else until a relief guard came up.

It not being a very healthy place, I crawled back into our lines, and as I made my exit I concluded that with the aid of the boys we would send them a *bona fide* ghost.

One of the boys had a large canteen, made of two quart pans that had been soldered together, and would hold a full half gallon.   It had been grazed by a bullet under its bottom and rendered useless.   I took this and cut a grinning mouth, with sharp teeth, large eyes and nose, after the manner of a pumpkin scarecrow of "All Saints' night."   Cutting a hole in the bottom large enough to insert my hand I made a regular " death's head " of it, and when a candle was inserted it was a hideous looking thing in the dark.

We took an old pack saddle and cut two pine poles about the size of a man's wrist and four feet long, strapped them to the horns of the X pack saddle and tied the " death's head " midway between them.   **We** then placed the saddle on the old mule, and spreading part of an old rotten tent cloth over the whole, we tied it fast. Gathering a lot of old rusty camp kettles and canteens from the battlefield of the year before, we fastened these on our ghost so as to rattle and make a strange, ghostly noise.

When all was completed to our satisfaction we led the old mule into the plank road and pointed her head in the direction of the negroes. One of the boys had just lit a fresh " conestoga," a cigar made from the whole leaf of tobacco without cutting, rolled and covered with a finer quality—they were sometimes nearly eighteen inches long, and would keep you smoking for half an hour or more. He had just lighted one and was standing close by, watching us prepare our ghost. As we were ready one of the boys pulled the " conestoga " from his lips, caught the old mule by the tail, hoisted it, and stuck the lighted " conestoga " under. She gave an awful squeal as soon as she felt the fire scorch, clapped her tail down and fastened it there, and down the plank road she went toward the negroes at a fearful gait, squealing at every jump, bucking high and making the camp kettles rattle at a telling rate.

We heard an awful stampede through the low-lying cedars and underbrush as she entered the negro lines, and now and then you could hear a fearful yell far away down her trail, but not a gun was fired in any direction. For twenty minutes after she left us you could still hear the cracking and crashing of the timber and brush in the direction of the Rappahannock River, as if a herd of cattle were on a stampede. About a dozen of us mounted our horses and followed in the wake of our ghost, and we passed long lines of stacked muskets in the road and hundreds of pairs of blankets, shoes and suits of clothing, just as they had been deserted by the fleeing negroes of Slocum's division. We followed our ghost for two or three miles, turned back, bent whole stacks of muskets against the trees, and set the cedar brakes on fire behind us. Thus " Jackson's ghost " drove Slocum's division into the Rappahannock a year after his death.

I notice that in " The Annals of the War of the Rebellion," Mr. Dana says of this escapade, that " Slocum's division, from some unknown cause, broke like cowards and deserted their lines." General Jubal A. Early, in his memoirs, says of the same incident, " When my men advanced the next morning, we found the field deserted, with the appearance of a sudden panic, their guns left stacked, their shoes, and blankets and knapsacks all deserted."

And our old gray mule and the boys around the picket post alone could have told them the cause.

I can shut my eyes at this distant day and drink through memory's cup that never-to-be-forgotten event, and the roar of that mighty host, as it rushed terror stricken through the thick, sharp limbs of the green and dead cedar trees, with a roar like a tornado ; and again, as we sent the scorching flames of a forest fire, with its lurid glare, on the wings of the night winds after them, it lent added terrors to their already tortured brains, and I suppose many of them never halted until they were safe in their homes, or the heart of some distant city.   As the years silently go down into the vales of the past, I can still hear and see it all.   I believe that if we had advanced upon the Yanks just after " Jackson's ghost " passed, we would have stampeded, driven back and defeated the whole of Grant's magnificent army, and sent it north of the Potomac, a shattered, bleeding remnant.   I know well that he would never have reached the environments of Petersburg, for he would have been driven back that night across the Rappahannock, and we would have had half his men prisoners or dead, and all his vast stores in our possession.

Day after day the steady roll of musketry along our whole line continued.   Grant, with his sledge–hammer, striking with his overwhelming forces, which were constantly pouring in from the recruiting stations of the North to take the place of those slaughtered along our lines, in a seemingly unmerciful way, by the rifles and rapiers of the immortal Lee. Each move of Grant was frustrated and anticipated hours ahead, until the Confederate veterans were weary of the terrible slaughter.

From Mine Run to Spottsylvania there was a dead Yankee left, with his swollen black face turned upward to the May sun, for every soldier that Lee had in his whole army.   This is no " pipe dream " declaration. The cold facts of the unbiased historian, when the final roll is called, will so reveal it.

At Yellow Tavern we lost our great cavalry commander, General J. E. B. Stuart.   On the Sunday morning just before the awful carnage at Spottsylvania I sent a bullet into the neck of General Sedgwick, the cavalry commander of General Grant, and avenged the death of Stuart.

I was with Barksdale's old brigade, and through my telescope I could see a body of officers, sitting and standing around a central group.   I saw a fine looking man, with a heavy beard, ride up, and instantly every eye was turned upon him, and obeisance reverently made to this later arrival.   I at once conceived the idea that this was General Grant.   I asked for permission to try my rifle at him, and after several refusals I was at last permitted to try.   The distance was great (twenty-two hundred yards), but I had confidence in my old Whitworth rifle; taking a careful sight, I sent my leaden messenger on its mission of death, and it entered General Sedgwick's neck just above his shoulder, and he fell a corpse from his horse.

At daylight on the morning of the twelfth of May, while a dense fog obscured everything, our lines were broken and Johnson's whole division captured by the Yankees.

I made my way down through the thick undergrowth, as near as possible to the place, and watched the enemy. I had not been in position more than half an hour when just behind me I heard the approach of a body of infantry.   I can safely say that at this moment, in all my experience, I never heard such an awful roar of musketry.   The air a few inches above my head was full of rifle balls, as thick as swarming bees.

I saw Major Rafe Bell, of General Nat Harris's Mississippians, cautiously leading his men into this awful storm of death, and as he came within a few feet of me he said, " It seems to me that I should go to the right here instead of the left."

" You are right, Major," I replied, and as I spoke he looked at me and said: " Who are you, sir? "

I told him my name and what I had discovered.   He was the only field officer in that brigade that I saw, and he was as cool as if on parade, giving his orders in an unexcited tone.   Like a great general he scanned every detail of the situation, and when we were in position and the word was given to charge, he swept the works clear of every Yank.

In this " bloody angle," at Spottsylvania Court House, I saw dead bodies piled in heaps one on the other, and I saw trees, twenty inches in diameter, cut down by rifle bullets; I saw piled around the stumps of these trees bushels of battered minie bullets.   This alone gives you some idea of the fearful rifle fire that raged in the " bloody angle " that day.

When we made the charge to retake the works I went in with Major Bell and we drove the Yankees out. When we were within twenty yards of them I was in full run, leaning forward, with my pistol in my hand, and a Yankee fired almost in my face.   The ball entered my left breast, grazed the heart, and passed out, cutting two ribs in front and one behind.   The shock was great, but I did not fall; the blow checked but did not throw me.   I fired as he was climbing the breastworks, and cut his backbone in two, killing him instantly.   As I rose the fortification just above him I received a ball in the thigh and one in the ankle.   I fell on top of the works, and several other bullets grazed me in different places.   I was not able to move, and lay for some time exposed to the terrible cross-fire.

Our men recovered and held the works until the Yankees again tried their flanking movement, and Lee headed them off.   I and all the wounded that could not be moved were placed in field hospitals with our surgeons and left on the battlefield.   Here a party of Yankee cavalry raiders found us, and with our surgeons carried us all to northern prisons.   With a good many others I was carried to Fort Delaware.

CHAPTER XIX

At Fort Delaware—On board the *Crescent*—In Charleston harbor—Under fire of our own guns—I agree to be exchanged for Major Harry White.

I SPENT a week or so in the prison hospital at Fort Delaware, and had kind attention from some visiting Sisters of Mercy and a priest from a Catholic school in or near Philadelphia, Pa.

Fort Delaware is on an island in the Delaware River, between Philadelphia and Capes May and Henlopen. After leaving the hospital, I was placed in the officers' quarters, where there were about a hundred men to a room, and the monotony of prison life again began. This I need not again recount, as one prison was but a duplicate of the other ; the only difference being the men who had charge. I must say that Fort Delaware, in her Captain Auhl, had the meanest commandant of all that I came in contact with, for he was absolutely devoid of any of the attributes of a gentleman or a soldier.

On the twenty-first day of June, 1864, General Jeff Thompson, of Missouri, General C. B. Vance, of North Carolina, Major W. G. Owens, of Harrodsburg, Ky., and myself, were taken out of the prison pen and confined in an inner cell, under ground, just beneath the " portcullis " of Fort Delaware, and chained to a swivel ring in the center of the cell. This cell was about eight feet square, and here we lay without even a shadow of light from the twenty-first of June until the fourth of July. A cup of water and a half a loaf of prison bread was our ration for twenty-four hours. And as regularly as these rations were shoved through a cat hole in the bottom of the cell door, and our empty cups of the day before returned, the Dutch guard would sing out : " We dakes you oudt ad sax o'glock, und shoots mit you." Old Jeff would hurl an oath of defiance at him every time it was repeated.

We were told by someone that we were held as hostages by the Yanks for something that our men were doing to the Yanks in Libby, or Castle Winder in Richmond, and we made no complaint.

After the lapse of a week our eyes became accustomed to the darkness, and we could discern small objects. We found a piece of board about six inches square, and with our finger nails we gouged a dent in its center and then a round ring, equidistant from the center. We would gather around this board and place two " graybacks " in the pit in the center, and watch the fight or race. If it was a battle, one or the other was certain to be slain, and if no battle, then a race took place for the outer circle. I had a champion fighter or runner, as the case might be, and I kept him, or her, stabled in the small bare place just above my ear, and while he or she lived I won most of the Confederate shin plasters that my companions had. I can safely say that I have been just as much excited at one of these races as I ever was on the race course, amid the waving hats and yelling crowds, anywhere in my own or foreign countries.

I missed my champion one day, and the boys said Old Jeff caught and killed him while I was asleep. Poor old Jeff, how my heart went out to him; he a prisoner and his devoted wife in a madhouse.

On the fourth of July my companions were taken out of the dark cell and their chains removed. An armorer came in and put a longer chain on my ankle and riveted it fast to the center ring in the floor. My rations were cut from twelve ounces of water to ten, and my prison loaf from ten ounces to eight. A pair of handcuffs were snapped upon me, and I was almost helpless. I made no effort to find out why I was thus treated, and bore it with Indian stoicism.

Once every twenty-four hours I would hear the guard come to the door and say, " You dere? "

I would say, " Yes, what do you want? "

" Dis your grub me haf."

As soon as I would push my empty water cup in reach he would fill it and send my bread through the same hole, then he would say that they were going to shoot me the next morning at six o'clock.

This life was very trying, and I wasted away under it, but kept my spirits up. The handcuffs I slipped off easily and never put them on until I heard the tramp of feet near my door.   I had no blanket, and the hard stone floor almost made my bones protrude through my skin. The " graybacks " feasted and multiplied rapidly, despite my all-day hunts and constant slaughter of them, and this was my sole and only employment, day in and day out.   I did not suffer from the intense July and August heat, as I was in a dark, cold cell and under ground.

At times the atmosphere was very heavy, damp and foul, but I would forget it, and shake off the depressing feeling, and turn my thoughts to the wide, wind-swept prairies of my native State, and let memory stray back over her flower-strewn hills and vales, and lose myself far from the " now."   The only sounds that came to my ears from the outside world was the boom of the morning and evening gun or a salute fired for some passing magnate, or some reputed victory over my own kindred in far-away Dixie.

Somewhere, far above my head, as the sun sank toward the equator, I could see a faint glow of light, as if the sun were shining through a hole.   This spot grew brighter, as the sun sank lower from the summer's solstice, and I used to watch for it to appear with all the intensity of my nature, and was as glad to greet it as a storm-tossed mariner would be to catch the gleam of a familiar light that pointed him to a haven of rest and safety.

To this day I know not what charges were preferred against me, and I knew not what hour I would be called to meet my doom.   I became callous to suffering, and prayed for death to end my sufferings and torture.   I longed for something to read.   I reviewed in detail every event in my life in all its minutæ.   I would lay for hours and catch the vermin that were sapping the life blood from my wasting frame, place them in the pit on the race board, and watch them combat or race, and exult in maniacal glee at the death struggles of each in their battles royal.

The dials of time in solitary confinement seemed clogged and hours stretched away into days, and days into weeks, and weeks seemingly into years. I could not lie in one position long at a time, as the stone floor would make my bones ache, and my flesh would become numb and dead. The odor of the putrid wooden sink that had not been emptied since my companions left me was, at times, almost overpowering.

My eyes had grown accustomed to the darkness and I could see the seams of mortar between the layers of stone in my cell. At times I would have cravings to live, solely to avenge my sufferings on my keepers; and I registered a vow daily, that never again would I spare a single one who should cross my path. I would have given several years of my life to be able to take a good bath, put on clean clothing and be rid of the " gray-backs," that so tortured my flesh and murdered my rest. I went so far one day as to ask the Dutchman, whom I could not see, only hear, to bring me a tub and water enough to take a bath or even enough to bathe my face. He only grunted and said that it was of no use to me. When he refused I felt humiliated, and I could have torn his heart out. I shut myself, as it were, in a shell, and never again did I open my lips to him.

The days crept slowly by, and on the twentieth day of August, just two months from my incarceration in that gloomy cell, its cell doors were thrown open, the handcuffs taken off, the shackles stricken from my ankle, and I was ordered to get up and follow my guards. I was too weak to obey, and I was roughly raised and placed on crutches, and after several attempts I was ordered by that miserable Dutch scoundrel, Auhl, to come on or he would chain and lock me up again.

With the most excruciating torture, every fiber of my body tingling with throbbing pains, by sheer will power I moved forward. I entered a blinding light, so intense and powerful that I was absolutely unable to see a step in front of me, and I fell heavily against some invisible impediment and received a severe shock. I was lifted to my feet by someone and my arm grasped by a strong, friendly hand. As I became accustomed to the light, I found that I was escorted by one of our own men, a Lieutenant Legg, of the Fiftieth Virginia Infantry.

I was one of a band of six hundred Confederate officers put on board a steamship called the *Crescent City.* We were marched aboard and down into the hold of the vessel, where it was very warm to me. At my own request I was placed on the top tier of the shelving that was to be used as bunks, and on the inside of the vessel's gangway away from the *slosh* of the waves on the sides. My feet were near a nest of boilers, but I heeded them not. As I lay on the soft, springy plank and the *darkness* enabled me to see, I felt a strange thrill of pleasure, and I lay in a dreamy, happy, trance-like state, and listened to the voices of comrades around me.

I don't think that I ever enjoyed anything more in all my life. The change, from that dark, loathsome dungeon of eternal solitude and misery, to this light-hearted, joyous throng was beyond compare. I did not care to talk, I only wished to hear the sweet murmur of their voices.

From them I learned our supposed destination, and heard of the exchange of my three companions, General Thompson, General Vance and Major Owens, and also that this was the twentieth day of August, 1864. My feelings were like those of some lost soul, I imagined, who enters the gates of Paradise after an aeon of suffering. The ship was a real Paradise to me. I cared not how long the voyage lasted. And to-day as I look back down the forty-odd years that have elapsed since that voyage I shudder at the horrors and tortures that my comrades endured. It lasted from the twentieth of August until the seventh of September, before our feet touched the shore.

Our fare was pea soup, very hot, and "hard tack." The air around us was stifling, and we had to blow with our breath to cool our drinking water, which would really scald you if you did not. There was but one small evaporator aboard, and this had to furnish distilled sea water, not only for us, but for the guards and sailors besides, and there was no ice in those days. There was but one small sink, on the the larboard side above the paddle wheel, with room for only one occupant at a time. The furnaces and boilers were only separated from us by a rough plank wall, that at times was so hot that you could not hold your hand against it. The narrow gangway, not more than thirty inches wide, was constantly crowded, with passengers to and from the sink, and this passageway was a reeking mass from those overcome by seasickness.

You can imagine our condition when you take in the surroundings. We had to lie down all the time, as our bunks were not of a sufficient height to permit a sitting posture, as the whole distance from floor to ceiling was not more than eight feet. The hatchways were kept battened down, and the unventilated hold was a sweat box, even without the heat of the furnaces to add to the horrors. The odors of the reeking, fermenting vomit, and the sweat of the human bodies that permeated the foul air, exceeded anything that you could imagine, and it was beyond my powers of description.

Strange to say, not a man died, and not one fainted or was overcome by his fearful surroundings. Hope of landing in Dixie and meeting the loved ones at home once more, held us spellbound and immune to all surroundings. The three tiers of human heads, with the perspiration trickling down from each pale, haggard brow, is a scene I can never forget, and it haunts me to this distant day.

Our ship grounded, one dark night, off Cape Romain, on the South Carolina coast, and we lay aground until late the next day. There was a stir among the prisoners, and some talk of capturing the ship, and going ashore to freedom and home; but nothing came of it, and the effort was weak hearted, as all were under the impression that we were going to Charleston to be exchanged, and if we attempted to escape and were captured, our exchange would be annulled; so the plan was not carried out.   But had we been able to look into the future and see the awful fate that was in store for us, we would have captured the ship, burned it, murdered the guards and thrown their carcasses into the sea.

I, on my upper bunk, could look down on the misery of my companions. I was not sick a moment, but steadily improved and gained strength as our ship sped southward.

We ran into Beaufort Harbor, S. C., on the twenty-ninth day of August, and we were all marched out on deck, new guards placed over us and our bunks and the gangway thoroughly cleaned, fumigated and deodorized. We could saunter around the decks and enjoy the soft balmy sea breezes and enjoy the distant view of the islands with the trees and houses.

I lay like one in a trance, looking up at the clear blue sky, the dancing waters, and the dark green of the forest in the distance, and as the night fell and the stars peeped out, I hated to retire to the hot stifling atmosphere of that awful hold. When we marched down the heat was not so great, for the fires were banked, the air was much purer and the foul scents dissipated. I felt truly thankful and was soon sound asleep.

For several days we lay off the shore in sight of Beaufort and Hilton Head, with men-of-war around us and in the offing. One day we were steamed up directly into Charleston harbor, and we thought the hour of freedom had arrived. I rested quietly in my bunk, and listened to the rumors brought by those who were allowed the freedom to visit the upper decks and gaze at all that was happening.

On the seventh of September we were landed on a sand bar on Morris Island and marched through deep sand for a mile or two, and placed in a stockade enclosure, about a hundred yards square, surrounded by black negro guards. Just behind us was Battery Gregg, Battery Wagner, and Chatfield. We were sheltered from the scorching rays of the sun by small fly tents, and our water supplies came from pits we dug in the sand.

In marching across the sands to our quarters in the stockade, I was so weak that I often fell, and the brutal guards, instead of lifting me up with their hands, would ram their bayonets under me and toss me up, prod me roughly, and say, " Keep up, you damn Rebel son of a b——, or we will stick our bayonets through you."

Slowly I made my way, and at last reached the enclosure. I gazed around as I dropped on the sand in front of one of the small " A " tents, allotted one to each four men, and all around the parapets of the enclosure I could see rows of surly negro guards, members of the Fifty-fourth Massachusetts Regiment under the command of Col. C. D. Shaw. Behind us on three sides frowned the guns of Wagner, Chatfield, and Gregg, all in our rear; in front was Moultrie, Sumter, Pickens, and the guns of Charleston, and some gunboats and floating batteries.

After resting and recovering my senses, I dug a pit in the sand, down to water, stripped, and for the first time since the twenty-first day of June, I bathed my hands and face and took a bath. I used the smooth white sand for soap, and for an hour or so I enjoyed the scrubbing, until my skin put on a ruddy glow. Then, in the bright warm September sun, I sat and washed and cleansed my clothing, rubbing and examining every fold and seam, until I felt that every vestige of vermin and their spawn had been obliterated. I laid each garment out separately on the warm sand, and rolled over and over in it, until I felt a tingling glow of reaction in every muscle. My comrades were amused at my performances, but said nothing.

When I was dressing, the huge guns of the batteries in our rear sent a volley of shells, hissing and humming over our heads, at the city of Charleston, and at Fort Sumter. Soon we saw the smoke curl up from these points, and right over and just beyond us our shells were bursting, in reply to theirs. The fragments of these shells would hum, hiss, and fall all around us.

We greeted these messengers from Dixie with wild shouts and clapping of hands; and instantly came a voice from our negro guards:

"You stop dat yellin' down dar, or I gwine to fling some bullits on you!"

Our laughter was over, for we realized our position at once. We were under the fire of our own guns, and those of the Yankees, for every now and then a shell from Wagner, Gregg, or Chatfield would burst just over us, and fragments would cut a tent cloth or tear up the sand near a group of us. It was as if we were supporting a battery without shelter in an open field. The Yankees would say, when their shells exploded in our midst, that it was a premature explosion, an accident; but we knew that they could not have so occurred, every hour or two, day and night, for forty-two days, without being intentional.

This ceaseless bombardment day and night banished sleep from our weary prison-racked frames, and kept a nameless, undefined dread hanging over each man.

I only stayed in the prison pen from September 7th until September 15th, eight days. Our rations for those days were these: Breakfast, four worm-eaten "hard tack" crackers, very rotten. Dinner, one-half pint of sandy pea soup, very watery and thin. Supper, all the ocean air you could inhale. Now this was the daily menu furnished us by the United States Government.

We answered to roll call three times a day, and were counted by the negro guards, and a little sawed-off Yankee lieutenant for a while took the report of our numbers as the negroes would give it to him. The absolute prison commander was a Colonel Hallowell; than whom God never created a meaner man. In a speech to us he said that if we obeyed the rules, he would treat us as gentlemen. We obeyed every rule to the very letter, and he treated us as wild beasts of prey.

On the fifteenth of September, I was sitting on part of a hard tack box, not a great way from the entrance, when a Captain Frank Bell, of the Invalid Corps, entered the stockade, and came directly up to me and said, "What is your name?"

I told him, and he said, " What is your rank in the Rebel army? "

I said, " I am a major in the regular Confederate army."

He then asked if I knew who was in command of the rebel forces in Charleston. . I replied that General W. J. Hardee was in command of the whole of the forces, and General Sam Jones, of the post.

" How long have you known General Hardee? "

I answered, " All my life."

" Have you any influence with him? "

I asked, " What kind of influence? "

He replied, " Have you sufficient influence with him to have yourself exchanged for one of our majors, who is now a prisoner in his hands? "

I replied that there was not a Yankee in Charleston that General Hardee would not exchange for me.

He then said, " Get your things, and come with me."

I told him I only had what I had on.

" Come on then," he commanded.

As he turned I said, " Captain, you will have to help me up."

He turned and said, " I can't help you much, as I am one-legged myself."

With his assistance we passed out the gate, and only a short distance off I saw a boat waiting for us. We were carried to a large ship out in the offing by a small steam launch, and on this larger vessel I was introduced to General J. G. Foster, major-general commanding that department. His headquarters were on board this vessel, lying off Hilton Head.

When I was ushered into his presence, he asked about the same questions that Captain Bell had, and I made the same answers. I signed a fifteen days' parole, agreeing to be exchanged for a Major Harry White, of a Pennsylvania regiment, who had been elected to some office, a Congressman I think, and they were anxious for him to be at home, and prepared for the next meeting ; or it may have been that he was only a member of the Pennsylvania legislature, of this I am not certain—anyhow, I well remember Captain Bell's saying that they were anxious to have him in the Assembly, and that White was a great friend of his.

Captain Bell was a captain, or had been, of the famous Buck Tail Rangers that Stonewall Jackson's men almost annihilated in the valley of the Shenandoah in 1862.

I signed my parole in duplicate, and put the duplicate in my pocket, and told the General that I would like Captain Bell to accompany me to the city of Charleston, and accompany Major Harry White back, as I was as certain as death of making the exchange. He agreed to my proposal, and after a short preparation, Captain Bell was ready, and we steamed away to the landing at Beaufort. Here we got into an ambulance, and with a driver, and flag of truce officer, we drove to the Pocataligo River, and met our pickets, and by them were escorted up to the railway station of Pocataligo. Here I met several men of the old 5th South Carolina Regiment who were with our brigade (D. R. Jones's) in the first battle of Manassas.

We were given transportation from Pocataligo to Charleston, on the railroad, and when the train came we got aboard. Just before entering the fortifications around the city, a guard halted the train, and an inspector came aboard and examined our papers. He informed Captain Bell that he could not permit him to enter the city, but that he could remain on the outside, and ample provision would be made for his comfort while negotiations were proceeding regarding the exchange. I told Captain Bell that I would not detain him long.

CHAPTER XX

At General Hardee's headquarters—I refuse to be exchanged for White—Confederate prison at Charleston—I am exchanged for Major Charles P. Mattocks—Yankees refuse to accept the exchange and I go back to Morris Island.

As soon as the train reached the depot I got in a hack and was driven to General Hardee's headquarters. As I entered, the General was sitting in his shirt sleeves with his feet upon the table perusing a paper. He looked up and recognized me, rose and said, " Lamar, I'm very glad to see you, and glad you have come, as I have much work in your line for you to do."

I answered, " General, I am a prisoner on parole only, and am here to see you about a special exchange of myself for a Major Harry White, of a Pennsylvania regiment, who I understand is a prisoner in this city."

He looked worried for a moment, and said, " They have quit exchanging prisoners, and I am afraid that I can't help you."

I pulled out my parole, and he read it carefully, and said, " Harry White; why, there is a letter from him now on my desk that I have not read; it is to a lawyer in Richmond."

I asked if I might read it, and he gave his consent, and handed me the missive to peruse. I took my seat at the table, opened and read it. It was to a cousin of mine, a former classmate of White's at some northern college.

I read it word for word, and the more I read the more contempt I felt, and the madder I got. I remarked, " General, I would like to make a copy of this letter, if you have no objections."

He seemed in a brown study, as my pen flew across the paper and he could see that I was mad. After finishing the copy, I wrote a postscript at the bottom of White's letter and I reproduce it for your perusal.

HEADQUARTERS OF GENL. W. J. HARDEE,
CHARLESTON, S. C.

Genl. J. G. Foster, U. S. A., commanding besieging
forces around Charleston, S. C.:

DEAR SIR: I positively and emphatically refuse to be
exchanged for this ——— ——— ——— a ——— ——— ———

Very truly yours,

I refolded the letter, and asked for a courier to send
it to Captain Frank Bell at the flag of truce station, to
be handed, sealed, in person by him to General Foster.

General Hardee said, "Why, Lamar, what is the matter with you?"

I replied that I would rot in a Yankee dungeon before
I would be exchanged for such a man. I then read him
the letter, and my reply, at the bottom.

He asked what sort of treatment we were receiving as
prisoners at the hands of the Yankees. I gave him a
full and clear account, and he said, "Don't be too hasty,
for I don't like the idea of your going back to such a
life as you describe. We have a good many prisoners
here in the city; go and pick out the sort of a one you
want, and I will send him through the lines to Foster,
and maybe we can effect an exchange yet."

I thanked him and said I would try. I got in the
hack, and told the driver to take me to the Yankee
prison.

As we were passing down the street, I caught a
glimpse of Lieutenant Harrolson, of our navy, whom I
had not seen for several years, and I hailed him and
asked where he was bound, and he answered that he was
on his way to see Captain Sharp, our naval ordnance officer. I asked him to get in with me, and I would drive
to his destination. I told him my mission was to the
Yankee prisoners, to get one for a special exchange for
myself, and he said that there was a crowd of them in the
Roper hospital wards, adjoining their office, and that I
might make a selection there without going out to the
general prison. This suited me exactly and I remarked
that I would get a wounded one, like myself, from the
hospital.

On entering the office, I was introduced to Captain Sharp, and was escorted into the prison hospital among the Yanks. Here I found the prisoners playing chess, reading books and papers, writing, or lolling on good soft mattresses; everything neat and clean, and here and there a Southern lady waiting on them, with tea, coffee, milk, and clean white bread, and beaten biscuits, carried on waiters by servants.

The contrast was so great that I asked one of these ladies if they were really Yankee prisoners?

She smiled and said, " Certainly they are, sir; did you never see one before? "

I answered, " Not like these."

I stood and looked at them for some time, then I said, " Boys, I am just from General Foster's headquarters. I am a prisoner in his hands and I am over here for the purpose of getting exchanged for some good Yankee major; one who will meet me on the battlefield and give me a chance to send a bullet into him; one who will serve his country to the end, and one who will tell the truth about us when he gets back home. Now I came down here to pick me out just such a man, but in looking at you all, I cannot make up my mind which of you to take, so I am going to ask you to pick one of your number, whom you know will fill all these requirements. Now select him as soon as you can, and send him up to General Hardee's headquarters, and we will send him to General Foster by flag of truce right away."

Now the reader of course wants to know why I refused to be exchanged for the one I was specifically designated for. In his letter to the Richmond lawyer, he promised that he would never, if exchanged, again enter the Federal service in any capacity, and that he would do anything that this lawyer would request, etc. It was the most woebegone, cringing, begging letter that I had ever read in my life; and it made my flesh creep, and every instinct of my soul to revolt. I would have been drawn and quartered before I would have accepted him as my equal in an exchange.

I reported to General Hardee my decision about the manner of getting a Yankee to send under a flag of truce, and he promised to give him a parole like mine, and send him through the lines as soon as he presented himself.

I felt so free that I drove down to a livery stable, mounted a horse and rode out into the country. I entered a dense forest, sat for an hour or two with my back against a large oak, and watched the birds and squirrels come down to the cypress brake and drink, and the scent of the woods was like sweet perfume to my weary prison soul. I rested my head on the root of a tree, and then I got up and took off my saddle, and folding the blanket between the roots of another large live oak, I lay down with my eyes toward the fleeting clouds, and for an hour or more I enjoyed the sylvan solitude as it seemed I never had before.

I did not return until the sun was sinking into the shadows of the west. Then slowly, and thoughtfully, I rode back to headquarters, and learned that Major Charles P. Mattocks, of a Maine regiment, had been chosen, and had been paroled and sent back with Captain Bell to General Foster. I gave myself no further concern about exchanges.

I had a good serviceable uniform made, and plenty of underwear and serviceable shirts, and several fine ones. I borrowed a good traveling bag from Lieut Harrolson, and paid a visit to some friends at Columbia. I enjoyed my fifteen days' parole with all the abandon I possibly could. I gave an account to the papers of our surroundings and treatment on Morris Island, and of our trip on the old Gulf Steamer *Crescent City*, from Fort Delaware, and I made an appeal to the citizens, and ladies especially, for shoes, clothing, tobacco, tea, coffee, sugar, and delicacies generally for our sick. I compared our rations with those I saw given the Yankee prisoners, both in their prison camp and in the Roper hospital. In a few days large quantities of supplies began to come into the provost marshal's hands for the prisoners on Morris Island, all directed in my care.

General Hardee informed me that the Yankees refused to accept Major Mattocks in place of Major White; and that he sent Mattocks through the lines three times, but was unable to effect the exchange. I felt the disappointment keenly.

On the last day of September I went down to the provost's office before breakfast, and informed him that I would leave that day for Morris Island prison, by flag. of truce, and to have all packages for the immortal six hundred Confederate officers ready, and I would take them. I had laid in a bountiful supply of clothing, tobacco, etc., for my individual use, and had these separate and distinct by themselves, while a car was loaded with the packages for the prisoners.

At ten o'clock our train pulled out for the flag of truce station at Pocataligo; I bade the waiting crowd good-bye, and back to the living hell I went.

When we reached the flag of truce station, the Yankee officer informed me that nothing would be received by him, except my own individual property; that such were his orders. I felt a pang of regret, as I had anticipated the pleasure my efforts, and the bountiful supplies sent by the ladies and the citizens of Charleston, would afford. But there was no alternative; alone I had to go, and the supplies were left in charge of the trainmen. All marked in my name were placed in the boat and we pushed off for Hilton Head.

How different were my feelings on this return trip! It is hard to even make a comparison. The outward, homeward bound from the terrible charnel house of the Yankee prison pen to light and freedom, I had enjoyed to its fullest but fifteen days before; and now, back to those same dark and well remembered horrors, had a depressing influence on my physical as well as mental faculties.

On that voyage all was hope and brightness; now only gloom and sad disappointment, and a giant despair held me in an iron grasp. By a desperate effort I shook off the shackles of thought, and assumed a devil-may-care attitude. I laughed, and entertained my flag of truce companions with jokes and yarns, until the decks would echo with their laughter, and I was glad that I was not alone with my own inner thoughts. When I clambered up the sides of General Foster's headquarters vessel, a peal of laughter from my flag of truce boat companions, and their " good-byes," still rang in my ears, and re-echoed as I went down the cabin stairs.

General Foster greeted me with, " Well, I see you did not have as much influence with General Hardee as you thought you had."

" How is that, General? "

" Why, you did not effect the exchange of yourself for Major White, as you thought you would."

" General, did you read Major White's letter that I sent you, with my postscript added? "

" Well, yes, I read them."

" Now, General, would you, as a man, have been willing, with all the facts and proofs before you, to be exchanged for this man? "

" Well, sir, is not that pen on Morris Island a miserable place to stay? "

" Yes, General, it is a hell on earth."

" Is not that old ship's hold another? "

" Yes, sir; it is a floating hell, and no mistake."

" Now Major Fontaine, you seem to be a man of intelligence and of plain common sense, fully able to see and comprehend the horrors of your surroundings and the exact situation, and it does seem to me, that being thus fully informed, I would have accepted an exchange of any man or thing, even a yellow dog, for myself, under the circumstances."

" Well, General," I replied, " that is the difference between you and me, and it is the true difference between a Yankee and a true rebel soldier. My honor is dearer to me than life, and I could never have held up my head and faced my comrades, and those I love best on earth, with the fact staring me in the face that I had cringed, or cowed, before the fate in front of me, and accepted a dishonorable exchange of myself, for one whom I did not consider my equal, merely for the purpose of escaping the fate that so many of my comrades were enduring. The thought to me, General, is so repugnant to my inner feelings, that I would suffer death by slow torture, rather than thus to lower the high standard that a true soldier should ever hold aloft."

He replied, " Well, I can't understand why you want to suffer, just because some of your friends do."

I said, " General, you look at it in a different light from me; I only see a so-called man, who has written a vow that if he is exchanged he will never serve his nation again, in any capacity whatever, no matter how much his nation may need him. Now, General, of what use is he to you, or your people, or your country; and must I give such a one liberty? No! a thousand times no. I have one great sorrow that will ever haunt me, and that is that my name is linked with his."

The General remained silent, and I think he saw the point and appreciated my feelings on the subject; I will give him that much credit anyhow, although his horrid treatment of my companions in the prison pen belied every attribute of a soldier or a man.

He was silent for some time after I had finished my defence, and sat with his hands folded. At last he said, " Have you any friends in the stockade? "

I replied, " General, every man in that pen under whose gray coat throbs the heart of a true Confederate soldier, is a friend of mine."

" Oh! I don't mean that; have you not some particular ones whom you think a great deal more of than of the others; can't you particularize? "

" Certainly, General, all of us have some companions that we think more of than of others."

" Well, give me their names."

I began at once to call the names of those whom I thought a great deal of and who were warm personal friends, and a clerk was making a list, as I named them. I had called about a dozen, when the thought flashed into my brain that this might be a trick to involve my friends in the same fate that had been meted out to me in the past, and that I had better not give him any more; so I halted.

He said, " Is that all the friends you have? "

I replied, " Is not that enough? "

And he said, " No, I want about sixty."

I then concluded that if we had to suffer, I would take those that had made themselves obnoxious to many of the boys in their daily intercourse, and let them share my fate. So I began and called their names until our roll contained sixty names in all.

After the roster was complete, the General said, " Captain Bell informs me that you admired an old churchyard and church as you passed through Beaufort, on your way to Pocataligo, and said that, if you had your choice, you would like to spend the balance of your days in a spot as quiet and beautiful as that old churchyard, and its surroundings. Now I am going to parole you and your congenial comrades, send you to this old church, and give you the freedom of its adjoining grounds. I will give you a guard of old disabled soldiers to protect you from all intruders; and I will allow you to trade and buy from the citizens any of the market products you may wish to add to your prison rations. I do this, Major, in honor of you, for I see that you are a man that will not betray a trust. Now you can go at once to your new quarters."

It would be impossible to describe my feelings as I bade General Foster good-bye, and I would have given much to be able to change the names on that roster, but I kept the secret in my own heart.

I was not required to give my written parole; the General said my verbal promise was enough for him while I was in the shadow of the old church and its grounds.

I went at once to my quarters, and found everything nice and clean; quarters were prepared for sixty men, and the pews had been converted into bunks.

The next morning my comrades all arrived. We spent a month or two in this delightful place. Our personal guards were real soldiers, belonging to the invalid corps, and had been crippled by our bullets. Capt. Frank Bell visited us often, and gave us the news from the outside world, frequently showing us maps of the progress of the war. These maps were issued weekly, giving the standing and advance of the Federal army, much as the weather maps of the United States do to-day.

I remember that a great serpent was coiled around the " so-called " Confederacy, and each day his coils grew smaller, and our chances of success less.   The places of each corps was designated, and its commander given.   The head of the serpent was just over Richmond, and its fiery tongue was touching Petersburg, while its fangs were exposed, ready to be driven into both cities.   These " war maps " were our constant theme of discussion and they did not bring much cheer to us.

I would often wander alone around the old churchyard, and read the names on the tombs.   One in particular had a strange fascination for me.   It was just a plain shaft with no name or date, but on it was carved in simple gothic letters, these words:

" STRANGER, STOP?   MY FATHER SLEEPS HERE."

It made a deep impression on me, and I can never forget it.

I shared with my companions all the delicacies my money could purchase; and the supplies that I had brought from Charleston.   Late in November I was taken with a wasting diarrhoea, and was sent to hospital at Hilton Head.   I was too sick and weak to pay attention to my surroundings; I only remember seeing some familiar faces that I had not seen since I left Morris Island on my exchange trip.   I remember seeing an armed guard at the door as I was carried into the room, and of seeing other sick men on low, hard rough-looking bunks.   I also remember being carried out one day in a cot by two rough-looking men and being placed in a boat, and of being lifted up on deck of a vessel and carried down into a large cabin, with small beds all in rows, with men lying in them.   How long I laid in one of these I have no recollection.

One day I recognized one or two of the men that were attending to me, and heard them speaking of how cold it was.   And then I began to feel the rock of the vessel and feel the jar of the ship, as it would jerk against the anchor chains.   I asked one of my nurses where we were, and he said that we were on a prison hospital ship, off Hilton Head, in the harbor.   I felt the slosh of the waves, as they pounded against the sides of the vessel, and I asked if I could get up and put on my clothes, as I felt that it would do me good. I was informed that they did not bring my clothes on board, and that they had never seen them.

One evening the storm increased, and Capt. J. J. Andrews, one of my nurses, came to me and said, " Major, it is a fearful night, half raining, and half sleeting; the wind is blowing a fearful gale from the northeast, and the tide is so strong that it is almost dragging the anchors, and they have taken the negro guards off of the upper deck."

I asked how far we were from the land, and he said not more than a mile or two, he thought. I asked if the tide and waves were going in toward the land, and he said yes. I asked if he would not throw me overboard, and he said no, that I would be drowned or swallowed by a shark as soon as I touched the water. I waited some minutes and listened to the war of the elements, and asked him again to aid me in getting overboard, as I felt that the winds and waves would aid me in reaching the mainland.

About nine o'clock that night, after begging him for a few more minutes and telling him that there was no danger from the sharks, as they had gone into deep water, he assisted me to the port hole, and raised the heavy wooden hinged window. With my crutches only to aid me, I plunged into the dark boiling waters, clad only in my hospital underwear, and was driven forward between Beaufort and James's Island, toward Pocataligo River.

The night was very dark, and I could see the lights at Hilton Head and on the vessels in the offing, as I would rise on the crest of a wave. I made but little exertion to keep afloat, and as the waves and wind drove me forward, I felt my strength and will power increase, and a sense of freedom came to cheer me. All night I was floating, and I drifted into a marshy, sawgrass channel. When the tide turned against the wind, I rested myself on my crutches by grasping the tussocks of sawgrass with them and holding on. I could not touch the bottom, nor could I raise myself clear of the water. The half frozen rain beat in my face all night and the air was so cold that I only exposed my face to it, and kept my body as deep as possible in the warm sea water, which here was tempered by the Gulf Stream.

When daylight came, I could not see anything but the tall sawgrass around me, and as the tide changed shoreward, I followed it slowly through the marsh grass, avoiding the open water, and keeping as invisible as possible. The second night the winds died down and the stars came out; the slosh of the sea lessened, and I would anchor amid the tussocks of grass when the tide was outward bound, and float with it when it went shoreward.

CHAPTER XXI

At Roper Hospital at Charleston—Reply to accusation of appropriating to my own use supplies sent to prisoners by me—Spend Christmas holidays at Montgomery—Assigned to duty around Petersburg—Rendered cripple for life.

On the morning of the second day, about ten o'clock, I saw the mainland but a few hundred feet away. All fatigue was banished, as my eyes caught sight of this longed-for goal, and with my crutches under me I turned on my back and headed with all my strength for the shore. I grounded near the mouth of a " rice flume," and the levee had to be climbed. It was a terrible struggle to reach the top of it, but when I did so I was amply rewarded, for there, stretched out before me, was a panorama that sent a thrill into my wasted frame. I could see the Confederate flag waving above some tents not half a mile away, and I could see a train of cars passing near the point. Down the levee, both to my right and left, I could see mounted pickets.

I took an inventory of myself; the sawgrass had nearly robbed me of my scant prison hospital underclothing, and my whole body was scarified by the sharp teeth of this seagrass. I felt the gnawings of hunger and a craving for water, and just under me, on the opposite side of the levee, was a ditch full of it. I rolled down the bank to it, and dipping my hands in, I tasted and found it cold and fresh. I bent down and stuck my lips in, and for a minute I drank all that I could hold. As I drew back I was challenged by a mounted Confederate picket. I was too weak to rise on my crutches and was shivering with the cold. The picket saw this and called for the corporal of the guard, and in a few minutes I was in the hands of my own people. They put an overcoat and some blankets on me and on a stretcher they carried me to camp, and then, closely covered, I was borne to the station house at Pocataligo and placed near a warm fire, and given a cup of strong coffee, which restored warmth to my body.

A surgeon examined me and administered some restorative, and in an hour or two I began to feel returning vitality. I asked who was in command of the post and was informed that Gen. N. G. Evans held the position. I asked if I could see him, and in a few minutes he came to my bunk and I made myself known. We conversed about the battle of Leesburg and other incidents, and I gave him an account of our prisoners on Morris Island, and at Beaufort and Hilton Head. He sent me a warm suit of underwear and a uniform, and forwarded me at once to the Roper hospital at Charleston.

I reached there that evening, and on the fifteenth of December I got out of my bunk and sat around in the room; on the sixteenth, I walked several hundred yards down the street, and saw several of our men who had landed on exchange from Beaufort the day before. The meeting was a pleasant one, and the past was like a dream. They told me my name was on the list of those who were chosen for exchange, and that they wondered why I was not on the boat with them. Two of them, Capt. J. W. Greer, of the 4th Georgia, and Capt. A. H. Farrar, of the 13th Mississippi, accompanied me back to the hospital.

The morning papers of the 16th of December had a card, signed by five of the officers whom I had selected to accompany me to the old church at Beaufort on parole, in which they stated that I had appropriated and sold for my own use all the stores and supplies generously donated to the Morris Island prisoners by the ladies and citizens of Charleston, instead of giving them to the prisoners. That I had had an ample supply of tobacco and various delicacies still in my hands when I was sent to the hospital at Hilton Head.

I answered this in the evening papers, giving details of the whole transaction, and calling on the provost marshal, to whom these donations had been originally consigned, and reciting that they were not allowed by the Yankee flag of truce officer to accompany me on my return, but were left in the train on which I had been sent to Pocataligo the morning of my return to prison; that only my individual stores, that I had paid my own money for, were allowed on the flag of truce boat.

At the same time I sent Lieutenant Harrolson and Capt. J. J. Andrews of Gen. P. D. Roddey's staff, to hunt these officers up, and direct them to apologize in the next morning's papers, and withdraw the charges, or they must meet me at six o'clock on James's Island and at sun-up settle the same at the muzzle of a gun, or the point of a saber or rapier.

Two of them came out in a card the next day and apologized, and said that they had learned from the provost marshal and from the railroad authorities that none of the stores were sent by me or had ever been forwarded until long after my departure; that they had been forwarded to Morris Island and turned over to the prisoners, and that they had seen the receipts for the tobacco, potatoes, etc. Three refused to retract. I sent each of them a separate challenge, and they accepted, naming six-shooters as the weapons of their choice.

Captains Andrews and Sharp, the latter our naval ordnance officer in Charleston, and Lieutenant Charles Harrolson accompanied me to the island, and at sun-up two of the three put in their appearance. One left the city that night and I have never heard a word from him since.

I took my place as time was called, and the seconds took theirs. At the word I sent a bullet crashing into my opponent's heart, and his pistol went off as the ball struck him. In a few moments I was ready for the second encounter, and as the word was given I tore his pistol hand to pieces, shattering the stock, rendering his gun and arm forever useless.

We returned to the city, and getting my transportation and a furlough from General Hardee I left on the first train for Montgomery, Ala., where I wanted to spend the Christmas holidays with my cousins, Major and Mrs. A. D. Banks.

I refrain from making public the names of these

officers who treated me so shabbily and who forced me
to a duel.   I do this out of my love and friendship
for every man who wore the gray, and out of respect
for their families ; but if any are curious enough they
can find their names and verify the statements here
made by examining the files of the Charleston papers
of this date in the public library of Charleston, as
did some friends a few years since at our reunion in
that city.

Upon leaving Augusta, Ga., a Mrs. Morrison, whose
husband was wounded and in the hospital at Columbus,
Ga., was placed under my protection, to escort to her
destination.   This I did under very adverse circumstances, over broken bridges and swollen streams, by
army wagons and on foot at times, followed by negroes
carrying her trunk.   But by dint of perseverance and
indomitable will power we landed safely in Columbus,
and she was with her husband and friends.

I reached Montgomery, Ala., and ate Christmas
dinner with Major Banks and Cousin Virginia and the
two children, Mary and Tommy.   I spent two weeks
here, then went on to Jackson, Miss., and spent the
rest of my furlough with my father at Belvidere, and
visiting congenial neighbors in the country surrounding.
At the expiration of my furlough I returned to Virginia, reported to General Lee and was assigned to
duty around Petersburg.   Here I remained, doing headquarters service, until the 27th day of March, when
I was wounded in the right ankle and rendered a cripple
for life.

I was furloughed and given permission to cross the
Mississippi River and remain until I was able to resume
duty.   I left on the 29th of March and reached Selma,
Ala., on the 12th of April.   Wilson's raiders were
in front of that city.   I met my brother as I was going
to a hospital to have my wound dressed, and he went
with me.   In the battle with Wilson I rode into the
fight and was again wounded.   My brother and one
of the men held me on the horse as we swam the river
and made our escape.

CHAPTER XXII

Lee's surrender—Refused a parole—Go to Yazoo Valley—
Make contract to gin cotton for Dr. Jiggets—Before
the Grand Jury at Yazoo City.

WE reached Meridian, Miss., a short time after, and
heard of Lee's surrender. The Yankees, under General
E. R. S. Canby, were near by, and the command we
were with was here paroled. But after my papers were
examined, General Canby sent me word that he had
orders not to parole me, as I had been wounded in a
fight before I was exchanged, and while I was only on
parole. I knew that this was a lie, and the general
said that if I would report in person to him he would
give me the freedom of the Federal camp. I wrote,
on the back of his note, and told him that I preferred
the freedom of the woods to that of a Yankee camp.

That evening, with two led horses, two of us started
for Jackson, Miss., and rode all night, spelling our
horses every hour or so, and by ten o'clock a. m.,
we were in the suburbs of that city. Here I found a
Colonel Risdon, the paroling officer, and with a squad
of Ross's Texans I applied for a parole, when I was
politely informed that they had orders not to parole
a man of my name.

I asked if I was the only man in the Confederate
army of that name, as I knew a dozen men who bore
the name of Fontaine, in various parts of our army;
that I had a father and two brothers, not far off.

He said, " Well, wait until the rush is over, and I
will examine into the merits of the case. I'm too busy
just now."

I stepped out and with a body of Ross's men rode out
to their camp, in an old field four miles from my father's
residence, avoiding the Yankee pickets on the main
roads leading out of Jackson.

I was at a Mrs. Ross's one day and she informed me that she had invited Colonel Risdon, the agent of the Freedmen's Bureau, out to dine with her that day, and that she wished that I would stay and help entertain them.   I told her that I was in camp with Ross's men, preparing to leave for Texas in a few days, and that Colonel Risdon had refused to parole me, and it was dangerous for me to put myself in his power.   She said that she would send and get some of the boys to be with me, and that he need not know that it was me, as her brother, Green Skipwath, was away, and she could introduce me as her brother.

I stayed, and met the agent and the Colonel and another officer.   They came with an escort of some half-dozen negro soldiers.   She had the contracts with her negroes signed and everything arranged.

After they were gone my negro came to the door and told me that the negroes in the yard had told one of the Yankee negroes that he had heard his mistress and I talking that morning, and that I had told her that I had not been paroled, and that I was going with the Texas men to Texas.

I did not feel comfortable after this news reached me. I went inside and told Mrs. Ross my predicament, mounted my horse and rode back to the camp and asked the boys if they would stand by me if the negroes were sent out to take me.   They agreed, to a man.

The next day I was again at Mrs. Ross's, and my horse was hitched in the back yard when my boy, George, came hurriedly in and said, "Master, the Yankees are coming, and they are all niggers."

I hurriedly mounted my horse and rode in a gallop out the back way to our camp, which was in the adjoining field of Mr. George Boddie.

About an hour after my arrival we saw them coming and we held a hurried consultation.   All the officers of the regiment were absent.   I went inside a tent and got my arms ready, and every man, some three hundred in all, was soon ready.

They came up, under command of a negro sergeant, and dismounted on the opposite side of a large gully that lay directly in front of our camp.   Our guard halted them and asked what they wanted.

The sergeant was very polite, saluted, and said, " We was informed dat you has a Major *Fountain's* in your camp, and de Colonel he done *saunt* me to bring him to Jackson."

" There's no such man here," one of the boys replied.   " No such man belongs to our command."

" De Colonel done told me to search ebry tent, and not to come back till I done found him."

" Well, come on and search," one of the men said.

With that they fastened their horses, and as the whole posse, some thirty in all, scrambled down into the ditch and were ascending the side next to us I looked down at them, and one negro, who knew me and lived in the neighborhood, and formerly belonged to Mr. Ben Whitfield, looked up and said, " Dar he is, dat's him."

All these negroes deserted right there, and they took refuge in the bottom of that ditch, and the banks, like the walls of the Red Sea, rolled over and hid them from all prying eyes, forever.   We hid all signs of their departure in the ditch, and a rain that night aided our efforts.

I spent several days in the neighborhood, listening to the gossip, and then went into the wilds of the Yazoo Valley.

I met a Dr. Jiggets, who resided near Livingston, in Madison County, Miss., and who had some three hundred bales of cotton in pens, to be ginned, and I took the contract to gin this.   But circumstances forced me to leave the country for a while and hide.   This I did, and on my return, when all was quiet, I fulfilled my agreement with the doctor.   I hired teams and hands, put an old gin of his in repair, and hauled and ginned and baled some two hundred and eighty-seven heavy bales, some weighing six hundred pounds or more, of which I got one-third.

The trouble was that the country was full of disbanded soldiers and deserters from both armies, and they would steal all the cotton that was ginned that they could lay their hands on, claiming that it was

" Confederate cotton," sold by the owners originally to the Confederate Government.

None was ever sold to our government until it was ginned and baled, as the government would not receive cotton in the seed, unginned.

As I ginned this seed cotton I hauled it direct from the gin to Satartia, on the Yazoo River, and shipped it by boat to Vicksburg. I took "bills of lading" from the boat, and the boat brought back receipts from the storage warehouse. I was constantly warned by parties that I would some day be caught on my way from the gin to Satartia, and my cotton confiscated by some of these restless, roving men who had no respect for law and order. I always attended my wagons on their trips to and from the landing at Satartia.

I used to gin from twenty to thirty bales before I made a trip to the landing, and I would sit on the front wagon and go into town with them. I was constantly on the watch for these cotton thieves, and carried a large double-barreled shotgun, belonging to a Mrs. Lewis, who lived in Dover, Yazoo County, and I had my drivers armed with six-shooters, and two other negroes accompanying each wagon. Often Louis or Dave Jiggets, sons of Dr. Jiggets, or some known friend would be with me, so it was not easy to take my cotton.

One bright, moonlight night, about midnight, I had about twenty bales piled around the press, which was an old tall, wooden screw, with long sweeping levers, like an exaggerated " A," to which were attached the mules that turned the screw down upon the lint, compressing it into the bale box. As I was standing near this press I could hear the rumble of wagons in the road leading from Scott's Ferry to Satartia, about a half mile north of the gin. I had seven or eight men at work at the gin stands and four nearly grown boys driving the mules that ran the gin stands.

The night was very clear and the moon shining brightly. About midnight I heard the big gate open, and the wagons coming toward the gin. I ran into the gin house, stopped the ginners, and putting them with their guns down where the mules were in a circle, facing the approaching wagons, I instructed them not to fire until they could see me shoot from the press. I hurried out and took my stand at one of the uprights, in front of the cotton bales, and waited developments. I had not long to wait before I saw several men in front of three six-mule wagons approaching along the narrow ridge road, between two deep gullies. There was not room for a wagon to turn or pass another in this narrow way. I waited until they were within fifty yards of me, then I halted the three men, who were in advance of the wagons, and asked what they wanted.

They replied, " We have come for that cotton, as it is Confederate cotton, and we are going to take it."

I replied that this was private cotton that I was ginning from the seed; that all Confederate cotton was ginned and baled before the government received it, and before the surrender; and that if they got it it would be over my dead body.

One of them said, " You are a liar, and you know it; so damn you, take that! "

A pistol flash followed his words, and the splinters from the post flew in my face, from the impact of the bullet, not missing me more than an inch or so.

I raised my old shotgun, with twenty number five buckshot in each barrel, and sent the two loads into their ranks, killing two of them and one horse, and wounding the other. The echo of my gun had not died away before my negroes from the circle under the gin stands poured a perfect hail of buckshot in among the drivers and the squad of men in the rear of the wagons, and I opened with my six-shooters on them. The drivers, who were all negroes, jumped from their seats, and the mules got into a fearful tangle, and we got every one of them. The men in the rear broke at full speed and never again came in sight.

I went up to the wounded man and found him in great agony. I had him carried to the house, staunched the flow of blood and had him cared for as best I could, and placed him under the guard of one of my negroes.

I had the captured mules released from their entanglements and placed in the stables.

At daylight I had a letter written and sent a negro mounted on a mule to carry it to the provost marshal at Canton. I also sent a note to Dr. Jiggets, telling him of the situation.

My negro had ridden but a short distance down the road when he met Louis Jiggets, and with him the provost marshal and about thirty soldiers. I made my report to the provost, and he took the mules, my wounded man, several of the negroes and myself, and carried us all to Vicksburg that day, as that was his destination. He reported the affair to General Slocum. I was questioned very closely by the General, and after examining the negroes thoroughly, he made me a present of one of the wagons, and six of the best mules, and sent us back to our gin work. We drove back over the same route the next day. The prisoner that I had shot was hung in Vicksburg a short time after. He was a robber and a deserter, by the name of Brooks, and had gained quite a notoriety.

I finished ginning without any other trouble, and when the last bale was shipped I went down to meet Captain Page, of the steamboat " *Emma No. 2,*" with whom I had done all my shipping. I saw notices posted at various places on the road, *that I was going to be shot at sight.* These notices were signed, " *By order of the Swamp Tigers.*" I stopped and wrote on each one a request to keep out of my way, as I did not wish to hurt any of them, but that I was ready at all times to defend myself, and had plenty of friends to aid me.

A mile or so from Satartia, on the morning I was to meet Captain Page, a large raccoon ran across the road in front of me, and as he was climbing a tree I drew my pistol and fired, killing him instantly. As I went to reload it, I found that the main spring was broken, and it was of no further service until I could have it mended. I only had a small derringer pocket pistol to fall back upon.

I rode into Satartia, and the " *Emma No. 2* " was at the landing. I went aboard and Captain Page took me up to his room and handed me $7,500 in very large bills, most of them $1,000 ones. These I put in an inner pocket of my vest. He also gave me a watch, with a long, old-fashioned gold chain, to be worn around the neck. This watch belonged to Mrs. Lewis, of Dover, in Yazoo County, and had been sent off for repairs. The boat was on its way to Vicksburg, and I gave the Captain my pistol, to have the main spring replaced, and to be left with Johnson & Co., in Satartia, upon the return trip. I tried to borrow one from him, to replace mine, in the interim, but he only had one. I tried Captain R. G. Johnson, and several others, but did not succeed.

I spent the day in Satartia, dressed in an entire new suit from head to toe. I folded my old Confederate hat into a small bundle, and placed it, with two pounds of candy, in my haversack. Dressed in a bran new suit, with an extra heavy overcoat and a fine white hat, at four o'clock that evening I mounted my horse and rode off up the river road toward Dover.

I stopped at the W. A. Gale place and took supper with an old friend, John McCutchin, who was in charge of the place. After supper I passed on up the hill overlooking the landing at Liverpool. Here the roads form a Greek delta, one going to Liverpool, one to Dover, and the other the regular Yazoo City and Satartia road. I passed at once into the Dover road. Nearing the narrow hills that border Anderson's Creek, the cane lies close to the trail or road, and two wagons can scarcely pass. When at this point I heard the trampling of horses behind me. I took my little derringer pistol from my pocket, cocked it and put my right hand with it in my overcoat pocket, and held it there. As the horses gained on me, I made up my mind that if they were friends I could lower the hammer and leave it there, as I shook hands with them, and they would never know that I had ever had any hostile intentions.

As they came in view I saw that one was riding a gray, and the other a dark-colored horse. I thought that I saw a pistol in the hands of the man on the dark horse, so, with my eyes glancing back over my right shoulder, I kept him in view. They came within ten feet of me, and the one on the gray spurred forward and said, " Where are you going? "

I did not reply at once, as I did not like the ring of his voice, and it was unknown to me. I turned half round in my saddle, so as to face him, and as I did so, he spurred right up against me, his knee almost as high as my belt, and I saw that he was a powerful built man, weighing about two hundred or more pounds, and wearing a short peajacket, or cavalry uniform.

As he almost touched me, he said in a gruff tone, " I want that watch! "

I made up my mind at once to kill him, and leap from my saddle and secure his pistol, which he held level with my head as he uttered his command. I instantly threw my left hand upward, as his knee grazed my side, and struck his pistol, and with my right hand I pressed my derringer above his belt and fired. My little mule gave a tremendous jump, and came very near dropping me on my back in the road. I grabbed the bridle as quickly as possible, and gave a hard jerk on the bit, and put my whole strength on it, and the reins snapped in two like burnt threads, and my mule dashed away like the wind, upsetting all plans to leap and secure the pistol of my would-be robber.

The force of my derringer rammed against the robber blew him out of his saddle, and his horse was jerked around by the bridle as his rider fell. I only had a momentary glimpse of this, as my attention was confined to the movements of my mule.

I heard a voice exclaim, " Sam, Sam, are you hurt? "

In the moment I saw the flash of a pistol, and then another, and another, until it seemed a continuous shower of bullets were following me. One grazed my left ear and clipped a lock of hair from the temple; one plowed across my right arm below the elbow, and one struck me a blow in the back, which gave me a shock.

The shower of bullets seemed to lend wings to my little mule, and she traveled with a speed I had never seen excelled. She dashed across Anderson's Creek and up the hill beyond, and as I came opposite Mr. Lacey's the front gate was open, a wagon just going in; my mule followed it and went right up to the gallery. Her race of over a mile had almost winded her. I dismounted as quickly as possible, and one of the boys took charge of my mule, and fastened her to the gallery.

As I came into the light, I looked down and saw that my shirt bosom was spattered with blood, as was my hat, and blood was trickling from my right arm, but the pain was in my back, and I thought I was shot through.

There were six or seven men sitting around the fire, smoking, as supper was just over, and the table not yet cleared away. I spoke to them and they asked me what was the matter; what all that firing meant. I told them and asked them if they would not go back with me and help kill or capture the gang. I explained that it would be easy to do, as they would not be looking for me to return, and that we could go afoot, make no noise, creep up, and surround them, and kill or capture the whole band, and thus rid the country of them.

I explained how I had killed one of their number by the name of Sam, but they refused, and said that they had had enough fighting, and didn't want any more.

I reloaded my little derringer, and asked if they would lend me a six-shooter, but they declined. I examined my wounds, and found only a scratch on my right arm below the elbow, a bruised place above it, and a small tip of my left ear bleeding. There was a bullet hole through my coat sleeve above the elbow, but it had not touched the skin. As I undid the belt, to examine the wound in my back, the bullet dropped to the floor from the clothing, and I found only a bruised spot where it had lodged in the clothing. The ball had passed through nine folds of my Confederate hat, made dust almost of the two pounds of candy and thus broken its force. The blood on my shirt front and hat was from the robber, and had been blown all over me with fragments of his intestines.

After bathing and bandaging my arm I went into the dining room and ate a biscuit and some potatoes and drank a glass of milk, came back into the sitting room, smoked and talked a while, and renewed my efforts to get the men to go back with me and capture the band of robbers, but they would not listen to the proposition. I procured a candle and went with one of the boys and mended my bridle, mounted my mule and bade them all good-night, although they insisted on my remaining until morning. I felt that it would be safer for me to continue that night than to postpone my journey for daylight; in fact, I did not feel safe with men who were adverse to ridding the country of a band of robbers, who spared neither man, woman nor child in their raids for gold, or gain, and I knew that I would be much safer out in the open, wide awake, and trusting to my own resources, so I rode away.

At two o'clock that night I rode into the yard of Mr. W. S. Noble, as I saw lights shining in the house. I dismounted and found the family all up, as little Willie Noble was quite ill. I related my adventures, and Mrs. Noble prepared me some lint and bandages and soaked them in boiling tar and turpentine water. After dressing my arm I continued my journey on foot to Dover, which was about half a mile away. I felt strangely safe as I entered my own room, and saw my array of guns and pistols all around me. I was soon in bed and sound asleep.

The next morning I ate breakfast at Mrs. Lewis's and delivered the watch into her hands and told her how the robber had demanded it of me. After breakfast I belted on my pistols and mounting my own horse I rode over to Dr. Jigget's at Livingston, and turned over his share of the money I had in my possession. I spent the night there, and the next day, with Louis Jiggets, I rode over to Belvidere and spent a few days with my father and his family.

Upon my return to Dover, in Yazoo County, I was summoned by Justice of the Peace Ne Smith to appear before the grand jury in Yazoo City. On entering the jury room I was certain that I saw men I believed to have been in the crowd who attacked me at the gin house the night I captured the wagons. I could not get this impression out of my mind, and when Mr. Joe

Mosely asked me about my encounter at the gin house these men left the room. When Mr. Thomas R. Holloman asked me to relate my encounter with the robbers on Anderson Creek hills several others moved out.

I told them that I believed a part of the jury before whom I was summoned belonged to the clique who had been terrorizing the citizens between this place and Vicksburg; that many of their names had been given me by parties, both men and women, who had been held up and robbed in the lower part of the county, and that though not personally known to me I could give their names, which I did, and it created a stir in the jury room.

I then asked them to give me a sheet of paper, and I would write a list of all, and attach my oath of affirmation to it. This I did and handed it to the foreman of the jury. It was handed around and read by every one present. And from that day to this I have never heard any more about the outcome of their investigations at that meeting.

I left the room and Mr. Holloman followed me and told me to look out or I might be assassinated on my way back to Dover. I told him that I always was prepared, and would certainly aid the good citizens of Yazoo County in ferreting out and bringing to justice the lawless element that had broken out among the disbanded armies of both the North and the South, and that I wanted it distinctly understood that I was on the side of the law-abiding people of the whole county, and was at their beck and call, day or night, so long as I remained in their midst.

I felt that these thieves knew that I would not hesitate to kill, at the slightest provocation, and that I was always ready.

I wound up my business transactions with Dr. Jiggets, and forwarded the proceeds to my old plantation home, with orders to my manager to put everything in first class condition; that I expected to return and spend the rest of my days in the quietude of my plantation home on old Caney Creek, in the land of my early childhood. But fate decreed otherwise.

CHAPTER XXIII

I teach school—My marriage—Make Austin my home—
The birth of our son—Surveying in Yazoo Valley—
Retrospection.

MANY of my old-time friends were forced into bank-
ruptcy, and guardian bonds, that I had signed for these
friends in the long years before, were thrown upon my
shoulders at this time, and my home passed from me
into the hands of strangers, and I was left without a
dollar or a friend from whom I could borrow.

I taught school for a while in the Dover neighborhood, and for a while tried to forget my condition. I
kept up my rifle and pistol practice, and on Saturdays
I would hunt or visit Yazoo City or some congenial
neighborhood. But I was restless, and for a while contemplated returning to the life of a sailor, and spend-
ing my last days on the wide waves of the restless sea,
as they were more in unison than my spirits.

While these thoughts held their revels in my brain,
I met, at a wedding in the neighborhood, the young
lady who had been so kind to me upon my escape from
Vicksburg, on the night of the surrender from that
terrible siege. From that wedding feast I returned to
my bachelor quarters, a new being. I determined to
change my plans and link my fate with hers, be it for
weal or woe.

I entered into the struggle with all the vim that I
possessed; and on the twentieth day of June, 1866,
the anniversary of that terrible day and night when I
pillowed my head on a dead Yankee on the battlefield
of Strasburg just four years before, I led her to
the altar, and made her mine forever.

In the following January we took up our abode
in the city of Austin, in Texas, and we spent many
happy days among the scenes of my early boyhood.
I was a recording clerk, and then a draughtsman, in

the land office under Captain Stephen Crosby, until the United States Government, by arbitrary power, displaced the local authorities and put carpet-baggers in our places.

I was disfranchised, and moved down into a cedar brake, about six miles above Bastrop on the Colorado River. Here I taught school for a while, and here my wife presented me with a splendid boy, and together we spent many happy days in our little cabin home, far from the haunts and sounds of the busy outside world.

The negro " Loyal Leagues " and their white social equals harassed the citizens, and kept every community in a stir. Our cedar brake was a haven for those whom the league were banded against. When the negroes would enter it, to bring some accused one before a negro justice or a Freedmen's Bureau tribunal, they invariably failed to report back again, and were marked as deserters, and when the white soldiers were sent, they reported the cedar brake as deserted and without an inhabitant.

Frequent riots would occur and clashes between the negroes and the citizens, and the slaughter of the negroes was invariably the result.

This kind of life became irksome, as I had a family now to care for, so I determined to return to my wife's old home and show our boy ; to leave the cedar brakes and wind-swept prairies behind us, and make our home in the jungle wilds of the Yazoo in the Mississippi Delta. We returned, and since that day we have made our home where the long gray moss, with its weird shroud, covers the hanging branches of the cypress, or out in the broken, cane-covered hills of Short Creek, or in the city of the Yazoo, with congenial friends.

For fourteen years I lived in the county, and was the county surveyor, and for thirty-six years I have aided in the surveying and laying out of the various lines of railroads that now traverse the Yazoo Mississippi Valley. My feet have trod upon every square mile from Horn Lake on the north, to the mouth of the Yazoo River above Vicksburg, on the south.

In the winter of 1888 we moved into the heart of the " Yazoo Valley," and built our home in the midst of a dense canebrake, surrounded by a beautiful holly grove, and near the heart of a large clump of mounds and ruins of the ancient mound builders. In these wilds, where the howling of the wolves, the cries of the wild cats and the scream of an occasional panther could be heard, a superabundance of deer, turkeys, squirrels, and an occasional bear, with the aid of our dogs and guns, gave us the choicest viands of the chase for our larder. We spent several years amid these wild forest solitudes, on Porter's Bayou, just below the head of Indian Bayou. Here, in this primal abode of nature, my friends from distant climes would visit us, and renew the memories and recollections of by-gone days.

In November, 1893, an early fire robbed us of all our household possessions, and destroyed all the relics accumulated from my world-wide travels. After the fire, we moved to our present home, in the little village of Lyon, and came out from the sylvan wilds into the great stream of progressive civilization.

And here, with my children and grandchildren around me, I sit in my great armchair, on the shaded gallery, with the balmy sea-born zephyrs, fresh from the Mexic Sea, fanning my brow; with the smoke curling up from my old meerschaum pipe, fragrant with the perfume of perique, I dream and retrospect.

Through the vales of memory I am again on the vast, wind-swept plains of the west, a wild, naked Comanche Indian boy. Again I touch the frozen shores of far-away Greenland and see the vast ice fields and mountains wrapped in their garbs of eternal snow and ice, gleaming in the ever varying hues of the grand aurora borealis, that vast arc light, produced by the meeting of the positive and negative currents of electricity, flowing upward from the equator, and meeting in battle array over the north pole, forming the sword of the Cherubim placed by Almighty God at the gates of the Garden of Eden to guard the way and warn man from trespassing upon this forbidden spot.

I hear again the thunder of the guns at Vera Cruz. I see again the beauties of the distant isles of the Pacific and Indian Oceans. I catch glimpses of the snow-clad peaks of the Andes and Himalayan Mountains. I hear again the awful crash of the exploding shells as I lay buried under the debris of the Malakoff, and I see the smoke of the guns at Balaklava and of Inkerman.

And again with my Bedouin Arabs, I cross the dead and parched sands of Sahara, with its wonderful mirages and desert horrors. And there looms into my memory's vision the great Chinese wall with its granite towers, stretching across wide plains, and deep foaming rivers, and ascending almost inaccessible mountain heights, guarding for twenty-five hundred miles the vast Mongolian Empire, built by people who were gray with age and knowledge before the foundation stones of the Egyptian pyramids were laid.

I glide along over the snow-covered steppes of Siberia, behind swift ponies, or the fleet-footed reindeer. I see the flat marshes of the shores around the capital of the Czar; the grand old castles and gloomy palaces and lovely vineyards and gardens of Germany, France, and England; the wonderful paintings and statuary of the fairyland of Italy, the vast churches and grand cathedrals that are scattered along the shores of the Mediterranean Sea. I hear the growl of the wild beasts of prey swelling up from the jungle wilds of Asia and the unexplored regions of Africa, and anon I catch the gleam of the yellow eye of the royal tiger, amid the tangled bamboo glens of Bengal, India. The deep bass growl and jarring purr of the tawny-maned lion of eastern Africa and the loud, hoarse trumpeting of the elephant seemingly swell upon the air.

Amid the dense forests of the Amazon I see twined around the trunks and limbs of trees, the huge vine-like forms of the boa constrictor, and listen to the chatterings of the wildly excited monkey tribes, as they discover their apparent enemy. Again I stray along the deep, gold-laden cañons of the Rio Madre di Dios that flows from beneath the beautiful Lake Titicaca, that rests and nestles at the feet of the snow-capped volcanoes in the Andean chain of mountains. I hear the soft sweet music of the dark-eyed maidens, as they touch the strings of their guitars, floating out on the still waters of Lake Managua.

Anon the visions drift away into the dreamy lands unreal, and I am again amid the shouting legions, hear the crash of musketry, the deep diapason of the guns hurling their missiles of death into the living masses of the charging hosts of Grant on the serrated hills of Vicksburg.

I see the folds of the Southern Cross with its white stars shining brightly above us as we charge into the hell of fire at Spottsylvania's " bloody angle," and the red fields of death, covered with the bleeding carcasses of men and horses. I hear the low, sad wails of the dying, and the death rattle in their throats.

And as the night spreads her shadowy mantle and the pale moon looks down on the red sands of the battlefield and the soft summer breezes kiss my forehead, my pipe slips from my fingers and rests upon the floor, and a sweet voice says, " Grandpa, come to dinner," and the past is in the infinite shades of the eternal past.

LECTURES ON
" AMERICA: THE OLD WORLD "
AND
OTHER SUBJECTS

AMERICA: THE OLD WORLD

Situation of the Garden of Eden—The glories of the
aurora borealis—North America undoubtedly the region
of the earliest civilization.

WHERE did God first plant the flora and fauna of
earth, and where was the *Garden of Eden?* In answering these great questions, that have puzzled theologians
and scientists throughout long ages, I shall endeavor
to give you a clear and unclouded answer, and prove it
by indisputable facts; and I shall be guided by my
own close, personal observations and explorations, and
not by any other authority. Long years ago, when
but a boy, I conceived the idea that the Garden of Eden
must have been planted in some region where the foot
of man has never since trod, and the question arose,
" Where was that spot? " The answer came, " It must
have been at the poles of the earth." These questions
came to me when I was but a youth, cruising on a whaling ship in that cold northern region of eternal ice and
snow.

In the winter of 1845-6 we were frozen in close to
an island in latitude 79° 10′ north and longitude 70°
40′ west, and on the 17th of July, 1846, we were anchored on the lee side of a grounded iceberg in latitude
74° 48′ north and longitude 66° 13′ west, and were engaged in cutting and trying out the oil of several large
whales that we had in tow. While sheltered behind this
berg the vessels *Erebus* and *Terror* of Sir John Franklin's fleet came in sight and " spoke " us, asking about
the seas and islands to the north and west of us, where
we had spent the winter. We gave them all the information that we had on the subject, they copied our log,
and we gave them a bountiful supply of oil for fuel and
lights.

I remember that they told us our ship had penetrated

farther north at that time than any other that they had a record of. After leaving us, they were in sight, going a little north of west, for fully twenty-four hours, and I think that we were the last that ever saw any of the crew of Sir John Franklin.

As I have said before, it was while cruising in this far off region of external snow and ice, in my budding manhood, that the idea entered my brain that it was here, in this cold bleak clime, that plant, bird, beast, and man first had their habitat. On every point of land my feet trod I saw vast quantities of the bones of great saurian monsters, and those of the monkey and elephant tribes, as well as of tropical birds, all in a fossilized state. I also saw the flora of the tropics, the orange, banana, and great palm leaves, all of gigantic size, frozen into stone. The fern leaves were from ten to forty feet in length, the oranges more than a foot in diameter, and the bananas larger and longer than a man's arm.

The great saurian monsters, sleeping under the "drift" of the "flora," and the great pachyderms could have lived in almost boiling water. The anthropoids were of gigantic size. I had a femur bone of one of these creatures that measured forty-nine inches in length; this would make the man-ape sixteen feet in height, as we now calculate sizes. These *Anthropoids giganti* had the dolichokephalic skulls and brain pans of the present negroes of the Congo and Upper Nile regions of Africa.

While viewing these monsters of the flora and fauna of that icy clime, I became satisfied that while they lived and where they lived, the present race of mankind, of the mesokephalic skull and clean white bones, could not have existed, for the lands were too hot. Well did I perceive that these monsters could not have lived amid the snows and chilly winds that howl around their fossilized remains.

On those bleak, barren, ice-bound shores, under the light of an almost eternal day, I examined every plant and bone with a keen and critical eye. I scanned every feature as they lay in countless thousands around me, until I silenced every doubt. Their size, color and component parts were as familiar to me as my A, B, C's, and I tried by every means at hand to compute their age, but in this I failed. However, I came to the conclusion that while they were on this earth, the man of the Eden Garden, the man of the " living soul," could not have been in existence. They were pre-Adamites and aeons of time must have elapsed before the Adamites could have wandered over the same lands.

I read daily and memorized every line and verse in the " Book of Books," given me by a loving mother's hand, from the first line in the Genesis of Moses to the building of Solomon's Temple. Again and again did I pore over its declarations about creation's dawn, and down to the deluge of Noah. Only one line, faint and indistinct, seemed to throw any light on the boundless sea of dark, unfathomable uncertainty that hedges around the description given by Moses, and this was the positive assertion that " the world was without form, and void." This was a clue, faint and indistinct, yet a something to build upon and reason from.

The clouds, floating in the ether above, were without fixed form and were void. The sun, moon and stars were all grand globes in the vaults above and below me, and were moving in regular defined orbits, obeying some great law. I had seen the molten lead poured from the towers, *without form, and void,* and seen it drop through space, and fall into the vaults of water below, each a globe, a miniature world. I had watched the cooks throw their slop water through the port holes out into the frozen air, also " without form, and void "; had seen it fall upon the snow and roll away, miniature worlds like our own. Every dewdrop clinging to a rose leaf or blade of grass; every bubble blown by a child; every raindrop falling through space, all represent miniature worlds.

Here was a solution, pure and simple. I had a foundation on which to construct the vast globe on which we live, and breathe. This old earth in the beginning was without form, and void, a mass of fiery, liquid matter, whirling through space, and the cold ether that fills all space compressed it with equal pressure from all

sides, just as it does the molten lead poured from the
shot tower, the bubble blown by a child, and the boiling
water thrown by the cook from the ship's side. The
raindrops falling from the void and formless cloud, the
red molten stars hurtling through illimitable space, are
all grasped by the same great invisible hand and compressed into minute or vast globes like our own.

This pressure fills all space; it has neither dome nor
foundation, and is a component part of eternity, because it has neither beginning nor end. It stretches beyond the limits of vision and is equal on all sides. Our
world is in the center of this pressure, and so are all
other worlds. The sun, moon and stars that hang in
this great, unfathomable sea of space were all fashioned
like our dewdrops, or our world, or the bubbles blown
by the child and are governed by the same laws. How
plain becomes the other descriptions of creation's dawn.
" And the spirit of God moved upon the waters." Here
that great power that holds the universe in place is
shown, and new and wonderful beauties break upon the
mind, and give us greater insight into the mysteries of
nature.

Is there in our midst a being of plain, common reason so dense that he does not know that all known substances, that are subject to heat, will first begin to cool
at the points farthest from the heat. Are we not aware
that all substances in liquid form, when thrown into the
air, will assume a globular or spheroid form? Now with
these facts—for they are facts beyond any cavil or
doubt—before him, can not any sensible or reasoning
being see for himself that it was thus our old earth was
formed? Formed, as Moses declares, from a mass, I
may say, of *floating star dust,* " without form and
void "? This great mass of molten matter, whirling
through the boundless ether void, under the binding influence of its two great powers, the sun that rules the
day, and the moon that rules the night, was held by
these two great luminaries in its present orb.

Thus in that far off frozen region we translated the
declarations of Moses. Proofs that this old world was
once a molten mass were ample. The igneous rocks—

medals of God himself—and the great masses of the
flora and fauna of a tropical clime, resting now on the
shores of an ice bound region, proved that this was once
a warmer clime than the tropics of to-day, and that
when they moved and had their being, the very earth
itself was hot.

The more I studied, the more strongly I became convinced that this northern shore of North America, at
the north pole, the farthest point from the direct rays
of the ruling orb of day, as well as at the south pole was
where our old earth first began to cool. And the older
I grow and the more I understand nature and nature's
laws, the more strongly confirmed in this reasonable
belief I become.

Now let us look at it in the clear light of unbiased
reason; let us review it in its every phase.

The poles of the earth are farthest from the direct
rays of the great solar heat of the sun; that body that
gives warmth and light to the entire world, and given
to us by God Himself to govern and rule the earth.
Hence the poles of this globe are farthest from the sun,
and would naturally begin to cool first. As soon as it
was cool enough at the poles, God would plant there
the flora and fauna of the earth. When I make the
declaration that it was at the north pole that grass,
birds, trees and animals first had their habitat, nature
and reason sustain my declaration, for there is no land
at the south pole. The continent of South America
only extends to Cape Horn and the continent of Africa
to the Cape of Good Hope; a boundless ocean rolls be-
.tween these capes and the south pole, and another ocean
rolls between the continents of Europe and Asia and the
north pole. It was upon this North American continent
alone that God first planted the flora and fauna of earth,
and only on this continent does dry land exist on which
God could plant the flora and fauna of earth; for they
do not belong in the water. These facts are so self-
evident that I need scarce pursue this argument
further.

Thus you can see that there was no place on the
European or Asiatic continent extending into the re-

gions of the north pole, on which plant or animal life could exist. The continent of North America alone presented the conditions necessary for the abode of plant and animal life, elsewhere all was a boundless ocean, uninhabitable to plant, bird, beast or animal, and it was undoubtedly upon the North American shore, at the north pole, that the first germs of life sprang into existence. As the earth cooled, plant and animal life grew and prospered, and followed the cooling earth down toward the equator. All this took place in the early tertiary period of the earth's creation.

As the earth became more cooled, the places of these tertiary birds, beasts, plants and animals, were taken by a more intelligent genus of animals and plants belonging to a cooler clime; and those of the quaternary period became existent; then came the intelligent anthropoids, and last, man. These followed in the wake of the croaking, blind, clammy, thick-skinned, heavy shelled saurians of the *hot age.* As the earth cooled, a greater variety of the flora permeated the land, and lent their beauties to the landscape, carpeting it with changing verdure.

In viewing those far-off regions through the dim glasses of the present over a lapse of sixty years, much has been forgotten of course, yet by brightening my memory from the observations of Kane, Greely, and others of a more recent date, they but fix the facts as I found them while upon the ground in person.

Let us look at that region when it was fresh from the hand of the Creator, and inhabited by primeval man. How beautiful it was! See it as the medals of nature reveal it in the days when its early, man-like inhabitants roamed its hills and valleys as shown to Moses, and spoken of in the sixth era after creation's dawn. Take it by eras in rotation. The first era after it was " without form and void," it assumed its globular phase and hissing, seething, whirling through the vast ether vortexes; it lights the distant dome of Heaven with sunlike radiance.

It would take an aeon of time for this great blazing, molten mass to cool, compress, harden and shrink to its

present 8000 miles of diameter. I repeat, it would take
an aeon of time for the outer crust of the great globe
to cool and shrink to its present diameter of 8000 miles.
In the second era, when the hot lands "heaved amain,"
and great chasms opened, and hills, mountains and valleys assumed form, and the other fluid molten stars in
red hurricanes of flame rushed through the interstellar
space, swift as the lightning's flash, and at God's command took their places in regular orbits, to travel their
allotted paths, under the "sweet influences of the
Pleiades," until time shall be no more. Our earth, too,
rushed through the vast chartless sea of space until
it felt the "binding hand," and yielded to the "sweet
Pleiadian influence" and rolled steadily into its allotted
pathway.

As time rolled by the internal heat escaped by raising
and bursting the cooling crusts of the earth. Volcanoes
lifted their towering heads above the undulating plains
and vomited forth their molten lava; the cracking earth,
with blazing torches, would fill the ether voids with dark
columns of smoke and poisonous vapor gases. All this
had to pass away, and ages elapse, ere fish, plant, bird
or beast could exist. That these features of nature
were facts in those far-away ages is amply proven by
the wrinkled brows of mother earth as we now behold
her, in the deep cañons and lofty mountains of this and
other regions of the globe. And these medals left us by
the hand of the great Creator give us much to contemplate.

The spawn of the first dawn of life, the testacea of
the protozoan era of cellular form, of grapholite or
trilobite, minutely revealed in the cooled strata of the
Laurentian era, corresponding to the Mosaic declaration
of the birth of fish and birds, and the waters were commanded to "bring forth abundantly—each after his
kind." This mandate issued by the Creator at the very
dawn of life, "each after his kind," has held all things,
having life in an even balance, and when controverted
or disregarded, has destroyed plants, animals and
nations.

Turn now again to that cold, icy region where I positively assert the earth first cooled, and plant, bird, beast and man primarily came upon the stage; let us reason together, and see if I am not right in making the declaration.

The land of the North American continent extends to the north pole—no other land or continent does. The poles of the earth are farthest from the heat of the sun that keeps light and warmth upon and with us; they are the coldest places, because they are farthest from the great solar heat, and would naturally be first to cool, as they are the most distant from the heat.   Of course it is but common reason for us to believe that God planted the flora fauna upon the earth as soon as it was cool enough to receive it.   The trees, plants, and vegetable matter, of course, were the first signs of life; then fish, birds, and the beasts, then came man in the sixth era—man of a low order of intellect, but a shade above the monkey tribe, with the long dolichokephalic heads, prognathus jaws, and small brain capacity, dark skin and woolly-haired, capable of standing a very hot climate.   They have heavy, tulip-shaped lips.   After them, in that far northern region, in the eighth era of the Mosaic account, came the later intelligent man, fair-skinned, with mesokephalic head, orthognathus or upright jaws, straight, slender bones with duties to perform, and it was into this man created on the eighth day, after the finishing of his work on the seventh, God breathed into his nostrils the breath of life, and that man became a living soul.   When nature was at its zenith of grandeur, God planted a garden there and placed the man of intelligence—the man of the mesokephalic brain pan, the man of the living soul—to dress it, and to keep it.

How beautiful this region around the north pole must have been, when in all its pristine beauty it bloomed, fresh from the Creator, planted by the hands of God! There was no night there; eternal day reigned.   Six solid months of sunshine, above the horizon; ninety-five days of twilight and dawn; forty-two days of soft moonlight, so brilliant that you could read the finest print by its gleam, and each star of the first magnitude revealed your shadow. Then, as the sun sank to the horizon's rim, the glorious aurora borealis blazed forth, more and more brilliantly, as the sun sank deeper into the shadow of the earth, until his face became entirely shrouded. Then the aurora disk became far brighter, and with ten thousand sparkling, changing colors per minute, it spread its variegated dyes over the entire polar region, in volumes of light so bright and lovely that neither pen nor pencil can give you a faint conception of its beauty and grandeur.

I have seen Louie in her wonderful serpentine dance with kaleidoscope lime-lights revolving and flashing upon her, and I have seen the revolving electric lights, playing upon the fountains, and millions of drops of water, each illumed with a different hue, all moving and sparkling, a living mass of indescribable beauty, but they all sink into insignificance when compared to that grand majestic, celestial fountain of light that flashes eternal above, and around, and ever guards the primal abode of man.

I have been impressed by and passed through many scenes of grandeur in my sixty years of wandering. I have felt the blasts of the tropical storms at sea; have watched the vivid flashes of lightning as they lighted the dark, boiling, pathless ocean, and felt the shock and deafening roar of the accompanying thunder; have heard the awful cry of fire a thousand miles from land; have watched the crash and heard the thunder of a thousand bombshells as I was sheltered inside of the Malakoff at the siege of Sevastopol in the Crimean war, and again upon the heights of Vicksburg, and at Petersburg, and in many of the battles of the Confederate war, but never have I had such feelings of awe, and demonstrations of grandeur, as I felt in my budding manhood, standing upon the frozen pinnacle of a grounded iceberg, gazing at the waving curtains of light, as they seemed to open and shut the doors of great caverns of light, seemingly hundreds of miles long, flashing and playing down the distant corridors and aisles of the grand auroran temple in that far-off frozen land, where the thermometer registers 90 degrees below the zero mark.   May I never view it again while life lasts.

It seems to me the greatest folly to attempt to reach the north pole.   It is tempting nature, and will be punished by death, for man cannot now exist where the foot of the man of the living soul first had his habitat, in that garden planted by creation's Master hand.

In the light of modern science I do not see how sane men can even dream that it is possible to penetrate to the north pole and live to tell the story.   The great maelstroms of electricity that flow up from the equator to the poles, meet here; the positive and negative currents in battle array produce the aurora borealis, and give us that grand display of light that is faintly illustrated in Edison's arc lamp; man cannot compete with this.   No being of earthly mold could possibly live where these great currents of electricity come together.   Once in their grasp man would be as powerless to extricate himself as he would be to scale with a pirogue, or dugout, the perpendicular falls of the Yosemite, or Niagara.

This aurora borealis is the flaming sword placed by the hand of God to guard the Eden Garden where first dwelt the sinless man of the living soul.   This flaming sword was not there until after the cooling crust of the earth had reached the equator.   The Garden of Eden was planted upon earth, and was in existence until, as I have said before, the cooling shell of the earth reached the equator, and the positive and negative electricity ascending northward met over this garden and produced the aurora borealis.   God warned Adam and Eve from this garden, and the language of the Bible is in these words: " So he drove out the man; and he placed at the east of the Garden of Eden cherubims, and a flaming sword, which turned every way to keep the Tree of Life."

Turning now to that long ago epoch, when the Garden of Eden was first planted, and Nature was smiling in the splendors and primal glories of creation's dawn, how beautiful, how grand must have been that region, fresh from the conception and hand of the Incarnate

God. Mind cannot conceive, nor words pen, nor pencil picture it. The tropical landscapes, spreading out on every hand under the warm sun of eternal day; the lovely, bright plumed song birds of every hue; the earth carpeted with the fairest and most fragrant flowers; fruits of every kind and flavor; trees robed in mantles of eternal verdure, waving their green foliage on the breath of heaven-born zephyrs, and filling the air with the sweetest perfumes, under a cloudless sky; with bird, beast, and the man of the living soul dwelling amidst the glorious, heaven-born surroundings, in perfect peace and harmony.

No chilling winds; no cold, cloudy, rainy hours; no storms of sleet or snow, no icy blasts sent their frozen breath against the forms of the man and his fair helpmate, to cause their forms to shrink and shiver from its boreal touch. Indeed this garden must have been, in reality, a paradise. Yes, a paradise, such as can never again exist on this insect-poisoned earth of ours.

Conditions have so changed that nowhere on the face of the whole globe can the Eden Garden be again reproduced. Where bird, beast, and man have multiplied by thousands, the insects and creeping things have increased by billions, and trees and plants have constantly decreased. The insects are the enemies of the whole fauna and flora of the earth and sea. They swarm around the tallest mountain tops, and penetrate the darkest caverns of earth, and sound the bottom of the deepest seas, until no place is exempt from them. They render life a torment, and destroy one-half of all the fruits of the labor of man in every clime.

Now let us resume, and recapitulate the cold, unanswerable facts regarding my original declaration that it was at the north pole, on the shores of the North American continent, that God first planted the flora and fauna of earth.

The geological strata of the formation of our continent is beyond question or doubt the very oldest. The igneous rocks prove that the whole globe was once a molten mass, in liquid form; it had to be a liquid before it could assume a globular or spherical shape from the ether pressure, equal on every side. It had to begin cooling somewhere first, and we are all cognizant of the fact that all known substances will begin cooling at the point most distant from controlling heat. Hence the sun, being the great fire that gives heat and light to all on this globe, and rules and governs it; and as this great governing sun is with us as it was at creation's dawn, and the poles of the earth are the most remote or distant points of our globe from it; hence they, the poles, would be the first to cool, beyond any controversy or doubt.

Now man, bird and beast, and the trees, fruits, and flowers have their habitat on dry land; and as we have shown from a glance at the common geographies of the earth's surface, and proven by personal explorations that there is no land for thousands of miles to the southward of the most southern points of the continents of Africa and South America, and but a few small islands in a boundless sea that rolls along the northern confines of Europe and of Asia, cutting them off from the north pole; it remains to be seen, that only on the North American shore, which stretches out its vales and mountain chains into the regions of this spot of cooling earth, could the first living land animals and plants have come into existence. Yes, the North American continent alone presents the physical conditions necessary, wherein the Great Creator could have planted the first flora and fauna of our old earth as we now know it. No other continent extends near enough to either pole to take from her this honor. That she was inhabited in that long by-gone age, when the earth was warm and genial where now eternal ice and snow ever gleams, is amply proven by the great storehouses of the bones of bird, beast and fauna, as well as the remains of all the flora of the tropics, now frozen into solid stone, to remain as monuments and imperishable medals, molded by the hand of God himself, to prove " the wonders of His works," and to show us that this continent of North America should be called the " Old World," instead of the eastern hemisphere being given that honor.

It was undoubtedly from this region of North

America that the migrations of men began, that peopled the whole western hemisphere and thence spread to Asia, Europe, and Africa. And it was on these shores that early civilization had its genesis, and that early civilization, which began on this North American shore, ended at the mouth of the Nile River, in Egypt, forty-two hundred years before the dawn of the Christian Era. Over the Garden of Eden to-day waves the grand aurora borealis, the *flaming sword* placed in the hands of the Cherubim to warn man away from his primal abode.

No living creature will ever again stand upon the spot where God planted the tree of life, and gave Adam, his last, his fairest, and best of all his created things, a heaven born " Woman."

WHERE DID CAIN GET HIS WIFE?

The sixth era of creation—The first men and women—The superior being of the eighth era—Adam and Eve—Cain's wife a creature of the sixth era.

THIS question has puzzled the so-called theologians and hide-bound ecclesiastical conclaves for many long centuries. Moses in his Genesis has attempted to embody a succinct history of the creation of man, as he gained it from Chaldean and Bablyonian lore, and from the priests and magi of Egypt. Moses was the lawgiver and leader of the descendants of Abraham, and was one of the greatest generals and lawmakers of any known age. Is there any reason why we should not pay attention to the Genesis of this great man?

Now in attempting to show who Cain took for a wife, I do not pretend to be wiser than the thousands of saintly priests or learned theologians, but shall bring reason and plain common sense to my aid, and lift the clouds and veils that have been thrown around the original declarations of Moses, and keep ever in view that mandate issued by the Great Creator, when fish, bird and animal first appeared on this earthly globe— that mandate issued alike to all—the atoms and molecules designed by God. He commanded herb, bird, fish and animal, and every creeping thing that contained life, to bring forth abundantly, each after his kind. Obedience to this law gives us the varieties of plants, fishes, birds, insects and animals that we are familiar with; each after his kind, in their glorious originality and perfection.

The controversion of this law and miscegenation of plants, fishes, birds or animals give us hideous monstrosities, abortions, and bastards—something not planned by the hand, nor designed in the wisdom of the Great Architect of the universe. With this prelude let us go at once into the principle of our subject.

294

In the sixth era of the creation, God said: " Let us make man in our own image, after our likeness." So God created man in his own image, male and female created he them. And God blessed them, and commanded them to be fruitful, and multiply, and replenish the earth. And he made them masters of everything that moveth or creepeth upon the earth. And he gave them of every herb, and tree, that had seed in itself, for meat. No tree or plant was forbidden these men and women of the sixth era of creation. There was no Garden of Eden tree for them. The Garden of Eden had not been planted. They had the fruit of every tree and plant that had seed in itself for meat. So how could they have been the man and woman of the garden?

For his especial command, in regard to herb and tree for meat, is in this plain, emphatic and unmistakable language as recorded in the twenty-ninth verse of the very first chapter of Genesis. And God said, " Behold I have given you every herb, bearing seed, which is upon the face of the earth, and every tree, in which is the fruit of a tree yielding seed: to you it shall be for meat." And in the very next breath, we find these words: " And to every beast of the earth, and to every fowl of the air, and to every thing that creepeth upon the earth, wherein there is life, I have given every green herb for meat, and it was so. And God saw that everything that he had made, and beheld it was very good." And the sixth era of creation was over. And in the seventh era God ended his first creative aeon and rested. It is thus expressed in the Bible language:

" And the evening and morning were the sixth day: thus the heavens and the earth were finished and all the hosts of them.

" And on the seventh day God ended his work which he had made; and he rested on the seventh day from all his work which he had made.

" And God blessed the seventh day, and sanctified it; because that in it, he had rested from all his work which God created and made."

In the above verses, copied from the exact wording

of the text of Genesis, I have closely followed it. And we find nothing in the sixth era, nor the ending of God's work in the seventh era, where he rested, to show us that the men and women of that early era were forbidden to eat of any tree or plant that had seed within itself, that grew upon the earth. Nor is there a mention made of a soul given to any being. These men and women in countless numbers made, created in the image and likeness of the Creator, were as soulless as the fish, bird, beasts or creeping things. And these men and women were commanded to bring forth abundantly—to be fruitful and multiply and replenish the earth. And they obeyed that chief mandate—" each after his kind." These men and women came into existence during the sixth era of creation. They multiplied and grew during the seventh, as did the trees, fish, birds and beasts and animals, while God rested during the seventh aeon of time.

Now these men and women of the sixth era of creation, made and fashioned in the image and after the likeness of God, grew, multiplied abundantly, and replenished the earth, as God commanded, and they subdued and had dominion over the fish, the birds, and the beasts of the earth. They were intelligent enough to make bows, arrows, spears and traps, that gave them power to subdue the beasts, birds and animals of the forests and jungles of the earth, and knew the use of fire. I have hunted and lived with these same creatures in the jungle wilds of Africa, where they live in a state of nature. They have no idea of God; no mode of counting or computing numbers, except upon the fingers; they have no written language or alphabetical signs; no idea of the potter's art. They are filthy beyond conception; know nothing of sanitation; have only savage, brutal, beastly instincts. They cannot be ruled by love—you have to rule and govern them by force. Gratitude is an unknown quality in their make up. They are the most perfect mimics on the face of the earth. They make no provision for the morrow; they live and breathe only in the now. They have not a single attribute of the white man, and only resemble him in size and a general outline of form. The dens of the lions, tiger, panther and cat tribes are models of cleanliness in comparison to the huts of the savages of the upper Nile.

Now in regard to the first men and women, they had no labors to perform; the trees and tropical plants yielded them a superabundance of all that was necessary to sustain life, as they could eat of every tree and herb that bore fruit and had seed in itself. They were not compelled to do any kind of labor, but lived a roaming, nomadic life, having only to stretch forth their hands and pluck the finest fruits for their sustenance. They needed neither clothing nor shelter, for the new earth was warm and genial; no heavy rains, no chilling blasts of snow and ice swept the land. They knew not how to sow, they only reaped of the fullness of the earth which brought forth abundantly. There was no incentive to work or toil. Not until the dawn of the eighth era of the world, that corresponds to the quarternary period of geology, did these conditions ever change.

Upon the dawn of the eighth era a new being was formed by Almighty God—a new man—a man of fairer mold—a man with a living soul—a man of intelligence —a man with a conscience—a man knowing right from wrong; far above the man of the sixth era.

This new man's arrival is thus announced in the Mosaic account:

" And the Lord God formed man of the dust of the ground, and breathed into his nostrils the breath of life; and man became a living soul.

" And the Lord God planted a garden eastward in Eden.

" And the Lord God took the man and put him into the garden to dress and to keep it.

" And the Lord God commanded the man, saying: Of every tree of the garden thou mayest freely eat: But of the tree of the knowledge of good and evil, thou shalt not eat of it: for in the day that thou eatest thereof, thou shalt surely die.

" And the Lord God said, It is not good that man

should be alone; I will make him an helpmeet for him. " And the Lord God brought every beast of the earth and every fowl of the air unto Adam to see what he would call them: and whatsoever Adam called every living creature, that was the name thereof.

" And Adam gave names to all cattle, and to the fowls of the air, and to every beast of the field; but for Adam there was not found an helpmeet for him."

For in all that host of men and women, bird, beast and animal of the sixth era of creation then existent, there was nothing after his kind; nothing of his pure bone, flesh and blood; nothing that would bring forth after his kind.

" And the Lord God caused a deep sleep to fall upon Adam, and he slept: and he took one of his ribs and closed up the flesh instead thereof.

" And the rib which the Lord God had taken from Adam, made he a woman, and brought her unto the man.

" And Adam said, This is now bone of my bones and flesh of my flesh."

She was after his kind. And Adam called his wife's name Eve, because she was the mother of all living (*i. e.*, mother of all those of the living soul).

This man Adam of the living soul we can readily see was of a newer creation. A far different being from the man of the first creation. This new man—this man endowed with the living soul—comes upon the stage after the Creator had rested throughout the seventh era of the world's geologic age. His female helpmeet was taken from his own anatomy and was " bone of his bone and flesh of his flesh," and she was the mother of all the future beings of his kind, " after his kind." The men and women of the first creation were of a lower order, and while made in the same form, size and shape, " each after his kind," they were not like the Adam creation of the later era. The first were created males and females in countless numbers, each after his kind, just as the birds, beasts and animals were, while the man of the living soul stepped forth pure, undefiled and alone

—fresh from the incarnate hand of God, and his wife Eve was a part of him, fashioned and molded pure and perfect, the last and fairest of all God's handiwork. When Cain, the first born of the two last beings formed on the earth, came into the world, the fair young mother exclaimed, " I have gotten a man from the Lord." Thus in the exuberance of her joy she named him a son of God, and from that far-away era to the birth of Jesus her descendants were called the sons of God.

Now as we become absorbed with the new order of beings, and their fall and expulsion from the Garden of Eden and the story of Cain and Abel leads us far away, we forget the multiplying thousands of men and women of the sixth day creation. I say we forget these beings and keep our thoughts with Adam and Eve, Cain and Abel.

Adam and Eve were expelled from the beautiful garden home and became pioneers in a strange, bleak land; cold winds and rain descended upon them and God clothed them in warm furs of animals. Cain became a tiller of the soil and Abel a keeper of the flocks—one a farmer, the other a shepherd—the heads of the two great industries that clothe and feed the world.

They offered voluntary sacrifices to God, their father. Cain brought the finest fruits of his fields, and Abel the first-born of his flocks. God had respect for Abel's offering, but not for Cain's, and this made Cain angry and he rose up and slew Abel. Now this all seems wrong, when viewed from our human standpoint. We think that God should have had as much respect for Cain's offering as for Abel's. Cain gave the choicest and best of all his field and garden products; yes, gave of the first and best; it was all that he had to offer, and who knew this any better than God, his Father?

In answering this question, I will merely say as a prelude to the real answer, that God requires of us a sacrifice of love with each offering. A something that touches the heart strings, the conscience, the living soul; a sacrifice that we can feel in our innermost nature. You never saw a child in your life to whom was given a bird, a kitten, puppy or pony or any living animal, that the child's heart did not stretch out and love it and cling to it as its very own.   This love increases and grows, and we have seen whole families distressed and grieved, and the child's tears flow and his little heart ache at the death of his pet.   Here lies the gravamen of Abel's offering that made it acceptable in the eyes of God.   He gave of the firstlings of his flock that he loved best, and it was a far greater sacrifice for him to give them up forever than it was for Cain to give up a few cabbage heads and potatoes, or other field or garden products. There was no love to give with these cold, inanimate objects; it did not touch a single finer fiber of the soul to part with them.   Hence no real, true sacrifice, in the full and inward meaning of the word, was offered.

It is true it was all Cain had to give, and no doubt he gave it willingly; but it did not require the tearing loose of the finer heart strings that touched the living soul and made each chord of love pulsate and vibrate like the strings of a harp. Cain was jealous of this and it made him angry with his brother.   And he determined to have his herds and flocks as his own, to monopolize the whole of them, and combine them with his farming operations in modern syndicate style.   So he slew Abel and took the herds and flocks and appropriated them to his own use.   The death of Abel left only the three beings of the living soul upon the whole earth.   These were Adam, Eve and Cain.   But there were countless thousands of the sixth era men and women on the earth and they had no fixed habitat.   They roamed the face of the earth and lived upon the herbs and fruits of every tree that bore fruit, and had seed in themselves.   They did not have to till the soil or labor to produce cereals and fruits for their sustenance; these all grew spontaneously for their use, as they do to this day in the tropics.

When the blood of Abel cried out from the earth to God his Father, God heard the cry and took the fields and flocks from Cain and sent him a vagabond and wanderer far out into the land of Nod to the eastward of Eden, among these prognathus-jawed and dolichoke-phalic-headed men and women of the sixth day creation. And fallen from his high estate he married one or more of these women, and of course as they were not " bone of his bone and flesh of his flesh," his progeny was not of his kind. They could not possibly be. Nor were his descendants like either parent, for God's laws were, by this union, controverted, and the children (as they do to-day) inherited all the mean qualities of both parents and none of the good.

Cain tried to civilize his wife's kinsmen, and at the birth of a miscegenated son, Enoch, he brought all of the kith and kin of his wife together, and built a city, and called it Enoch. And many of this miscegenated race intermarried and begat a new race entirely; and this race of half-breeds spread rapidly over the earth. This breed changed the shape of the heads and jaws, and the color of the two races, and gave a brachykephalic skull and jaw, such as we see to-day in the Chinese; and they, in remixing, gave the red or brown color. I mean by this that the men and women of the sixth era, mixing with the miscegenated race of Cain and his Nodite wife, gave us the brown or red man. Their pictures are seen on the walls of caverns on the Cumberland River in Tennessee; at Palenque in Mexico; on the walls of the cliff-dwellers of the Zuni Plateau in New Mexico and Arizona; in Hondurian cities and along the Andean range of mountains as far south as Lake Titicaca; among the ruined cities of most of the islands of the Pacific, and throughout China, Persia, Arabia and Egypt as well as on the pottery on the banks of the Ohio and Mississippi valleys. These all point with un-erring fingers to the miscegenation of the two races that were in existence when Cain took his Nodite wife. These pictures have been viewed and commented upon by every anthropologist and archeologist that has ever given a page of his history to the world.

The picture is as universal as that of the flood in all countries and all climes, and among all peoples. I shall give you a word painting of it. You see a group of four men standing in a row. The front man is pure and white, a well-dressed son of God. Just behind him is the thick-lipped, woolly-haired negro, with the prognathus jaws and dolichokephalic head. Behind him is the

blended white and black, making the yellow man. And
behind the yellow man is the blended yellow and black,
making the brown or red man. Thus we see in that far-
off age, the Nodite woman and Cain made the miscegenated yellow race. Now the yellow and white race again
blending makes a man or woman of a fairer hue, while
the yellow and yellow mixing retain their yellow, and so
on through all the various so-called races of the earth.

Now returning to Biblical lore. Seth took the place
in Adam's family vacated by the death of Abel. Adam,
after the birth of Seth, lived eight hundred years and
begat sons and daughters, and when Seth was a hundred and five years old he begat a son called Enos. And
Seth lived eight hundred and seven years after the birth
of Enos and begat sons and daughters. And so on for
ages, these sons and daughters and grandsons and
daughters of Adam increased rapidly, and the miscegenated race of Cain swung around into view. These sons
and grandsons, named by Eve " The sons of God," saw
this mongrel race of Cain were fair, and they took wives
from among this race, and again controverted the laws
of God and disregarded that mandate given to all creatures, that they should each and every one beget like
and like, " each after his kind." And he repented him
that He had made the man of the living soul; so He
determined to destroy every miscegenated creature, bird,
beast and animal and man on the face of the globe. But
in looking over the situation he found one pure and
perfect family, namely, Noah and his sons and his own
wife and the wives of his sons. These were pure and
perfect types of the man of the living soul. And the
Bible declares that Noah was " perfect in his generation "; no mixed or contaminated blood here.

If these black people were not already in existence,
right here we would have learned this fact from the lips
of God. They were here in countless thousands; soulless
beings, just above the brute creation, in the form and
pattern of the man of the living soul, but of a darker
hue; a simple anthropoid, who would pass away as the
beasts of the earth. The production of the red, white,
black and ringed streaked and striped cattle are ac-

counted for in the Bible, and the cause given by God Himself.   And is it not reasonable to suppose that if Shem, Ham and Japeth had been respectively the red, black and white sons of Noah, and father of the Indian, negro and white races, that God would so have declared? And if Mrs. Noah had been the mother of three sons, at one birth, one a thick-lipped, woolly-haired, dolichokephalic-skulled, prognathus-jawed negro, one a brachykephalic-skulled, long-haired, red Indian, and one a fair-haired mesokephalic-skulled white man, and neither after the father's likeness nor after her kind, the miracle would have been mentioned in the Holy Bible and commented upon and explained, as was the red, white, black, streaked and striped cattle.   Surely what appertained to the highest of God's creation—the men of the immortal soul—were of more importance to the human race than were the mere brute creation.

With the first great law of " like shall beget like, each after his kind," staring him in the face, would not old Noah, a man perfect in his generation, have been surprised and wondered how he could have been the father of three sons of such distinct and different anatomical forms and features?   And would not his wife, and the attendant women of that age, have been equally puzzled to know how she could have given birth to these three totally different beings?   There would have been mention made of it, just as of the cattle and confusion of tongues.   If we give credence to the Bible, there was no way for Noah and his wife—pure and perfect in their generation—to have been the progenitors of the white, black and tan races of men.   Theology must look to another source, for Shem, Ham and Japeth were pure white men of the living soul, and inheritors of all that that means, and being such, only through corrupting God's laws and miscegenation with the beings of the sixth era of creation could they have been begotten of the brachykephalic yellow and red races of the earth, and only by this corrupting mode did the yellow and mixed races come upon it.

Now prior to the flood of Genesis, man was strictly a vegetarian; only the unclean beasts preyed upon flesh.

After the flood, man became a flesh eater and an unclean animal. For a confirmation of this view see Genesis, 1-29, and Genesis 9-13; as I assert nothing in this work that is not susceptible of absolute proof, by sacred and profane history and by the medals of nature, as revealed by the fossilized remains of the flora and fauna.

So God gave the earth once more a chance to carry out his original designs. He commanded Noah to take into his ark for preservation of all the clean beasts, birds and animals, fourteen of a kind, seven males and seven females, and of the unclean, only two of a kind, one male and one female, so as to keep seed upon the earth, and Noah did so. And after a stay of one year and one month in the ark, Noah opened the doors thereof, built an altar and sacrificed a part of the birds, beasts, and animals that were in it with him as a burnt sacrifice to Almighty God. This sacrifice would have destroyed whole tribes and species of animals, birds and beasts, if he had only had one pair of each with him in the ark. And the very means he employed to preserve them would have been destroyed and annulled. And it was after the flood that God gave to the sons of Noah dominion over the whole earth and over everything that dwelleth thereon.

Now the miscegenation of the men and women of the sixth era of creation with the men of the living soul of the eighth era of creation brought about the destruction of the world, as is shown by the Bible. God created the men and women of the sixth era without souls; and the men of the eighth era could not give or create what God did not, nor could they by any manner of means give a living soul to their descendants of miscegenated breed, for " like " here did not " beget like, each after his kind." God created the black and white race, but not the yellow, red, brown and tan. And all the mean and vile traits that lie dormant in the man of the living soul, and in the sixth era men and women, crop out and predominate in the miscegenated races; none of the good of the two races abide in the miscegenated descendants. Yes, every mean quality of both parents is concentrated and magnified in this miscegenated offspring, and is forever cursed. Now the miscegenated races continue on the same plane; " like begets like, each after his kind," with them as with any animal, bird or beast, and any of the yellow, red or black or white tribes will again miscegenate indefinitely; thus peculiar tribes or races of men are formed.

It is the same with animals as with men; the law of " like begets like " once corrupted goes on unchanged to the end of time. The hairless, naked, worthless pug-nosed pup of Chihuahua, Mexico, will miscegenate with the massive St. Bernard, the Newfoundland or the intelligent collie, and breed on and on until the land is full of a mongrel breed of worthless curs, with not one attribute of the parent stock apparent. So with man. This law once corrupted sinks the whole nation. Sacred history is pregnant with warning of this corruption. And the progeny of the negro and white man were called bastards, because they were not begotten, " each after his kind "; these children thus miscegenated were not allowed in the temples, nor to touch any of the holy things belonging to them, even for ten generations. (See Deut. 22 :12.)

We need not go to sacred history for a confirmation of the assertions here promulgated. The world is full of the facts. The curse of nature and of nature's God follows the corruption of this great fundamental law, given at creation's dawn, when the great Architect said, in unmistakable tones, " Let the whole earth bring forth abundantly." The plants, the fish, the insects, the birds, the animals, the cattle, the beasts, and man and everything that creepeth on the face of the earth, " each after his kind."

According to the Bible, Cain, the oldest son of Adam, the first son of God, the first-born being that came in the likeness of the man of the living soul; the first inheritor of that precious soul that gives us eternal life; this man, this Cain, this first son of the living God, disobeyed this mandate of his father, and chose a wife not of his kind. He took a Nodite woman of the soulless beings, the woman of the first or sixth era of creation, and this first corruption of that law brought about the Noahian deluge, with which God cleansed the earth of this abortive crew.

There is no way to dodge this solemn truth, and profane history confirms these facts of the Bible, despite the clouds and darkening mists of corrupt priests and ecclesiastical conclaves thrown around them in the dark days of ignorance and superstition, when the mighty, sacred stream of religion was in its early childhood. The powerful searchlight of modern science, backed by the permeating Roentgen rays of unbiased reason, but the more fully confirm these sacred truths.   They will forever shine like glittering stars above the darkening cesspools of ignorance, superstition, infamy and earthly corruption, until the purifying fires of destruction shall again turn this earth, at the last day, into a molten mass again, " without form and void," to whirl through space until purified by fire and again be regenerated and born anew.

THE MOUND-BUILDERS

Civilization first attained along the range of the Andean
  Mountains—From here spread to the shores of Asia and
  Africa—Negroes the Mound-Builders under taskmasters
  —The potter's art—Life of the Mound-Builders.

WHO were the Mound-builders? They were negroes,
under the supervision of white men, or white masters, to
direct and govern them.

In my earlier explorations among the ruins of the
ancient people of the earth I had conceived a false
idea of where the oldest ruined cities were to be found,
and I wasted several years of valuable time, and much
money in making journeys and examining closely, in
person, the tumulii of Baalbeck, Palmyra, Babylon,
Nineveh, and those of Egypt.

I read various histories of these ruins, my curiosity
was aroused to the fullest extent, and I determined to
see them with my own eyes and judge for myself. I
was unable to find a work, by any explorer, that gave
me any information about that part of the continent
of Africa that lies south of the states or kingdoms that
border the Mediterranean Sea, so I determined to approach Egypt from the west, and go far down south,
beyond the confines of Morocco, and turn east across
the Great Desert of Sahara, and strike the Nile River,
far up, in the Nubian desert.

I landed at Sallee, a port on the western shore of
Africa, about 125 miles south of Tangiers, and on camel
back I took the road in an easterly direction to the city
of Fez, the capital of Morocco.

The city lies on the banks of the Wadi Sebu, in latitude 34° north and about the fifth meridian west of
Greenwich; it is an old, dilapidated place, seemingly
several thousand years old, from the tumulii and ruins
that are apparent on every hand. Here I fitted out
my desert " kit" and became a part and parcel of a

great desert caravan of about 5,000 people of all kinds and nationalities, and for five months we left the known world behind us and buried ourselves in the Great Desert of Sahara.

For 300 miles our path was over mountains and through valleys of wild grandeur, and at times we were 11,000 feet above the level of the sea, and our camels suffered from the sharp rocks cutting their feet. The whole region to the oasis of Tafilet is one of gloomy grandeur. The first oasis at which we stopped for a rest of a week was Ferkla; here there were some rich lands and fertile spots, but as a whole the region is barren and God-forsaken. The whole region, as far as the eye can reach, seems to rest under a curse, and only where the influence of the wadis, or rivers, is felt, is there any signs of vegetable life; where there is moisture it is wonderful how productive the land is.

But I did not set out to give you a description of the country or to recite my adventures while crossing the great sea of sand that rolls from the Atlantic Ocean to the valley of the Nile in far-off Egypt, as it would take too much time and space.

We entered the valley of the Nile near the north end of the Nubian desert. Part of the great caravan, of which I was a member, turned south to Khartoum, and we north, down the Nile.

I gazed at the massive temples and statuary of Karnak and explored miles of the painted and decorated mummy vaults and tombs of the ancient residents of early Egypt. While contemplating these great masses of colossal statues and sculptured, pillared temples, the work of a people more than six thousand years ago, I saw that they had been civilized many an aeon or centuries of time before they could have constructed such works as I saw here. Yes, they could not have builded such works as these without the experience of many centuries of teaching, and under the instructions of those who had combined wisdom and knowledge, gathered from a long line of highly cultured and gifted ancestors.

I found that I was on the wrong track of archaic

ruins; I would have to hunt another and an older region to find the beginning. Here I was really at the mouth of the first great stream of early civilization, a civilization that really came to an end rather than began more than six thousand years ago. There was no childhood of art or religion here; everything was perfected, yes, hoary and gray with age, when these builders laid the foundation stones of the pyramids.

From whence came the ancestors of these builders, for they had to have them? And their ancestors had to have teachers; they did not spring into existence fully taught, armed and equipped for such work as I saw here on every hand. I found that in Egypt, Arabia, Persia, or any part of the so-called " Old World " I could not find the first ruins, nor the beginning of an early civilization; everything here indicated that I was at the mouth of the stream; yes, a stream that was drying up and evaporating centuries before the birth of our Saviour, or the dawn of the Christian era, at least 6,000 years ago. I was well aware that it would take the ancestors of this six-thousand-years-old civilized people several thousand years to reach the point of civilization that I beheld here amid the ruins of Palmyra, Baalbeck and Egypt.

They had an ancestry, they had a beginning, and they had teachers. They did not spring into existence by magic in a single year, nor a single century. It took aeons of time for them to attain their civilization and to teach their children. Where did they begin and whence came they? I determined to trace them to their source; and I firmly believed it could be done. I was alone in my endeavor, and the results I will give you, and let you be the judge.

I sat for hours on the great pyramid, the great work of a people, who, six thousand years ago, were in their glorious zenith of civilization—a civilization that the new nations of more modern Europe and America will never reach for another thousand years. As I sat on a stone on the flat top of the great pyramid in the soft, clear atmosphere, so transparent that the eight other mounds in this group, and the lion man-headed sphynx, a thousand years older than the pyramids, seemed almost in reach. I looked down from my four hundred and eighty feet of elevation above the desert sand upon the dim, unreal past and I felt an inspiration not of this earth. I could see Abraham and his descendants passing by, for they, too, looked up to my perch in that long ago time. I could see the children of Israel, as they toiled under their Egyptian taskmasters, making brick for the residences of the rich citizens of the worshipers of Osiris. I could see the vast armies of Darius, of Cyrus, of Alexander, of Caesar and of Napoleon, passing by. I could see the laden vessels of these bygone people bearing the rich stores of their granaries to the distant continents and islands of the world; to the city of Rome, alone, they bore annually twenty million bushels of grain. Now all are gone and only the still, voiceless desert, with its recent horrors over which I had but a day before passed, stretching out until lost in the dim maze of the horizon.

It is worth all the toil and dangers of sea and desert to live but a few short hours upon the apex of the great pyramid and let its inspirations drift you back through the countless ages of history that are familiar themes to this vast pile of inanimate stone. It is no easy matter to realize that here on this great mass of rigid stone you are standing upon a work of man, made and built forty-two hundred years before the dawn of the Christian era. You seem to be, as it were, snatched up to some vast height that overlooks the plains of time, and see the centuries mapped out beneath your feet. The mind, in contemplating these vast, mysterious, hidden vaults of time, seems to sink into the shadowy vales of the infinite, and there is no place of rest in the seething maelstrom of thought, that, like the simoon's blast, hurtles with its dust and desert-parched sands around you. No place of rest save in the gloomy vaults of oblivion beyond the lethean river that flows along the shores of eternity!

But laying aside these vast speculative themes, awakened by the contemplation of the grand, gloomy and beautiful ruins of ancient Egypt, let us turn to the

questions now uppermost——Who were the ancestors of
these builders of the mounds and pyramids of Egypt?
And from whence did they come? They had a beginning and they had a long line of gifted ancestry, ages
before they could attain to the height of civilization
that we see displayed in the ruins around us. There
can be no doubt about this fact. It did not take me
long to come to this conclusion. I saw that I
was at the mouth of the great old river, the very end
of the great stream of civilization, a stream that evap-
orated into a sea of ruins more than fifty odd centuries
ago. Where was the source of this great, grand old
stream? Where its head? Where the springs that once
furnished its living waters? These were the burning
questions that fired my youthful heart; that let inspiration into my soul and bent my will to undertake the
solving of the almost unsolvable task. I fully realized
the difficulties I would encounter in the effort, but with
ardor and determination I bent my will to accomplish
the undertaking and I am fully satisfied now. Just
past the seventy-sixth milestone of life, I can rest and
say that I have drank deeply from that hidden spring
from whence flowed the ever-broadening river that laved
the very foundation stones of ancient Egyptian civilization.

To take you, gentle reader, over twenty-seven years
of wanderings horse-back, mule-back, camel-back or
afoot over and across every continent and great isle of
the globe, and by pirogue, dug-out, skiff, yawl, sail or
steam vessel across the pathless seas, and still and foaming rivers, would tax your powers of endurance beyond
the limit. For it takes inspiration, a will, a firm resolve
to weather the storms and dare the dangers that ever
beset your way.

On the southern shores of that great pleistocene sea
that stretched from the Rocky Mountain chain on the
west to the Appalachian chain on the east; that covered
the great plains that lie between, and of which the
great lakes of the northern boundary of the United
States are left as debris, I found along this southern
shore and upon the islands that dotted this great inland

ocean the first relics of the ancestors of the civilized people of ancient Egypt.   Here and down the valley of the great river that flowed southward and drained the surplus waters of the great ocean into the Gulf of Mexico, as the St. Lawrence now drains the Great Lakes, I found the first signs of a civilized people.   Each tributary of this great river, flowing from the Rocky Mountains east and southward, and forming the Appalachian chain, west and southward, contains numerous tumulii of the beginning of early civilized man.   As I explored these regions east and west of this great oleographic plain and proceeded farther and farther southward, their marks of true civilization gradually increased and greater improvements would appear, slowly, but with an ever upward and onward tendency to improvement, as marked and as distinct as the growth of plant, flower, animal or child.   I had found the head of the stream, and floating down the current with wind and wave in my favor was easy, and I enjoyed it.   Each new discovery, each new ruined city proved I was right in my surmises.

I wandered among the mounds of the Miami valley in Ohio; along the caverns and tumulii of the Cumberland; into the wild jungles of Yazoo valley, which in the vernacular of the Indians is called Yazoo Okiniha, or, translated, the river of ruins, and not the river of death as some translate it; over the wonderful buried cities of Arkansas; far out into the mesas of Arizona and New Mexico; down into the ruined cities of Mexico, Guatemala, Honduras, Nicaragua, Panama, Colombia, Equador, Peru, Chili and the whole slope of the Adean chain of mountains to the great Lake Titicaca, the highest and most beautiful lake in the world.

I followed the great macadam and asphalt road, sixty feet wide, for fifteen hundred miles, with its continuous walls and beautiful ruined cities.   I penetrated into the great tunnels, dug through solid mountains, fifteen miles long and thirty feet wide, paved with hexagonal stones, nine inches on each side and thirty inches long, fitted as smooth and close as sheets of tissue paper, along which flowed the pure waters of the mountains through these artificial aqueducts, for four hundred and fifty miles, into their cities. I saw trees whose concentric rings proved them to be from fifteen hundred to two thousand years old, tearing up the mosaic work of the city pavements and standing upon and piercing the walls of these deserted cities. These trees were turned into agate and quartz of variegated hues. I saw the sculptured busts of bird, beast and man ruined and overturned by these now petrified forests.

The question naturally arises in the mind of the explorer and scientists, When and at what age were these cities the abode of civilized man? When were they built, by whom built, when deserted, and for what cause? Let us answer these, *seriatim.*

Ages must have elapsed since these cities were deserted before the seeds and sprouts of these monster trees could have taken root in the cracks and fissures of the solid walls and pavements of these cities; the dust of ages accumulated and the stones disintegrated by the slow action of the winds and rains and the plural processes of the combined forces of the elements of nature so that their tiny roots could find sustenance sufficient to feed the gigantic bodies and wide spreading limbs of these monsters of the forests, now ten and fifteen feet in diameter and towering two to three hundred feet above the tessellated pavement and sculptured gates and doorways of the now ruined cities of the ancestors of the ancient builders. And ages have elapsed since death and decay seized their massive trunks and hurled them into their silent graves, crushing the pavements, sculptured walls, carved temples and palatial homes in their fall. And how long did they lie on the top of mother earth before each minute particle of their vast trunks and limbs was disintegrated and frozen into a mass of solid crystallized agate and flinty quartz? The mind of man is staggered in contemplation and gasps as the centuries roll before him.

No living explorer with a single spark of poetry or sentiment in his nature and one gleam of unclouded reason in the finer fiber of his brain can wander as I did for four long years among the ruins of the prehistoric

people, and not feel and realize that these builders were
as far in advance of the civilization of the people of this
generation as the ancient builders of the ruins of Egypt
are ahead of the nomadic tribes that now fasten their
desert-bred horses to the shafts of their spears stuck
in the sands that whirl around the great sphynx under
the shadow of the pyramids.   He cannot gaze at the
intricate tracery on the moulded pottery, the finely
chased and graven vases of gold and silver, the deli-
cately chiseled statuary over the gateway and on the
walls of Cuzco, Titicaca, Granchimu, Teahuanaco, Tu-
loom, Chichen, Itza, Uxmal, Mayapan, Mitla, Copan,
Palenque, Labna and a thousand other minor cities
throughout Mexico, Central and South America, without feeling that he is standing amid the ruins of a people
who had attained unto a higher plane of civilization
than we, the boasted denizens of the twentieth century
of the Christian era.   He must feel that here, amid these
beautiful ruins, were born and taught the ancestors
of those people who laid the foundation stones of the
sphynx, and reared the mighty pyramids and temples
of Egypt.   For this land was hoary and gray with age
before the valley of the Nile lifted its form from out
the depths of the Pleistocene Sea; while the Andes, with
their hoary heads lifted high toward the azure zenith,
blazed in the glorious light of the Southern Cross, and
that shining symbol lent its grandeur to the scene revealed to the eyes of these first people of a civilized
world ages before the land of Egypt came up out of the
sea bed or the walls of the Dead Sea were raised.   The
very winds teach us these facts.   They are the hand-
maidens of geology.   They are ancient and faithful
chronicles and when rightly consulted will reveal to
us truths that nature has written upon their wings in
characters as legible and more enduring than she has
graven geological events on tablets of stone.
    The hoary-headed Andean Mountains lifted the seas
that rolled over the African continent, sank the Dead
Sea, parched the Saharan desert, and lifted the land
of Egypt from its ocean bed by the agency of their
winds.   To-day you can see the dust of the Sahara upon

the plants and rocks of this great mountain barrier; this huge elevation dividing the southern half of the entire globe. And this huge backbone of the earth had to come into existence before the winds, the hand-maidens of geology, could lift the African continent to a habitable land for bird, beast or man. I repeat, that it is along this range of mountains, with its lovely plains and valleys, that civilization first attained its zenith, tens of thousands of years ago. And from here it spread across the isles and waters of the Pacific west-ward to the shores of Asia and Africa.

This civilization peopled India, China, Persia and Arabia and ended in Egypt six thousand years ago. The pathway is strewn throughout the entire line of march with their ruins, ever increasing in beauty and grandeur and massiveness, as time and experience taught them. It is as easy a matter to follow them, when you get into the current of the stream, with wind and wave in your favor, as it is for a locomotive with its grooved wheels to roll along the two steel rails.

As we have followed the prehistoric people from the shores of the great inland ocean that lashed the feet of the Rocky and Appalachian Mountains, south-ward into the lower part of South America, and thence to Asia, and left them at the mouth of the Nile in Africa; in theory let us turn back and see what proofs we can introduce to confirm our theory.

This great inland ocean that we have described as covering the plains and valleys between the Rockies and the eastern mountain ranges of the continent of North America, had its grand southern outlet through a gap at Tower Rocks, above Cairo, and lakes Superior, Michigan, Ontario, Erie, etc., are now the debris of this ancient ocean. It was drained by a great river, a grand Mississippi, of which the present Mississippi is but a pigmy of its giant ancestor; only in the time of the fullness of rainfall does it pretend even to swell to a shrunken representation of its forefather. When the great dam that held the waters of this inland ocean in abeyance was eroded or worn away or suddenly burst by an earthquake or other cause, by the centrifugal force of nature, a great cataclysm rushed down the valley and poured its waters into the Mexico sea, where Baton Rouge, the capital of Louisiana, now stands. The present serrated hills were then a level plain in the valley of this great river, and it was inhabited by an industrious agricultural people, steadily advancing by slow steps into civilization.

Now to my mind, the writer of the book of Isaiah was familiar with this great catastrophe, learned from the records kept by the immigrants from these shores to Egypt, centuries after it occurred. The reference I refer to can be found in the eighteenth chapter of Isaiah, beginning, " Woe to the land shadowing with wings," etc., etc. Now the North and South American continents are the exact shape of bird wings, the tip of one wing touching the shoulder of the other, and Isaiah, as he spoke, had to look directly westward beyond Ethiopia or Africa, to bring America into his vision. At that time the lands had been spoiled by the rivers, and millions of the people drowned and the fowls of the air and the beasts of the earth had summered and wintered upon their decaying carcasses, and to this day, from Memphis to Baton Rouge, on ten thousand hills, you can find hundreds of acres of their human bones lying in heaps six feet thick, or scattered over vast areas. This, I say, may be a reference in written history of those long ago days. It is certainly enough to make our scientists and men of brains pause and take a passing glimpse at the medals of nature left for our observation by the Creator of all.

Now, I gave you the above merely to show how we may get support from others to corroborate our own views, and this method is too often followed by writers and scientists who draw their observations from others, and crowd their works with footlines and make their pages bristle with quotations. I make the assertion here that the mounds of North America were built by the thick-lipped, woolly-haired, prognathus-jawed negroes, with dolichokephalic skulls, and they did not build these mounds voluntarily, but under taskmasters. They were forced to do the work, just as the slaves of the Egyptians were, by the superior race of the mesokephalic and orthognathus-jawed. The bones found in the acres of them I have examined are as different in color, size and shape as the bones of the grey or cat squirrel and the red or fox squirrel.

The pictures upon the pottery and tombs from West Virginia to Lake Titicaca, India, Persia, Arabia and Egypt; yes, from the caves of West Virginia to the sepulchral vaults of Egypt, always show a crowd of these negroes under the supervision of one white man, who is generally sitting down with a wand or rod in his hand, directing the negroes in their work.

The polished stone implements known to archæologists as neolithics (in contradistinction to the paleolithic or cracked or splintered arrow and spear head weapons of warfare) are the oldest. They were made by these industrious agriculturists and used for domestic purposes, long ages before the rough splintered arrow heads and javelin points and rough battle axes came into use. These ancient Mound-builders polished their stone morters to grind their corn and wheat, and to curry the hair from their skins for clothing and to mix their colors. They mixed their clay first and shaped their pottery inside of woven baskets of willow and cane and burned them over open fires. This was the archaic beginning of the potter's art, and is the very first sign of a real civilization. These ancient burnt pastes of clay inside of wicker or basket work are something I have found nowhere else on earth except in the valley of the Mississippi and its tributaries, and I have been a close hunter after them all over the world.

Now by observation and constant search we follow the evolution of the potter's art in the tracks of the early Mound-builders. As I have said before, the kneading of the mud into the wicker work and hardening it in the sun and over the fire is the very first step. Then comes the second stage, in which they plastered mud over the gourds, apples and pears and fruits of various kinds, roasted the clay in the fire, and removed the mould from the inside. Then they made various kinds of moulds of wood, bark and straw and burned them in the ashes, or roasted them I may say.   The third era shows the irregular hand-fashioned pottery of grotesque form, with walls of irregular thicknesses, and made of, several kinds of clay, all burned in open fires.   Then come the figures of gourds, pears and various fruits and vegetables of a mixed kind, baked in an oven.   Last comes the smooth, beautiful pottery, turned upon a wheel, and moulded and smoothed by a machine.   These all have a trade mark, the oldest an ordinary cross, with each arm of the cross bent in at right angles to the center; another trade mark was a design now known as a Greek scroll.   In these wares are found the shells of a bivalve, now geologically extinct, ground up and mixed in clay before baking.   Finally comes the colored and glazed pottery.

Now, in the lapse of years, we find that not until this later stage of the potter's art did they attempt to make human figures, and to place animals, birds and flowers upon the burnt clay in different colors.   Soon after this era, migration from America began to move westward toward the shores of Asia into Africa.   But I did not set out to write a dissertation on pottery, porcelain or ceramic art.   You can get a better one from your encyclopedia.

The Mound-builders were not a warlike or nomadic people; they were purely agriculturists.   They hunted and found the most productive spots on the face of the globe.   They knew the rich lands from the poor, and on these rich new lands they planted their colonies and cultivated them much as we do to-day.   The rich delta of the Yazoo in the valley of the great Mississippi was one vast garden spot; not a foot of it was waste land. They used the waters of the New Mississippi, after it shrank to its normal proportions, to irrigate and keep fertile the already rich alluvium they found here in their migrations south.   They furrowed every foot of it; dug over ten thousand miles of drainage, irrigation, and navigable canals, from east to west and from north to south, crossing and intercrossing each other in thousands of places. So perfect was this canal system throughout the delta that, though thousands and thousands of years have elapsed since they were dug, you can to-day enter any one of them and by following its channel go to any part or plantation within its confines.

So densely was this delta populated that there is not a square of one hundred acres in extent that does not contain a pottery kiln where they manufactured their ware, or a residence mound. There is not a natural stream in the delta west of the hill drain of the Yazoo proper and the Mississippi River; all are artificial, and the work of negroes, under the supervision of their white taskmasters. The bones of these negroes, where they still exist, are found in countless thousands in burial grounds along the high banks of the ancient shores of the Mississippi River. In front of my own residence on the eastern shore of a natural depression extending for miles north and south of me, is one of the ancient cities of the dead. In walking a few hundred yards along this front after a rain you can gather a pocketful of their teeth and find whole jaw bones and skulls of this protruding-jawed nation. Here and there, separate in a pottery coffin, is found the frame of a white man, but never near the bones of the dolichokephalic breed.

On the west side of the Mississippi upon the old bank of that stream, above the highest waters and opposite the widest part of the Yazoo-Mississippi delta, once existed the largest city in the universe. It covered Drew, Desha, Ashley and parts of other counties, and fully twenty millions of these busy Mound-builders once had their homes here. The Mississippi River and the Gulf of Mexico furnished them fish, the Yazoo delta was their garden, and the valley lands of the river and the rich prairies of Arkansas and Texas gave them their bread. Their mounds to-day yield many relics of those long-ago vanished people. Their colonies spread to the Zuni plateau to the west and down into Mexico in the south, and on and down through Central and South America, as you can see by following the ever-increasing and ever-progressive traces in that direction. Try to trace them in any other way and you are going up stream against wind and current. Follow them as I have, and each day's journey will show you that I have solved the problem of the early Mound-builders.   Each day's journey toward Lake Titicaca in South America shows you plainly the evolution of civilization.   It had its birth on the southern shore of that great North American island ocean ages ago, and it ended at the mouth of the Nile four thousand years before the Christian era.

The testimony of the rocks, the testimony of the fossilized remains of the earth, the archæology of pottery, all point to North America as the earliest habitat of man.   The prehistoric ruins of over two thousand cities give us the earliest history of civilization's genesis on this same continent, and some bold Columbus of Peru or Chili first discovered Asia and Africa in an American-built ship.

Why need we speculate on the ability of these builders of the magnificent temples and cities of America, whose zodiacal stones and telescopic tubes turned to the heavens show us that they were far in advance of us in the knowledge of movements of earthly and heavenly bodies.   We can see the great aqueducts of these people passing through tunnels fifteen miles long and thirty feet wide, paved with stones of hexagonal shape, thirty inches deep and polished and fitted so close that no water has leaked through them for a hundred centuries.   Who can see the great walls built up from the depths of chasms a thousand feet deep and more than twenty-six hundred feet wide; who can see the great pyramids built of earth and stone, three hundred feet high and covering more than one hundred and sixty acres, with grand and beautiful temples upon their tops, and their interiors filled with thousands of vaults of their mummified dead; I say, who can see these wonders and doubt but that these people of that far-off civilization had sense enough to construct vessels, the equal of any that Columbus or Cortez possessed, or that we used less than a century ago?

They built structures impervious to fire, with walls so massive and thick that they could not be heated to the melting point, hence were indestructible by heat and as impervious to the corroding tooth of time as the mountain chains.   Were we to now leave our cities and dwellings in all their pomp and splendor, ere the lapse of a thousand years not a vestige of their splendor would be left visible to the eye of some future archæologist.

In the 19th chapter of Job, 23rd and 24th verses, we see that at the time he wrote, and his is the oldest book of the Bible, he was thoroughly acquainted with the printing of books and the art of moulding type in lead, then in rock moulds after their forms had been graven on the stones, just as we do now.   Hear what he says: " Oh, that my words were now written; oh, that they were printed in a book.   That they were graven with an iron pen and lead in a rock frame."

I believe that for ages this race navigated the seas as we do to-day, and that they and their negro slaves populated all the great islands of the Pacific ocean; that the great stream of immigration flowed westward from the shores of America, and kept up constant communication with Europe just as we do to-day.

The grandest graveyard and the greatest monumental city of the dead that I have ever seen on the globe lies between Australia and South America.   It is twelve miles long and seven miles wide, and has steadily grown smaller and smaller through countless aeons of time.   This graveyard is more than a thousand miles from any other land and is called Easter Island.   It is claimed by Chili, and is but a speck on the map of the world.

On this island are monuments in the shape of a man —not one, but countless thousands—some not more than two feet high and others thirty-seven feet high, carved from a rich lava stone, quarried from the small volcanic mountains on the western end of the island. These monuments are too old and too much worn by the plural actions of the elements and time to allow one to decipher any inscriptions upon them.   I spent several months wandering among them in the vain endeavor.   Some yet lay in the quarries ready to erect, but they rest now, as their builders left them, ages ago. As the sea encroached upon these monuments they tumbled into it, and the beaches of the whole island are covered with them and are whitened by the countless thousands of yet undecayed human teeth. The bones are but dust and cannot be handled or measured, but they belong to an orthognathus-jawed white race. And this race understood the higher branches of dental surgery, for I found bridge work, and teeth so perfectly crowned with a porcelain substance that you could not, with the naked eye, discern the junction. You could pick up a hat full of them in a day's search on the beaches. On the breast plates of these great statues of men and women you can trace faint outlines of men's faces, pictured in the sun, and from this fact I conceived the idea that they were sun-worshippers.

I believe that early man was a sun-worshipper, from the facts I shall here present. "On the first day God made the light. And on the fourth day the sun and moon were created." God made two great lights, the greater to rule the day and the lesser to rule the night. Now without these lights nothing could exist on this earth, and God has promised that the power of neither sun nor moon shall injure the children of earth, in these words: "The sun shall not smite them by day, nor the moon by night." No pure-blooded man of the living soul with an unsullied conscience need fear either. (See Psalms, 121-6.)

Easter Island is in latitude 27° 8' south and longitude 109° 25' west, more than 2,500 miles west of Chili and over a thousand miles from Pitcairn's Island, far out of the usual tracks of vessels, in the desert sea, as it is called by sailors. After a careful survey of it, I came to the conclusion that this island was once in the direct pathway between America and the western world, or new world, as I shall call it. That these ancient Americans, these civilized people, these early Mound-builders carried their religion and their works of art to the new world, we have many proofs. In Mexico and other South American states and throughout Central America there are regions covered with pyramids, of which those of Egypt are the exact patterns, and after having visited Egypt and gazed at her pyramids, then at those of America, you feel that the builders were one and the same.

One of the most striking *facsimiles* of a statue can be seen at Siva and Parvati on the Island of the Elephants, between Bombay and the mainland, about seven miles from Bombay.   Here is an artificial cave, whose mouth is sixty feet wide and eighteen feet high; you enter and see carvings of colossal elephants.   One carved elephant stands at the mouth of the cave and is now rapidly decaying, and farther inside stands the statue of the father and mother of the human race.   It represents the binding of the soul of man and woman into one, when the two are made one at marriage.

The ancient Aryan Hindu believed that at death the souls of the man and woman blended and became one, just as two drops of water run together and become one.   The woman could not marry again at the death of her husband and he could not enter into the bliss of Paradise until her soul joined his and became one. This statue commemorates this event.   One half of it is man, one half is woman; the two making a perfect being.   Drop a veil over one half and only a perfect man is seen; shift the veil and hide the man, and the perfect woman appears.

In the winter of 1860 I came upon a similar statue, carved in solid iron granite in a great niche in a ruined temple in the wild and unexplored region near the mouth of the Ulna River in Honduras, about forty-five miles due south.   The work was rough and worn by the hand of time, but it was one and the same in every particular.

Far up in the wilds of the Gangri Mountains, in a rocky glen of a spur of these mountains connecting the Gángri with the Himalayas, I have wandered among my Zuni plateau cliff-dwellers.   The style of their houses and their pottery utensils were so perfect a reproduction, that I could almost hear the voices of my little Comanche playmates with whom I roamed, a captive, in my early boyhood.   The finding of this statue—this sculptured form of Siva the man, and Parvati the woman—on the Island of the Elephants on the coast of India in latitude 18° 57′ north and longitude 73°

east; the sight of the similar Honduran Siva and Par-vati statue of a colossal size, overlooking the great plain of Sala in latitude 15° 20′ north and longitude 87° 40′ west in far-off Central America—almost at the very Antipodes; and the tracing of the cliff-dwellers of the Zuni plateau of Arizona and New Mexico, to the Gangri on the headquarters of the Yang-tse River in far-off China—all this evidence confirms my theory.

In the ancient ruins of the cliff-dwellers of China I noticed an improvement in the stucco work on the walls and ceilings in their rooms, as well as the softer tones and colorings of the glazing of their pottery ware. The stucco work on the walls and ceilings was exceedingly smooth and fine, showing that it had been made with tools or moulds, while that in the caves on the Zuni plateau was coarse, uneven, and plainly showed the finger prints and other hand marks of the artisans. Many of the designs in the two localities were identical, the scrolls and patterns being of wonderful similarity— almost as close as the letters of a book.

These facts—the silent medals of a pre-historic peo-ple preserved in unyielding stone—speak louder to us than any chronicled story penned by living man; they are silent, voiceless and unchangeable through count-less centuries, and they plainly show us that at that day there was a grander civilization than we, with all our pomp and splendor, can ever attain, for these are works that cannot be duplicated by hirelings, but only by slavery or forced labor.

WHAT BECAME OF THE MOUND-BUILDERS?

Miscegenation the true causes of their disappearance—
Moses and the Israelites—A warning to this nation—The
Negro.

WHAT became of the Mound-builders? They migrated, and their descendants set their slaves free, and
then miscegenated with them and begat the yellow or
mixed races we now see scattered over the earth's surface.

The above question and the answer is in accord with
the medals of nature, and the proofs recorded in both
sacred and profane history, and is deduced from more
than three score years of close personal observation
and study, and an experience on most of the great islands, and among the people of nearly every clime
under the sun.

Yes, the true cause of their disappearance—robbed
of clouds and seen in the light of truth—was miscegenation. They mingled their pure Aryan blood with
their slaves, lowered their brain capacity, and changed
their clear, rosy-white complexion, soft yellow hair, and
finer fiber of mind and body, to that of the cloudy, flat-
nosed savage, yellow, or red man, where every beastly
instinct and desire that is inherited from both parents
is fostered and exaggerated, and every good quality is
thoroughly obliterated. Yes, this miscegenated race
retains every mean quality of both parents, and eschews
all of the good; they are an accursed race, and can
never rise to the level of the pure-blooded white man.

These miscegenated beings can never plan, build or
produce the great works of the pure Aryan or Anglo-
Saxon. They have not the brain capacity and they
are a cursed race. Instead of building and beautifying
a country they tear down and destroy, and spread ruin
and desolation on every hand.

Who can read ancient history and not be impressed
with the terrible doings of these yellow or red savages?
They spread their poisoned spawn over the earth in
countless numbers, and seem to multiply as do the insect
world; they are the offspring of sin, and as such they
are sent as punishment to us.

When Moses led the children of Israel out of Egypt
into the Holy Land he was driven back by the warlike
hordes who inhabited that region, for his men were not
soldiers, they knew nothing of the use of arms, they
had been slaves too long under their Egyptian taskmasters.   Moses saw this as soon as he attempted to
enter the land of promise, so like the great general he
was, he led his people back into the wilderness, and for
forty years, or a whole generation, he drilled and hard-
ened them until he had one of the best armies that ever
trod the earth.   They were desert-born and desert-bred,
capable of standing any kind of fare or fatigue, and
when he again led them up against the owners of the
land, these owners were as chaff before the wind.

Who can read the Biblical account of the sacking of
the cities of the promised land by these desert-bred
soldiers, murdering of the male defenders and the ap-
propriation of the women to gratify their beastly lusts
and desires, the liasons of King David and the lecherous
personality of the Wise Man, without finding a cause
for the lowering and fall of the chosen people of
God? Yes, a cause for their fall from the high plane of
the rulers of the earth to that of homeless wanderers,
without a country, without a land, from the fall of
their beautiful temple to this day. Not only were they
barred from their sacred tabernacle and holy of holies
for ten generations, or for three hundred and thirty
years, but almost two thousand years have elapsed, and
many more will roll away ere the curse of Pariah will
be removed, and they can again build their altars and
firesides in the land of promise.   Such is the decree of
fate; such the decree of nature; such the mandate of
Almighty God.

Not only the Israelites, the chosen people of God,
but every other people and nations of every clime under

the sun have suffered from this miscegenation. It is to-day sapping the life blood of the people of this proud, beautiful republic of the United States, and if we do not take cognizance of it soon, we, too, will follow the fate of the Mound-builders, the Egyptians, the Greeks and the Romans.

Their examples are before us, and as surely as the seasons obey the equinoxes of the sun, and seedtime and harvest, and cold and heat, summer and winter, day and night follow, will this nation be in peril, and sink into oblivion, for and by that same great overshadowing cause that is the prime factor in the death of all nations.

To-day we are living under, and are governed by the laws of Moses, of the ancient Greeks and Romans; they still find places in our common law books. In this, the twentieth century of the Christian era, we still use these laws as text books in our common schools and colleges, because we can find no better or grander similes than are given in the Homeric poems, those of Virgil, and the fiery orations of Demosthenes, Cicero and Tacitus. They fire the brain and lend grace to the tongues of our youths.

Surely these people of a bygone age must have had wonderful brain capacity, chaste and beautiful ideas, and grand modes of expression, thus to hold us spellbound in this far-away age. Who were they? We see their sculptured forms and painted likenesses, still clear and distinct, upon the walls of their homes in the land of their nativity. Yes, almost speaking likenesses, they look down upon us in all their godlike grandeur, just as they appeared in life, two thousand years ago. And they were men, men of the white race, men of brain, men of pure mesokephalic skulls and straight jaws, with fine white bones, slender and fair.

And who are the descendants of these great men? Who inhabit their old homesteads? Who are the inheritors of their estates? Let us look at them closely. The average Greek of to-day is a brachykephalic-skulled being with yellow, red or swarthy skin, long, coarse, black or kinky hair, with thick protruding jaw and soft nose, somewhat flattened. And what of the descendants and inheritors of the noble Romans? Where and what are they? One simple word tells the tale, " Dagoes."

What brought about these conditions? What sank these grand, great nations to their present level? There is but one answer; they set their slaves free and then miscegenated. They attained their greatness through the labor of their slaves. Under the management of overseer, or taskmaster, the Grecian owner had ample time for study and recreation, without having to labor with his hands to procure food and clothing for the sustenance of himself and family. His slave labor produced this in superabundance.

These conditions changed when he set his slaves free, and his downfall was assured when he mingled his pure Aryan blood with that of these low dolichokephalic-skulled, prognathus-jawed, thick-lipped, woolly-haired black Africans. It needs but a glance at these people to convince anyone with ordinary intellect that I am right in my declaration, that it was the sin of miscegenation that caused this great change in these once noble people.

The pure-blooded white man steps out on the stage of life the highest and the brainiest and most capable of attaining to the loftiest planes of all the arts of civilization ; he alone is able to command and compel the lower beings to obey his mandates. All other races are subservient to him and have been since God gave him the power, as he left the doors of the Ark, upon the subsidence of the deluge.

He stands upon the most elevated plane of humanity, and will so stand as long as he keeps his blood pure and uncontaminated. Riches and power and true glory are his for all time if he but obeys the mandates of God. When he corrupts these mandates by debauchery, and disregards that law, given at creation's dawn, that " Like shall beget like, each after his kind," and, with his wealth and power, furnishes a harem, as King Solomon did, of many wives and concubines of every hue and blood, and leaves a progeny behind who are merely the offspring of sinful lusts and beastly desires, Almighty God curses this progeny with every vile instinct of both parents, and cancels every one of the good. This debauched progeny thus cursed, begets only the low born, " each after his kind," until but a few generations elapse ere the nation is sunk into oblivion. Yes, into the dark vales of unenlightened savagery, from which no power on earth can ever lift it again.

This poisoned race, this scum of the earth, is omnipresent in our midst, and we are constantly inviting them from the overcrowded cities of Europe, Asia, and Africa, and by mixing our pure, white, Anglo-Saxon blood with this lower element, we are lowering our brain pans and our standards of civilization, and inviting self-destruction.

We are catering to a cold, half-bred, half-civilized people, whom we could not in a thousand years bring to perfection.   One drop of this soulless, miscegenated race of mixed blood has leavened the whole, and it is not in the power of man to create what God has not.

Our laws are not stringent enough. Some of our States permit the union of the pure-blooded Anglo-Saxon with the thick-lipped, woolly-haired black negro, only a shade above the chattering monkey, and not half as sanitary.   Again they permit their bastard-born progeny to enjoy all the privileges of the most favored of the land.   This is against the laws of God, and we as a nation must in the end suffer for it.

These " bastards," for they are bastards; they are not begotten " each after his kind," as commanded by God, neither in the image or likeness of father or mother, but are merely " go-betweens," neither white nor black, but yellow abortions, children of sin, and cursed as were the offspring of Cain whose sins brought about the destruction of the world by a flood when the earth was young, to purify it from this very sin committed by Cain.

How foul and abhorrent to the father and mother of the pure-blooded Anglo-Saxon is the idea that their gentle, delicate, fair-haired, blue-eyed daughter is wed to one of these black brutes, with his thick, long, narrow skull, protruding, beastly jaws, fresh from his African wilderness. Does it not send a shudder through your inmost fiber, even to contemplate the idea; though he may be the son of a pure-blooded African chief, or a jungle king.

The cold, repugnant horror of the thing is the same. The mulatto breed, that spring from the union of the black and white, will continue to propagate a yellow race throughout infinite ages; because the immutable law of Nature works the same in tree, plant, fish, bird, beast and man alike, and the qualities inherited from their parents descend to their offspring through all time. None know this better than our skilled gardeners, poultry fanciers, the breeders of cattle, sheep, dogs, and the race and trotting horses of our common country. We can plainly see that the miscegenation of the white and black beings of earth in the mould of man, does and will produce every race on the globe; yes, every variety of the *genus homo* on this old earth.

Take the white and black, mingle their blood, and you get a yellow being; neither white nor black. Mingle the yellow and black and you get a red or brown; now mingle the white and yellow and you get a being neither white nor yellow, but of a muddy hue. And so on, until you produce all kinds and classes, as well as shades of people; and these will beget like and like, " each after his kind," through infinity, after the tenth generation.

These beings thus begotten invariably inherit all the mean and none of the good qualities of their primal progenitors. I am able (by long years of travel, and residence among these miscegenated beings, in many climes and countries), and I positively assert that I can take a dozen members, both male and female, all perfect representatives of their people or tribes, selected from all parts of China, Japan, the various South Sea Islanders, the Manchurians, Eskimos, Terra del Fuegans, Arabs, Bedouins, Peruvians, Mexicans, North American Indians, Hindus, Egyptians, Greeks and Dagoes—yes, from any part of the earth—dress them all alike, or stand them up in a state of nudity before a congress of the most skilled anatomists of the whole world, and they could not tell but that they all were of the same parentage and from the same country, judging entirely by their anatomy and color, size and general characteristics.

It is an impossibility to distinguish a particle of difference in any one of them, for I tried for twenty-seven years faithfully to do so, with everything in my favor, and I could find none. So I feel safe in saying and in declaring that there is none. I visited the frozen shores of Greenland, of Siberia, of Terra del Fuego, and all the coasts and interior regions of North, Central, and South America; and the same in Africa, and Australia and many of the great islands of the Pacific Ocean; and amid the mountains and plains of Asia, and I think that I have a right to express my conclusions.

It is not a fact that climate changes the color of a people, for if this were so, the yellow and black and red Eskimos of Greenland, and the yellow, red and dark-skinned natives of Terra del Fuego should be the whitest on earth. Every condition for bleaching and whitening them exists in these cold, cloudy, snowy, icy regions. I cannot help giving an incident that will convey an idea of the denizens of that cold, damp country that surrounds the south end of South America.

I was on the Beagle Channel, in that region of almost constant rain or snow; for one or the other seems to be falling fully half the days of the year. I was making a survey of the surrounding country, which is but a rocky, wooded, slippery, broken, worthless waste, and we were in constant contact with the miserable, half-starved men, women and children that inhabit that God-forsaken land. I have seen the naked women sitting upon the shelving rocks that dip into the sea, nursing their babes, not a week old, with the snow falling upon them, and making a stream down their breasts, as the babe drew its sustenance from their paps. They were as contented and happy as their more favored sisters of a warm tropic clime.

These people often suffer from hunger in its worst form; they live upon fish, and prefer the blubber of a spoiled or rotten whale to any other delicacy on earth.

I gave a rotten, worm-eaten ham, that weighed sixteen pounds, to a boy of not more than ten years of age, and at one sitting he ate the whole of it, and I believe that he would have eaten more if it had been offered him. They kill and eat their old men and women in times of famine. I saw plenty of dogs among them, and I asked why they did not eat them instead of their grandmas and grandpas. They replied, " Old man or old woman no good; dog catch otter." And it is thus with most of these people of the yellow, red or black tribes of earth, but especially so with those who inhabit a cold, bleak, inhospitable clime; they are prone to become cannibals to sustain life.

There is a fact about the negro, the yellow and the red and brown men that I have not seen commented upon; they cannot distinguish between right and wrong. In other words, they have no conscience—that still, small, that divine spark, inherent in the soul of the pure-blooded white man, which enables him to distinguish right from wrong in its minutest form; that dictates what to pursue, and what to shun, and when we are guilty of wrong doing, haunts our sleeping or waking dreams, and disturbs our every thought.

This " soul fire," this flame breathed into the white man when he was first created, yea, first wakened from creation's womb, is sadly lacking in the yellow, red and black races all over the earth. That soul fire was made alone for the pure white man ; and he can only convey it to his kind. That *something* created by God for him alone, he can convey to his own pure-blooded offspring, bone of his bone and flesh of his flesh, a true reproduction after his kind, but he cannot convey this living soul to the low, dolichokephalic-skulled, prognathus-jawed negro, nor to the brachykephalic-skulled, yellow or red man ; for they are not each after his kind, and are not like Noah, " perfect in their generation." They are the offspring of two distinct races of mankind, neither " after his kind," and it is impossible for man to create what God did not, and what God has positively forbidden. Yes, it is against the law of God, and man's sinful lusts and desires cannot overcome that fiat of

" omniscience." Every command and law given us since creation's dawn has been fulfilled, and every trespass thereof has been punished.

The pure, white, mesokephalic races of earth are followers of the meek and lowly Jesus, and at the command of Christ, they have preached His name and doctrines to every nation and people on earth, and to-day in every land and clime the spires of the temples of the living God point to heaven. But in no yellow, red or black country has Christ been universally accepted; while you cannot find a white country or a white people on the face of the whole globe which does not universally accept Him as their Lord and Saviour.

Does not this fact alone speak louder than a trumpet's blast, or the roar of a cannon? The yellow, red or black races have no souls, and neither can the white man give them one. They cannot conceive or understand the meaning of the hidden or invisible things taught by the followers of Christ. It is beyond their comprehension, for they only understand those things that are visible.

These are cold, real facts. They stand before us now, and have so stood since Cain mingled his blood with that of his Nodite wife, and begat the first miscegenated being or bastard of the conscienceless breed that ever trod the earth.

There is no truth more firmly held than " like begets like, each after his kind." I well know that many who read this work will think that I am prejudiced, and am radical in my views, especially on this subject of " the living soul "; but I am not. They think it a dangerous theory to promulgate, and I know that the great band of Christians, who compose our so-called foreign missions, will bring all their " big guns " to bear on me, but I will not flinch, for I know that I am right. The cold, naked facts are ever before me, in all their stern reality.

I am opposed to foreign missions, and look upon them as a colossal humbug, so far as converting a nation of yellow, red, black or tan people to the worship, or the understanding, or the comprehension, of the true mean-

ing of the Bible as given to us, is concerned, and I think
it a sacrilege to even try to make these soulless beings
pretend to comprehend it.   I do not pretend to say that
these earnest but mistaken missionaries do not do these
poor benighted and soulless savages some good by teaching them to wear clothes, to cleanse their bodies, and to
live in sanitary surroundings.   Thus far they civilize
and make them better, but outside of this their life's
work is a dismal failure.

The parrot and jackdaw can be taught to mumble a
prayer, and a monkey, dog, horse, elephant, or other
animal can be taught to go through the act of devo-
tional kneeling, as if in worship of a divinity.   And
these yellow, red, black and tan anthropoids are on an
exact and even plane with beasts of the forest; their
worship is only a mimicry, and is in reality a sacrilege,
a sacrilege of the most holy of holies, a mockery of the
most sacred things bequeathed to the men of the " living soul " by their great Creator and His crucified
Son.

You may belt the earth, as I have, and wherever the
white man has his habitat, there you will find the Christian religion is supreme, and the crucified Christ is their
guide.   For a thousand years the white man and his
ancestors have been trying to bring the black, yellow,
and red and brown into the true fold of the Redeemer
and they are no nearer now than they were a thousand
years ago.   They are of course better off and better
cared for under the refining influence of the Christian
men and women, than they would be in their native wilds
and jungles and living on doodle bugs, roots and
reptiles.

But you can never make a pure white man of a mixed
race; and the great danger to the white race will come
when this miscegenated race shall have become so white
that they cannot be distinguished from the pure blood
only by the closest scrutiny.   The world is full of these
miscegenated and mixed races, and we can see how they
have destroyed nations that were once civilized and enlightened.

We can look back down the dim aisles of time and see

the beautiful ruins of the Aryan cities and kingdoms of ancient America, of Japan, China, India, Persia, Arabia, Egypt, Greece, Rome and Spain, as shown by their sculptured busts and paintings; all these were once under the reign of the pure white Aryan, but they are now peopled by hordes of miscegenated yellow, brown, or red half-civilized, conscienceless semi-barbarians, knowing and caring as little about the magnificent ruins around them as the nomadic red men of our western plains, or the black, woolly-haired, tulip-lipped cannibal of the jungles of the Congo.

Were it not for the God-given instinct of the females of the pure Aryan white race, that warns them against lowering their progeny to a level beneath them by contact with the males of the plane under them; were it not for this very attribute, born with the immortal soul and inherited by every pure Aryan white female, that mother instinct that protects their young even at the sacrifice of life itself, there would not to-day be a pure white man on this earth.

The male of any genus of man, bird, beast, or animal cares little about the color, or kind of female momentarily his partner, or that he may form a temporary alliance with. Nor does the color or condition of his progeny that may spring from this alliance deter him in the least from the gratification of his sinful lusts or beastly desires.

The same mother-instinct that guards the pure white woman and keeps us white, is also present in the females of the lower orders of the black, yellow, red or brown, and is just as strong; but she uses it to lift her progeny to a higher plane, yes, to a higher, grander plane than the one she herself occupies. The white man stands upon the very highest of all the planes of humanity, hence the black, yellow, red or brown woman is ever ready, yes, constantly seeks to be the companion, momentarily, of the white male in every country under the sun, for she feels that her offspring from this union will have a whiter, softer, fairer skin, and stand on a higher plane than she herself does. And as I have before remarked, this instinct in the woman guards her, protects her offspring and keeps us white, for if the white female were as lewd as the males of her race, there would not be a white man in America to-day. We would all be the offspring of soulless sin.

In every yellow, red, black or tan country in the world, if you, being of the male gender and of the white race, are an invited guest of the head of the family, or of the chief or patriarch of the tribe or camp, the women of the household are a part of the hospitalities extended to you. This is a universal law, and it holds good in all lands and climes inhabited by the colored races. You can take China, Japan, Manchuria, Hindustan, Arabia, Egypt, the islands of the Pacific, the regions of Africa, North, Central and South America, including Mexico, and it is the same.

We can plainly see in the miscegenation of the slave and her master, the absolute primal cause of the decadence of the nations. Sacred and profane history teach it to us in their every page, and the medals of nature and the testimony of the rocks and of the ruined cities of the whole world confirm it. I reassert, that it was not plague, pestilence, nor famine, battle, murder, nor sudden death, that destroyed the ancient Mound-builders, the builders of the pyramids of Egypt, and the other magnificent ruined cities of this and other lands; but the miscegenation of the white and black races.

It is not necessary to prolong this argument to any greater length, nor to add further proof to my theory. The personal observations of countless thousands of thinking travelers around the world bear me out in my contentions. You can see right in our midst, and call to mind, yes, in your own memory, some well-known family that has fallen from its high estate by the marriage of one member of it to one of an inferior grade. It is the same with cattle, horses, dogs, birds, and the whole brute creation.

These mongrels are on every hand; the mean qualities of their parents cropping out in their progeny in an exaggerated form. The bastard of the Bible was a miscegenated being, not begotten after his kind, and this soulless creature was not allowed in the temple, nor was he allowed to touch any of the holy things, no, not even to the tenth generation. It takes ten generations for the miscegenated breed to attain its equilibrium, in other words to attain that point where like will beget like, each after his kind. And this means from three hundred and thirty to four hundred years.

It cannot be too strongly emphasized, or kept before the eyes of the civilized world, that we must be ever on guard if we wish to keep our present standard of civilization up to the high mark set us by our pure white forefathers, and continue on the same plane. We are surrounded on every hand by a thick-lipped, woolly-haired, black, dolichokephalic, prognathus-jawed race, and their miscegenated descendants, and they are ever on the increase; this corroding dross, this baleful, poisoned, blighting, accursed cloud, hangs like a dark incubus over us.

Yes, this corroding dross, this deadly scum, is festering and polluting our whole body politic, and if not brought to a standstill, and destroyed, or curbed in some way, it will wreck our civilization and place us on the list of the departed Mound-builders. For the blight to us is like the withering blasts of the simoom of the Sahara desert to the tender herb.

None know this better than those who live in the great " black belts " of the earth, where they are in constant daily contact with this negro anthropoid, and none understand less and have less appreciation of the danger that surrounds them than those who only here and there come in contact with a few isolated wanderers. From these specimens they get only a very faint idea of the real negro, for these wandering specimens are the greatest mimics on the face of the earth and the most deceptive.

The facts are before us, that these anthropoids, made in the image and after the likeness of the white man, have been under the influence of the white man and his civilization, all over the world, for tens of thousands of years, and yet they nor their descendants have ever profited by this contact in the least degree when that contact ceased.

Education only makes them weaker and shows their short-comings in a more glaring light and a more pronounced form. Full and absolute freedom is a curse to a negro; he must have a taskmaster, someone who has the power to make him go and do; remove this power and you spoil a good laborer and a faithful worker.

England, a century ago, after civilizing, Christianizing, and thoroughly educating them to their full brain capacity, set them free and built them cities, towns, schools, and churches; the whole Christianized people of the world lent them aid. And what has been the outcome of this costly experiment? Their schools, colleges and churches are in ruins and the abodes of bats and owls, and their towns and cities have gone to decay. The proteges of the most civilized and powerful people on earth, they are again back upon the same low plane from whence they sprung. It is argued by some that it was the curse of slavery that sank them into their present state; but this is an absurd fallacy, and I deny it emphatically. Where are they the most degraded? Where are they only one degree above the gibbon monkey? Where are they the freest people on the face of the earth? I answer, in the wilds of the African jungles, their native habitat.

Yes, here they are only a shade above the brute creation, and no chain of slavery has even fettered limb or thought since the dawn of their creation. They are as free as the birds of the air or the wild beasts of the plains. Yes, there in the land of their birth in the jungles of Africa, they have always been free. And yet for ten thousand years they have not advanced one step upon the plane of civilization; they are to-day just as they were when Noah turned them out of the Ark, not one sign of improvement in any form; just as creation's dawn beheld them, they remain.

They live among the animals, and are a part of them; they have never tamed an elephant, or horse, and made him bear a hurden; they have never made a garment to cover their nakedness, they go in a state of nudity, and plaster their hair and bodies with mud to protect themselves from insects—the swine do the same; there are no mounds, no walls, no ruins of any kind, erected or planned by these free-born sons of the African wilds; no letter, figure or symbol or sound ever recorded by these low-born, stationary people, who have been free, and yet in contact with civilization and civilized men for for more than 4000 years.   As yet they have never advanced one step in any direction, save when compelled by the lash of a taskmaster.

They are at constant war with one another, but it is not a war for betterment of government, not to rid the land of a tyrant king; but war for the same causes that impel the brute creation to fight one another.

It is a notorious fact now present before the civilized world, that when these creatures are taken from their jungle wilds and taught by civilized men, given the books and arts of the nations who invented them, and taught the use of fire-arms, and then returned to their native land and tribes, they only retain that which is most low and brutal of all they have been given by their civilized teachers.   They seem to forget the good, and only retain the bad.   When they reach their old homes from the land of civilization they direct their superior knowledge to their own aggrandizement, and not for the betterment of their kindred, or their fellow-beings.

The negro in his native state has never invented anything; they are wonderful imitators and mimics, equaled only by the Japs and Chinese.   The latter stand above them on a far higher plane of humanity, as they possess a far greater brain capacity, and have one half of the white man's blood in their veins.   Yet the negro is far more gentle, docile and obedient in every respect, and really less brutal and savage, than the Jap or Chinaman, for these miscegenated beings retain all the mean qualities of both the negro and the white man, and none of the good.

The negro is not of a progressive, but of a defacto, stationary race.   We have only to view Hayti or Jamaica, under the rule of these anthropoids, to prove the facts of our assertions.   The helping hand, and the example of every civilized and Christianized nation of earth, have been stretched out to aid them and to look after their welfare, but they have only sunk lower and deeper into the shades of ignorance and superstition.

We have had a whole century of experience and practice before us. Under the rigid rule of the Egyptians, the Greeks, and Romans, and I may say Spanish masters, and then under the French and English, and lastly under our own Southern guidance, they were the happiest and most care-free beings on earth. They had good, well-ventilated houses, well-cooked food, and warm sanitary clothing, and a master's hand to guide them and minister to their every want. Under these conditions they prospered, and were a source of wealth, profit, and pleasure to themselves and to their masters. They could imitate every movement of " Old Massa " to perfection, even to the intonation of his voice, and followed in his footsteps in the most minute manner.

Now who can say that these creatures were not benefited by the guidance, example, and teaching of their Southern masters? Let us survey the environments of these thick-lipped, woolly-haired, black savages, as they appeared to us when freshly landed from the jungles of Africa, a few short decades ago.

We took them from the decks and holds of New England ships, manned by New England sailors and owned by New England merchants; I have myself bought them from these New England blockade runners, when the poor black creatures were unable to walk from being cramped up in the hold of the vessel so long hiding from the cruisers of different countries, and only paid one dollar per pound for them. They were naked and emaciated; many hardly able to raise themselves to a sitting posture, much less to stand. Now I took these poor creatures, nursed and clothed and fed them, and taught them how to work, to talk, and to wear clothing, and as far as lay in their power to be civilized Christians. At least I taught them to imitate, and to go through the form of worship and to practice the modes and customs of civilized beings.

For two hundred years the planters and citizens of the South pursued the same course with these savages and their progeny, and at the close of the great Confederate war, when these slaves were forcibly taken from us by the armies of the North and turned loose upon the world to wander at will, they were not the same low savages that were brought from the jungles of Africa.   But they were the most civilized black savages that have trod the earth since the Egyptian era of the Pharaohs, and the most Christianized since the birth of Christ.

Now, after a lapse of forty years, these same savage beings are sapping and lowering the brain pans of the very people, and their descendants, who set them free. Viewing all the facts, in the light of modern research, with the ever-present and visible truth before us, and the fate of Egypt, Greece, Rome, and Spain staring us in the face, cannot an intelligent, enlightened and observant people see the true causes that led to the overthrow, not only of these more modern civilized people, but to those far away Mound-builders of the old world in North America, and also her younger colonies in India, China, Persia, Arabia, and Egypt?

Can these yellow and red survivors, who now lead nomadic lives or live in tents and huts, construct such massive temples and beautiful statuary as did their pure-white, civilized ancestry?   Have they any of these proud, god-like forms or creatures before them as models from which to fashion their modern statuary?   Look at their present work and see the answer graven there.   Behold the hideous images of the yellow, savage Aztecs, and under them the chaste and beautiful carvings of their ancestors, before miscegenation spread her dark corrupting blight over the land, and left it an accursed and ruined region.

To me it is passing strange that among the thousands of learned ethnologists who have written tomes upon the subject of the different races, so-called, of men who have peopled the earth, not one, in the past twenty centuries, has ever advanced the true idea of the exact cause of the decay and the destruction of the nations.

They have been too easily led astray by the thoughts and reasonings of those gone before.   If we will only look at the real cause which I assert, how easily and how plainly do the facts present themselves to the thinking, reasoning mind. We can look around, right here in our midst, and see Indians, Chinamen, Japanese and mixed men of every nation; all born here, reared and living in our midst, whose parents and ancestors, for ten generations back, have never come in contact, nor been in any way even associated with one of these yellow foreign-born people. And yet the most skillful anatomist, upon a close and careful examination, would pronounce them full-blooded offspring of one of these yellow, foreign-born people. After the black and white once mix, and the yellow tinge is made permanent, then the equilibrium of nature is attained, like begets like, each after his kind, to the end of time; and they only change from the infusion of a darker, or a whiter blood into their veins. This readmixture of darker or whiter blood continued through ten generations attains its equilibrium, and a higher or a lower order or race is placed upon the earth, having a higher or lower order of intellect, as this progeny is nearer or farther from the intelligent white man or negro.

There is no process of reasoning that can controvert this fact. A thousand generations will not remove the taint of negro blood in the veins, and restore to purity the polluted miscegenated race. Nor can it ever again sink to the level of the negro; for each drop of white blood raises the intellect of the lower order of humanity and each drop of negro blood lowers it. The progeny of the negro and the white race, as I have before remarked, are the true bastards, the originals of Biblical lore, because this offspring is not like either parent, and is not after either kind, neither white nor black, but a separate and distinct being, hence being equal white and equal black, a product in which nature has assimilated an exact division of both. Being so begotten, this creature is a " child of sin," and inherits only the vicious and mean brutal instincts of both parents, and not one of the good. It is produced contrary to the mandate of God; that mandate which commands every created thing that creepeth upon the earth to bring forth " each after his kind." And this creature is but an abortion—a mixed " thing," neither white nor black, and not after either kind.   Nature fashioned him as near as it was possible, by mingling the two in equal proportions, but he is like neither parent.   With these facts before us, can there be a doubt in the minds of anyone that miscegenation alone was the true cause that destroyed the Mound-builders?   It was the chief factor in the destruction of India, Persia, Arabia, Egypt, Greece, Rome, and Spain.   A yellow race now occupies and roams amid the ruins of these once highly civilized and enlightened people.   And we found a savage yellow people in possession of the homes of the ancient American Mound-builders.

THE DARWINIAN THEORY

The survival of the fittest—Empedocles precursor of Darwin—Darwin theory tenable up to the eighth era of creation—" The Immortality of Love "—Darwin theory not in conflict with the Mosaic account of man's creation —The blessings of God—Eternity.

Is Darwin's theory of the descent of man consistent with the Mosaic description of the creation, and is it tenable?

Before giving my answer to this, I will remark that Darwin had (if I may so call it) a master analytical mind. He delved far into the hidden mysteries of nature, and drank deep, until intoxicated with his draughts—then drank and sobered up again.

No closer observer ever put his thoughts upon paper. Yet Darwin forgot his Great Creator, the Mighty Ruler of the universe, trusted all to chance and made the law of selection, and the survival of the fittest, his deity. On this hypothesis he based all his arguments. Tyndall, Huxley, Schmitt, and others followed, all in the same path. They all forgot that Master Hand that fashioned the universe, set the stars in their paths, and created boundless space, all subservient to His will.

They forgot that it was at His command the worlds sprang into view. Our minds are too weak even to grasp a momentary conception of the vastness of His power. Is there any limit to the boundless space beyond the stars? If so, who set the boundary lines, and can the boundary lines be set? We know that there is a boundary to our vision, but what an illimitable space there is beyond it. As with our vision, so with our minds. We have not the vision to penetrate, nor the mind to contemplate this vast boundless ocean of interstellar space. Nor can we comprehend the power or majesty of the Great Ruler who has his residence somewhere in the illimitable regions beyond our earthly vision.

We cannot grasp nor comprehend the things that lie

beyond our mortal minds. Our Creator does not give us that power. We cannot wing our way to the distant stars and planets that glitter and shine in the vaults above us, each a far greater and grander world than the one we inhabit; yet our thoughts can fly, in a moment, to the most distant one that twinkles in our vision's range. This is our God-given privilege, as this is a part of our being, conferred upon us when we were given a part of Him, upon the eighth era of creation's dawn; yes, when we became partakers of His kingdom, through the immortal soul that He breathed into our bodies.

This mind, conscience, immortal soul, was not given to any of the countless thousands of the fourth, fifth, sixth or seventh day creatures of this world; only to that one lone man that God placed in the Garden of Eden, to dress and to keep it, and to us, his pure-blooded descendants of the now present, bright eighth era.

How long these days, eras, or aeons of creation were, we do not know, nor can we compute. Countless millions of years, as we now reckon time, may have elapsed between each period. We may have been testaceans, mere testa, so minute that millions of us could have rested upon the point of a pin, in that first era of our creation, and happily lived and loved in the protoplasms of our shells, and densely covered the protozoan plane. And how small the deposits were from our decaying dust may be seen on the present bed of the ocean; where the accumulations do not exceed an inch in a hundred years, and in places not the hundredth part of an inch in a century.

Now, when we see these deposits of the testaceans, several thousand feet thick, and remember that they only formed at the rate of an inch, or the hundredth part of an inch, in a century, we can readily see the vast unending line of centuries that have marched by with ceaseless tread since our testacean ancestors first breathed and clung together in that dim and far-off era.

And this testacean or monerian age had to pass to that of a higher Molluscan era; and in the order of the Mollusca we can find the picture, the outline, the embryo of every bird, beast, or animal on the face of the earth.

Every pattern is shown, even of the whole order of the Reptilia. The patterns shown are all in embryonic form, from the univalve conch to that of a man. The primal egg cell is there as well as the foetus, and it is not impossible, nay, is it not more than probable that from these early Mollusca all living creatures may have had their beginning; may have sprung, and been guided and governed by cogenital surroundings of air, food and water, as well as climate.

It would take too much time and space to go into the microscopic changes that lifted the testa from the protozoan plane to the man of the present era. To carry him through the fish, bird and animal kingdom, up to the high plane of civilized man, is an unending task that only God can perform. But the Mosaic periods of the creation point to the different eras of their growth; and when we view them in the light of clear, cold science, we have to acknowledge that there is much of truth in Darwin's theory.

But Darwin was not the first, by thousands of years, to advance the theory of the descent of man from a conch, or the order of the Mollusca. The scholars and wise men of the Chaldeans and Egyptians, and the historians of those far-away days advanced and advocated the idea that all the fauna of the earth had their birth in the sea.

The Assyrians regarded the Polyps, or male Argonauts, the common Nautilus, or Portuguese Man-of-War, as the ancestor of man; and who after living for an age in its shell at sea, abandoned it and crept out on the land on some propitious shore, and transformed itself into a bird, beast or man, just as it felt inclined, and as the surroundings and conditions suited.

The historian and scientist Empedocles was the precursor of Darwin, and Empedocles gathered his ideas from the myths and the mythological lore of those ancient people. He believed that all animals, birds, beasts and men were born and came up out of the sea; that the polyp sailed over the waters of the ocean, and gathered those parts of himself that belonged to the peculiar head that his shell presented; if his head was that of a bird he began and gathered the parts belonging to a bird, and if an animal, he would gather those, and if a man, he only gathered the components of a man.

It is a singular fact that the heads of these little sailors do bear wonderful likenesses to various birds, beasts, as well as to men. I have handled hundreds of them, fresh from the sea, and have been struck with the strange resemblances they would present to men, birds and animals that I was familiar with. You can take a hundred of them fresh from your net and examine their faces carefully, and no two will be alike; you can distinguished the different kinds of men, birds and animals that you have ever seen on the face of the earth, and the likenesses are so very perfect that you are astonished.

You have a creepy feeling, as you look at a polyp, and remember what Empedocles says about it; that it sailed over the seas and gathered from it the different parts of its body that suited its face, and then sailed to a clime and shore that was best and most congenial to the perfect development of the being that its face indicated; here it would leave its shell and crawl out on the land, and in a hidden, secluded spot gradually assume the shape and life its creator intended.

Many men retain the brutal instincts of their faraway ancestors, be they bird or beast. You have seen men whose faces resemble those of the lion, the eagle, the fox, the vulture, the dog, the parrot, or the monkey; they are common; and these very resemblances crop out and come to the fore upon any and every occasion. They intrude themselves upon every observant person.

Do we get these habits of ours from instinct, or from cultivation, or do we inherit them from our polyp ancestors? We see and feel them, know that they are present, yet from whence do they come?

Some may answer that they are God-given. This I do not deny. Others that all things are possible with Him; this too is so; yet the Great Creator never controverts His own laws, nor does He do anything that He would have to correct; He makes no mistakes, for

He works from a perfect principle, hence all His works are perfect, and will so remain until the end of time.

I am satisfied that much of Darwin's theory is tenable up to the eighth era of creation; but since that long-ago period there has been no other development; no new creation. God ended his work on the eighth day with the creation of the pure white female, as recited by Moses. Yes, He ended His work with the man of the living soul and his helpmate Eve, she the last and fairest of all His handiwork.

Now for a higher and more perfect creature than Eve, we will have to look to a purer region and planet than ours, beyond the stars, where love, the great and best attribute of man, is the primal power that love is immortal, as declared in the Bible.

Darwin has brought our forms from the lower order of the Mollusca atom in the testacean cell, into the broad open plain of the eighth era of God's work. When he brought the man of the living soul up from the dust of the earth and placed him in the beautiful Garden of Eden to dress and keep it, the Great Creator spread before this man of the living soul the beauties and splendors of earth for examples to teach him how to dress and keep his earthly habitat. He spread carpets of flowers over the plains in all their variegated hues and tints. He put his bright rainbows as arched doorways, and he painted the clouds in ever changing hues, and hung them as canopies and curtains of beauty above him; thus by daily and hourly teachings showed him how to make his home beautiful. Yea, commanding him to beautify his early home, to dress and keep it; not only for his own individual benefit, but for the passerby. Yea, to dress and keep it beautiful and bright, befitting the example set him hourly by his heavenly Father. And we should consider it a sin not to copy after the work of the Great Architect, so truly and abundantly set before us.

Where is the being with a spark of the immortal soul glimmering in his bosom, that can gaze at the peaceful glow, with all varied hues and cloud dyes dancing in the west as the orb of day fades in the shadows of evening twilight, and not feel the presence of that Master Hand that fashioned all things for His glory? And who can watch the forked lightning's flash and hear the deep thunders roll and crash in the ether vaults above without knowing in the inmost recesses of his heart that there is a great governing power, a power beyond our mortal ken, that set these physical forces of nature to work, and who holds the universe in the hollow of his hand?

Where is there a being with reason, conscience, thought and an immortal soul, who does not at times, while viewing a lovely landscape, perusing a pleasing book, or listening to some grand old song or hymn, drift away to a dim, unreal past, and see, hear, or feel that he has heard, seen or felt these same realities thousands of years before in a different stage of life and in another form? A trance, a dream, a momentary vision flits by and gives a glimpse we know not how, or why or when.

Is this the germ memory given to our spawn that was fashioned by the Divine hand when He laid the Tremadoc beds of our earth at creation's dawn? Have these germs in embryo state kept these memories alive during the long aeons of time that have circled away since those far-off eras of our past existence? Have they been borne as spores of atomic dust o'er continents, seas, and isles by the gentle winds or storms, those fleet hand-maidens of God's messengers of our planet, and the fair ambassadors of changing climes and seasons? We know they visit all parts of the earth, we know not whence they came, or whither they go. They fill all space and the electric force pervades all nature and per-meates the atomic germs of all life. There is no vacuum, for it is abhorrent to nature and nature's God.

The more we study nature and comprehend the won-ders revealed, the nearer we approach perfection. We harness the elements and make them our servants. Wind, lightning, heat and water do our bidding. They are dutiful servants and cruel masters. By their aid we conquer a barren waste and make it bloom and prosper. We catch the rays of the sun and by chemicals transfer the shadowy images of things for our picture galleries.

By the aid of the electric spark we converse with the denizens of distant continents and isles. And by chaining these same elements great burdens are lifted and borne over land and sea, guided and controlled by a single hand. With our breath we can speak against a sensitized, chemically prepared plate of glass and with the sound of our voice produce upon its face beautiful flowers and forms, thus showing how the Great Creator, with His breath, called things into existence at His will.

It is an ancient truism, "where there is a will there is a way," and none knows this better than the close student of nature. Have the will, then seek the way. All great inventions for the benefit or destruction of man have thus been brought about. The mind is centered on one thought and the will is bent to carry or perfect that thought and render it visible to the eye and touch.

We cannot fathom the depths or look into the inner workings of nature. The thoughts that come to us are moulded by a higher power that we know not of. Our great armored vessels, the rawhide shield of the savage, are but the reproductions of the bony coverings of the armadillo, the turtle and the crocodile transferred in a different form to subserve the same purpose and lifted to a higher plane. Try as we may, we find nothing new under the sun. All has been created and adopted in some form ages and ages agone. We make nothing new, only improve the old, and make it more adaptable to our present use. We have garnered only from a bygone age the accumulated wisdom that has been stored away in the minute cells of gray matter of our brains; and as necessity, the mother of invention, called it forth, do we apply it.

We see birds and animals perform feats and do things seemingly from instinct that closely resembles reason, and we sometimes think that they are endowed with this higher faculty of the human mind. I have watched the bower birds build their beautiful dance halls, smooth the floors and carpet them with variegated fragments of colored leaves and shells, and have watched the females arrange themselves around the walls, to see the males dance and caper and show their gaudy feathers and bright plumage in all their glory for their admiration.

I have seen the birds of paradise and the lyre birds clear the jungle grass from spaces several hundred feet long, making open roads, wide and clear, for the females to stand and view with unobstructed vision their flights from one hanging limb to another at the farther ends of these roads, and seen them sail from one to the other, in graceful flight, whirling and displaying each tinted plume and feather to the admiring gaze of their watching female friends, and then sail down and receive the plaudits and caresses of the chosen one.

For hours I have gazed at the pheasants, the peacocks, prairie chickens and the wild turkeys strut and spread their tails and gay plumage to their females; and the questions would naturally present themselves to the mind of any observer, do we possess the same attributes as these birds, in a more exaggerated form, or have we simply imitated them? Yet there are millions of our people who have never witnessed nor even read of these bird dances, and who, thousands of miles away from the habitats of these winged denizens of the wilds of forest and plain, amid the busy crowded marts of trade and commerce, mimic their every motion and act, and would fly if possible.

Is it not highly probable, yea, possible, that our atomic-germs had to pass through the thousand different stages, from the monerian to the plane upon which we now stand, before we were sufficiently educated for the purpose of our Great Creator? We had to have a beginning, and we slowly and constantly ascended from that far-off protozoan plane to the " Now."

To stand on this intellectual plane, in this broad reasoning era of the eighth day of creation, and understand in a manner the workings of our Creator, we had to rise through vast aeons of change. To make my meaning clear, I present you the following as an exemplification of my views. It will give you my ideas fully, and is addressed to my wife, with the love of the ages.

THE IMMORTALITY OF LOVE!

Sweetheart, did you know that scientists say,
  By a process weird and strange,
We sprang from conches, to Catarrhine monks,
  And thence to Man by law of "change"?

That somewhere, in the aeons agone,
  In an age that no one knows,
Our microsomes and chromosomes
  From protoplasms rose?

When testa on the protozoan plane,
  We dwelt in cellular forms
As grapholites, or trilobites,
  We felt azoic storms.

How we clung to each in that Laurentian age
  And grew in lapse of years;
How at a stroke our senses woke
  In thrill of hopes and fears,

When we were tadpoles, or boneless fish,
  In Paleozoic time,
And side by side on ebbing tide,
  We sprawled through ooze and slime;

Or fluttered with many a caudal swish
  O'er depths of Cambrian fen;
My heart was rife with joy of life,
  I loved you even then.

Then mindless we lived, and mindless we loved,
  Mindless at last we died;
And deep in rift of caradoc drift
  We slumbered side by side.

The ages came and the ages fled,
  The sleep that held us fast
Was riven away in newer day,
  Our night of death was passed.

We woke amphibians, tailed and scaled,
  As drab as dead man's hand;
We lay at ease 'neath Trias trees,
  Or trailed through mud and sand;

Croaking and blind, with our three-clawed feet,
  Writing a language dumb,
With never a spark, in the empty dark,
  Or hint of life to come.

Yet happy we lived, and happy we loved,
  And happy died once more;
Our forms were rolled in clinging mould
  On neocomian shore.

The world turned on in the lathe of time,
  The "hot lands" heaved amain;
We caught our breath, from womb of death,
  And crept into life again.

We left our tails and our saurian scales
  In the Pleocene main,
And caught in rift of glacial drift
  We sank to sleep again.

Thus life by life, and love by love,
  We passed 'round circle strange;
And breath by breath, and death by death,
  We followed the law of change.

Until light and swift through the jungle's rift,
  We sped in airy flight,
Or breathed in balm of fronded palm,
  And slept in moonless night.

There came a time in the cycle of change,
  From out the mindless voids,
The shadows broke and we awoke,
  Changed into anthropoids.

And oh! what beautiful years were these,
  Our hearts clung each to each,
Our life was filled, our senses thrilled
  With first faint dawn of speech.

Then I was thewed like an auroch bull
  And tusked like great cave bear,
And you, my sweet, from head to feet,
  Were gowned in glorious hair.

And deep in the gloom of a fireless cave,
  When night fell o'er the plain,
And moon hung red o'er river bed
  We crunched on bones of slain.

While dwelling thus on the cavern wall
  The levin flash would play;
Fair reason came with subtle flame
  And woke a newer day.

I watched the lightning shatter the seared pine,
  And fire his lofty dome;
I caught a spark from blazing bark,
  And lit my cavern home.

I polished a stone to the cutting edge,
  And shaped with brutish craft;
I broke a shank from woodland dank,
  Fitted it head and haft:

I hid me close by the reedy tarn,
  Where mammoth came to drink;
Through brawn and bone I drove the stone
  And slew him on the brink.

Then loud I howled through the moonlit waste,
  Loud answered our kith and kin;
From west and east, to bloody feast,
  The clans came trooping in.

O'er joint and gristle and padded hoof
  We fought and clawed and tore,
And cheek by jowl, with many a growl,
  We talked the combat o'er.

I carved that fight on a reindeer bone,
  With rude and hairy hand;
I pictured his fall on cavern wall,
  That men might understand;

For we lived by blood and the right of might
  Ere human laws were drawn;
And the age of sin did not begin
  'Til our brutal tusks were gone.

Time sped on in the law of life,
  'Til o'er the nursing sod
The shadows broke, our souls awoke,
  In strange dim dream of God.

And that was a million years ago,
  In age that no man knows;
And here to-night in raiment bright
  We sit where lamplight glows.

Your eyes are deep as the Devon springs,
  Your hair as dark as jet;
Your life is new, your years are few,
  Your soul untried, and yet

Our trail is on the Kimmeridge clay
  And scarp of Purbeck flags;
We have left our bones in Bagshot stones
  And deep in coraline crags.

Cities have sprung above the grikes
  Where hairy cave-men made war;
The engine shrieks across the creeks
  Where mummied mammoths are.

Our life is old and our love is old,
  And death will come amain;
Should it come to-day, what man can say
  We shall not live again?

Despite the blights, we will climb the heights
  That shade our dim pathway,
And rise again to higher plane,
  When rid of mortal clay.

God wrought our souls with the Tremadoc beds,
  And furnished wings to fly;
He sowed our spawn in the world's dim dawn,
  I know they cannot die.

Then as we go to luncheon here,
  O'er many dainty dish,
Let's drink anew to time when you
  And I were boneless fish.

That all things on this earth are subject to change, we are all aware, for it is subject to direct proof; time never pauses in his onward flight, and we see his ravages on every hand. There is nothing surer than that all things must change, either for better or for the worse. As we change from the lower to the higher order, we approach nearer to the attributes of our Creator; we gather more and more wisdom. We had to pass through all the forms of the animal kingdom before we were fitted to understand God's laws.

The Son of God, born of the Blessed Virgin, had to take upon himself the sinful form and spirit of man, and feel all his weaknesses and changing nature before He could accomplish the work of redemption, the work His Father set Him to do. Is not this a living, a real proof set before us?

No man is employed by another to take charge of any business, and perform the duties required, unless he is familiar with what he has to do. And he has first to learn those duties before he is competent to perform them, and someone must teach him first, and give him understanding.

And it is my opinion that thus God has created and taught us and raised us from the lower to the higher plane. He has raised us from the lower order of the fauna, up through all the grades, to the present high plane of intelligence, and when we leave this mortal frame that we now inhabit as man, the atomic spark, the living soul, will take its place in the vast interstellar regions of space to do the bidding of our great Creator. We are educated on earth so as to be prepared for the performance of those duties. He shall assign us in the next stage or plane that He places us upon. I think he prepares us here for our future duties just as the child is prepared by his teachers to take his place in this life. So God, by lifting us up from the protozoan plane to our present place, has carried us through the various grades of life, and fitted us for His great work in the vast worlds and starless voids that surround us. And having passed from the A, B, C of the Mollusca to the X, Y, Z's of the differential and integral calculus of our graduation in this the high plane of reason and intelligence of our eighth day of change, we are now ready to be sent as ministers, ambassadors or servants to do His work, when we are lifted out of the shell that confines our immortal souls.

We are of the earth earthy, but when we rise from this bed of clay to a newer, we will ride on the wings of thought far swifter than the rays of light can travel, and with our knowledge of every creature of earth, perfected from having ourselves inhabited their forms in bygone ages, we can better understand and obey His orders.

This, to the man of reason, seems but a clear exposition of the facts, and it does seem to me that the deeper we delve into the hidden mysteries of nature and the clearer we understand them, the better we are educated and fitted for the life yet to come; and as we have toiled here and lifted ourselves above the undulating plane of humanity, so God will lift us to higher and fairer realms in the great beyond. So I think it our duty to ever try to excel in whatever walk or calling we may pursue on this old earth, so that we may take our place as near the throne of our Creator as possible and not be forced out to the far-off confines or frontiers of that unknown region that lies beyond the ken of mortal man.

Darwin's theory of our descent from the protoplasm of the Mollusca in the whole is not in conflict with the Mosaic account of man's creation, and if he had followed the dictates of reason, and given heed to the still small voice within every man's heart, that atomic living spark, that part of the immortal God, the Divine Creator, known and recognized by every living, conscience-bearing human of the eighth era as the soul; that atom that joins us in an unseverable bond to our Creator and makes us a part and parcel of Him, his work would have been complete.   But he laid this aside; he forgot the Divine Ruler, and trusted to the law of chance, just as the gambler trusts to the turn of the card or the drop of the dice.

As we journey down life's pathway we should delve deep into the mysteries of nature that surround us, and try to drink fitting and beneficial draughts and prepare ourselves for the eternity beyond.   Look at the bright side, find good in all mankind, and keep the bright spark of charity in our souls burning with an ever-increasing ray; we may have faith and hope, but charity alone and unaided covereth, with her broad mantle, every sin.   The Bible says it covereth the multi-tude—not a multitude of sins.

Let us pause in life's race, brother; look up at the sky light;
   Don't blink at God with the eyes of a mole;
Come from the gloom of a self-shrouded twilight
   Into the broad open fields of your soul.

Gaze on the stars, heed their beautiful story,
   List to the wonderful tales they can tell;
Think on their cause, don't beshadow their glory
   With narrowing thoughts of a man-fashioned hell:

Say to your brothers and sisters, " I love you ":
   Fill up your life with generous deeds;
Climb to the heaven of beauty above you,
   But not on a ladder of meaningless creeds.

Walk in the sunshine, grow in its gladness,
   Gather life's joys as you journey along;
God will not curse, with an infinite madness,
   Souls that are filled with an infinite song.

That Being that brought us up from the Tremadoc beds, through all the different phases of life, spread the broad, beautiful fields of earth before us, set the stars in their pathways, carpeted the valleys and plains with the bright flowers of every hue and color, and canopied the heavens above in clouds of ever-changing dyes, is certainly endowed with wisdom and power beyond our mortal ken. He has brought us up from the low, mindless voids, and passed us through every stage of existence to fit us for our future duties on far-off stellar shores. Yes, He thus educates us here to fill our places and perform our several and various duties and allotted tasks in the Great Beyond.

He has given us a free hand and let us choose our own pathways on this old earth, and we should bend every energy of our minds and souls to understand and make returns to Him for all His goodness, mercy and the blessings. extended and bestowed upon us during our brief sojourn on this transient earthly shore. God would n[ ] [p]assed us through so many changing [ ] many aeons of time, and given [ ] ducation, had He not [ ] perform our duties [ ] that our possession of [ ]. For this immortal [ ] ncarnate God Himself, [ ] us at creation's dawn [ ] ever die or perish. It [ ] ven, that home not made [ ] for us when He gave us [ ] cation was not given us [ ], but for all " eternity." [ ] perfect.

[ ] mprehend the meaning of [ ] ning and no end. As an [ ] humming-bird that floats [ ] of [ ] rth to take an atom of the [ ] ear it to the most distant star that [ ] vens above us and be a million years making a tra[ ] o and from that star; when that bird, with its tiny beak, shall have borne the world away eternity would not yet have been begun.

Is it not reasonable to believe that God, in His infinite judgment, goodness and mercy, knowing all things and contemplating the fields of that vast beyond to which we are to be assigned to perform our duties, has not brought us up from the lowest stages of all animate matter, and so prepared us to take our places in that great beyond; so educated us as to fit us to fulfill every duty He should call upon us to perform?

This education given us in this frail life is to last us through all eternity, and not merely for that short space of time that it would take the humming-bird, with its tiny beak, to bear the world away to that distant star. We have nothing, you and I, to do with our coming into this state, and we have nothing to do with our going out of it, for God alone governs this advent and this exit. He knows our beginning and our end. He has fashioned us for His own ends. He works from a perfect principle, hence all His works are perfect. We, knowing that He is all powerful, and cognizant of all things, should, in common reason, at least, assume that He would wish us fully equipped, and would so equip us, so educate us, and fit us to perform the duties allotted to us in that vast field He has stretched out in the great illimitable space around us.

He has lifted us and brought us through all the stages of life, from the testaceans of the lower protozoan plane, up through all the various stages of the kingdoms of the animate beings of earth, with the view of fitting us perfectly to do His bidding in the life to come.

Let us take these higher, loftier, and holier views of evolution, as it relates to the whole order of the universe. The creation of new stars in the boundless space that surrounds us is but a repetition of what is revealed by our microscope when we attempt to search each drop of water that makes the great seas, whose waves lash the shores of every continent and isle of our earthly abodes. These microscopian atoms of living animalculæ that inhabit and fill every drop of water that compose the great seas and oceans that roll around us, but aid in declaring the glory of God, while the firmament showeth His handiwork.

The flaming meteors from the firmament that we float in, speed with swift wings into our habitat, and with fierce heat dive into our earth and cool and leave for our admiration a drop of star-dust, in the form and shape most pleasing to our wondering minds; and we polish and gather them to our persons, and let them sparkle on our fingers, to remind us of that star-dust from whence they sprang. These diamonds scintillate and sparkle for our delectation, ever reminding us of the glories and the grandeur of our future abode that may be ours when we rise again, cleansed and purified from the dross and scum of our earthly abode, and tread the pathway of the angels, beyond the regions of the " milky way " that stretches across the vision in the domeless beyond.

No mortal mind can contemplate the wonders and glories of that great beyond. We can only catch a dim, clouded view of the bright, gleaming stars around us, each a grander, larger globe than ours, and we see these same stars, or worlds, nightly, canopying the most distant ranges of our vision and gathering into groups or constellations in the vast unbounded regions beyond. In contemplating these same islands of stars in that vast ether ocean may we not dream that they are but the beginning of the evolution of the stars themselves, the gathering together of the " star-dust " of this really " boundless ocean of space," yes, of every luminous, visible and invisible body, as is shown to our wondering gaze in that mysterious " milky way " and mythical " pathway of the angels," into one great, grand whole? May not, I repeat, this " star-dust," as the time rolls on, gather into one great globe, or world, and by " cohesive force " draw all stars and worlds that now exist, from the most minute to the largest, and weld them into one great globe or world, on which the Supreme Ruler of the universe shall have his abode, and reign over a domain and people, perfected and taught, from personal experience, from having passed through every form and phase of evolution?

Yes, when this great world of the future, built, framed and rejuvenated from all the perfected parts of every star, and peopled by beings evolved from the *best* of all living men and women, and purified of every stain and made perfect by the great " I Am," then, indeed, will these living souls, selected and purified by God Himself, be prepared and fitted to take their places, and be the companions, ministers and servants of the " King of Kings," in that vast, eternal habitat, capable of understanding and comprehending *all things,* and able to fly on the swift wings of purified " thought " to the most distant part of God's realm, to do His will.

And the beings who have been the most observant and have closely studied the laws of nature and of nature's God, and delved the deepest into the hidden mysteries will be chosen, in the natural order of reasoning, to be with Him in person, and remain in closest harmony and communion, while those least fitted for these closer duties will be relegated to the outer confines and more distant regions, away from the splendors of the palace and paradise of the Great God-Head. Yes, those best educated and best suited, who have passed from the lowest cell of the protoplasm of the protozoan testa, through all the various shades of evolution, and studied every phase of life in that state where God placed them, will occupy the highest office in that evolved world, and dwell in perfect peace and harmony with their Great Creator throughout the endless aeons of eternity.

THE END

ImTheStory.com

CPSIA information can be obtained at www.ICGtesting.com
Printed in the USA
LVOW12s0340270713

344935LV00006B/66/P

9 781313 559911